AMERICANA LIBRARY

ROBERT E. BURKE, EDITOR

THE TERRITORIES
AND THE UNITED STATES

1861 - 1890

Studies in Colonial Administration

By

EARL S. POMEROY

With a New Introduction by the Author

UNIVERSITY OF WASHINGTON PRESS

SEATTLE AND LONDON

PREFACE

MY primary debt is to Professor Frederic L. Paxson of the University of California, who guided my graduate studies and the preparation of the doctoral dissertation on which this volume is based. I hope that his influence may be evident here in some measure.

I wish to thank the custodians of the various collections cited in the bibliography. In particular I am indebted to Mr. Arthur V. Sullivan of the Treasury Department, whose willingness to share his knowledge of his files made working there an unusual privilege, to Mr. Charles R. Beard of the Department of the Interior, who allowed me free access to the then unclassified records of the department, and to the late Miss Edna Vosper (Mrs. Stephen Decatur) of the National Archives. Professor Clarence E. Carter of the Department of State, whose monumental series of *Territorial Papers* is revealing a clearer picture of the earlier territories than we now have of the later, gave his good counsel and encouragement on several occasions. Professor John D. Hicks (then of the University of Wisconsin) read an early draft of the manuscript.

For financial aid I owe thanks to the Native Sons of the Golden West, who, at the recommendation of Professor Herbert E. Bolton, gave travelling and resident fellowships in 1938–40; and to Dean W. W. Pierson and the Smith Graduate Research Fund of the University of North Carolina, who financed two trips to Washington at a time when the University was unable to pay salaries in full.

The chairmen of the Beveridge Committee, Professors R. H. Shryock and A. P. Whitaker, and the Committee's technical editor, Miss Bertha E. Josephson, have been tolerant and ready in offering the fruits of their wide experience to an unpracticed author pressed by other duties. The staff of the University of Pennsylvania Press made wise and helpful suggestions on matters of expression and form, and edited painstakingly.

I completed the manuscript substantially as it is here during the year 1941–42, while at the University of Wisconsin, making some changes in matter of form in the year 1943–44, while at the University of North Carolina. Since the manuscript was submitted, in 1942, much has been published which I would have cited or cited more fully if I had assembled this study in 1946 rather than chiefly in the years 1938 and 1939. Still Professor Carter's volumes of documents of the early territories are the best introduction in printed form to the government of the later territories.

My own concern with this topic grew out of a feeling, as a graduate student, that I could best approach certain political events and developments in the West after exploring, over a fairly broad area in time and space, the administrative conditions of the units which framed the frontier West. Further, it seemed that those conditions constituted a legitimate division of the history of American government and American liberty, whose chronicling is the first privilege and duty of the American historian.

EARL S. POMEROY

The Ohio State University
March, 1946

CONTENTS

INTRODUCTION TO THE 1969 EDITION

MOST books about the territories of the United States, including my own, have concerned themes that J. Franklin Jameson defined many years ago. In his early years as director of the Department of Historical Research in the Carnegie Institution of Washington (1905-28), he "had been greatly struck," he said, "by the multitude of inquiries... from western states concerning documents of their territorial periods...." He saw such concerns of Westerners as parallel to the interest of historians of the thirteen original states in securing archival materials from Europe. "The archives of Washington stand, to the history of all the newer states, in the position which the archives of London, etc., stand to that of the Old Thirteen."[1] Perhaps Jameson's own project of many years of collecting the records of the Virginia Company prepared him for this colonial orientation of Western history. When he planned the *Calendar of Papers in Washington Archives Relating to the Territories of the United States (to 1873)* (1911) that David W. Parker edited for the Department of Historical Research as the first in a series of calendars of archival materials in Washington, the assignment of the volume went first to a colonial historian, one of Jameson's students at Brown and then at Chicago, Marcus W. Jernegan; Parker was a Canadian, whose other work concerned foreign affairs rather than the West. Writing the preface, Jameson described the volume's orientation:

The interest of historical writers at the present time is, and in the immediate future it will apparently continue to be, greatest in respect to those papers which have to do with the territory as a whole, as an administrative unit, as an organic body of population on its way to statehood, and which accordingly have to do, in one sense or another, with its government and its constitutional and political history.[2]

Historians welcomed the volume, although Justin H. Smith regretted the political emphasis, observing that students of the West were

[1]J. Franklin Jameson to Senator Carl Hayden, April 16, 1937, in Elizabeth Donnan and Leo F. Stock (eds.), *An Historian's World: Selections from the Correspondence of John Franklin Jameson,* Memoirs of the American Philosophical Society, XLII (Philadelphia: American Philosophical Society, 1956), pp. 364-65.

[2]David W. Parker (ed.), *Calendar of Papers...* (Washington, D.C.: Carnegie Institution of Washington, 1911), pp. 3, 5.

interested also in social and economic history[3]—in themes, that is, such as Jameson himself later turned to in his *The American Revolution Considered as a Social Movement* (1926).

Jameson continued to support the political-constitutional emphasis when, as chairman of a committee of the American Historical Association on Documentary Historical Publications of the United States, he promoted the legislation by which Congress authorized collecting and publishing the documents that appeared as *The Territorial Papers of the United States* and provided that Parker's *Calendar* should be the basis for the work. The editor of the series from 1931 to 1961 was Clarence Edwin Carter, who had made his reputation as a historian of British rule in the colonial West. Carter prepared twenty-six volumes, which set a standard for historical editing; he stated the editorial principles that his successor has followed; he helped a long succession of students.[4] Carter worried about the enormous bulk of material that for lack of space and time he could not publish, and in 1955 he announced an experiment of reproducing by microfilm nearly all of the documents relating to Wisconsin Territory in the National Archives; after his death a committee of the American Historical Association recommended microfilming documents for all the remaining territories, in order to present more than a small sample of the whole range of Western materials and in order to complete the project within this century.[5] But substantial research has rested on Carter's published volumes.[6]

I do not know how much Jameson or Jameson and Parker influenced what I did, let alone what others did. Jameson was in Washington, advising researchers as he did for thirty years after, although Parker had not begun work on his *Guide,* when Charles Henry Meyerholz prepared the study that he presented as a doctoral thesis at Leipzig in 1907, on "Federal Supervision over the Territories of the United States."[7] My first visits to the National Archives and to

[3]*American Historical Review,* XVII (1911) , 413.
[4]Philip D. Jordan, "A Dedication to the Memory of Clarence Edwin Carter, 1881-1961," *Arizona and the West,* X (1968) , 309-12; Clarence E. Carter, "The Territorial Papers of the United States: A Review and a Commentary," *Mississippi Valley Historical Review,* XLII (1955) , 510-24; Clarence E. Carter, "The United States and Documentary Historical Publication," *ibid.,* XXV (1938) , 18-19, 20-22.
[5]Carter, "Territorial Papers," pp. 519-21. The committee reported in 1963.
[6]Francis S. Philbrick and Jack E. Eblen, for example, depended on them heavily. Cf. Philbrick's massive introduction to *The Laws of Illinois Territory, 1809-1818,* Collections of the Illinois State Historical Library (Springfield: Illinois State Historical Library, 1950), vii-cccclxxvii; and Jack E. Eblen, *The First and Second United States Empires: Governors and Territorial Government, 1784-1912* (Pittsburgh: University of Pittsburgh Press, 1968) . Eblen calls attention to several unpublished theses on territorial government and politics.
[7]Charles Henry Meyerholz, "Federal Supervision over the Territories of the United States," Zwei Beiträge zur Verfassungsgeschichte der Vereinigten Staaten,

archives still at the departments in 1939 showed me how small a sample Parker had taken even for the first twelve of the thirty years I chose to concentrate on; I simply went through everything I could find. The Old Files room in the basement of the Department of the Interior building was such a rich chaos of registers, volumes of fair and press copies, and vertical Woodruff files with letters enclosed in faded red tape and brittle rubber bands that no guide could have helped much; the archives at the Treasury and in the custody of the Department of State were in such good order that a published guide to a portion of them was for the most part superfluous.

Parker had overlooked some of the series that are richest for his and Jameson's theme, such as the appointment papers in the Department of State. Yet they had defined a theme, and definition was important in approaching the mass of documents, whether it was implicit in their plan or merely in the documents themselves. The analogy of British colonial administration was obvious enough to anyone who worked at the major graduate schools where British and colonial approaches still overshadowed purely American and Western approaches—Max Farrand at Princeton, Carter at Illinois, Meyerholz at Harvard—or anyone who read in English constitutional history, which after F. W. Maitland increasingly became administrative history.[8] Even from the time of the Spanish-American War the resemblances between European and American colonial responsibilities and systems came to seem clear enough so that politicians looked more suspiciously at residents of the continental territories who, like the Filipinos and Puerto Ricans, spoke Spanish; and in 1899 B. A. Hinsdale brought out a new printing of an old book on the territories with its title revised to correspond to a changed point of view: *The Old Northwest: The Beginnings of Our Colonial System.*[9]

Beiträge zur Kultur- und Universalgeschichte, VI (Leipzig: R. Voigtländers Verlag, 1908), 83-246. Meyerholz apparently was the first scholar to use sources in archives at Washington on territorial government, citing in his chapter on "Executive Control over Territories" (pp. 195-220) correspondence in series of the departments of State and Interior.

[8]Note the doctoral theses by Max Farrand, *The Legislation of Congress for the Government of the Organized Territories of the United States, 1789-1895* (Newark, N.J.: W. A. Baker, 1896) , and Clarence Carter, *Great Britain and the Illinois Country* (Washington, D.C.: American Historical Association, 1910) . Farrand, like Meyerholz, also studied at Leipzig. In the 1930's, to a student of William Alfred Morris and George H. Guttridge, both inspired teachers, the administrative themes that they and other historians of the Middle Ages and of the eighteenth century were developing suggested analogies in American government more interesting than the themes of most American constitutional historians.

[9]B. A. Hinsdale, *The Old Northwest: The Beginnings of Our Colonial System* (rev. ed.; Boston: Silver, Burdett and Company, 1899) ; cf. his *The Old Northwest; with a View of the Thirteen Colonies as Constituted by the Royal Charters* (New York: Townsend Mac Coun, 1888) , which is essentially the same. Frederick J.

The basic system of government over the territories between 1861
and 1890 was not essentially different in framework or mode of administration from the system of government over the territories in
the years just preceding.[10] By the 1840's and 1850's it had become
a system for organizing the participation of the population in government rather than one for restraining it. The territories that Congress
created between 1861 and 1868, however, remained territories for
unusually long times—with New Mexico and Utah (organized 1850)
and Nebraska (organized 1854), an average of about thirty years,
against an average of less than thirteen years for the earlier territories.
Even Nevada—a territory under that name for only three years—had
been under territorial government for eleven years when Congress
separated it from Utah, against totals of six years for Tennessee (as
Territory South of the River Ohio) and eight for Louisiana (as
Orleans). The differences in time of exposure to ordinary territorial
government would be much greater if one discounted the transitional
phases of initial organizations, the preparations for statehood, and the
first stage of government (which did not apply to the later territories)
when legislation was by governor and judges, rather than by an
elective legislature. The people between the Rockies and the Pacific
(excepting California and Oregon) waited for statehood for as long
as sixty-two years and no less than twenty-three. Territorial government may have lasted long enough for them to warrant their making
more adjustments than Middle Westerners had made, and at least
it found them in more extended experiences in which historians may
profitably observe them.

They lived subject to politicians in and from the states at a time
when the differences between territories and states—in geography, in
economy, in price level, even in religion—were greater than they had

Turner called attention in 1901 to the essentially colonial character of territorial
government. "The Middle West," *International Monthly*, IV (1901) , 795. The first
substantial treatise on the government of the insular and continential dependencies
was William F. Willoughby, *The Territories and Dependencies of the United
States, Their Government and Administration* (New York: The Century Company,
1905) . Willoughby was treasurer (1901-7) and then secretary for Puerto Rico
before he went to Princeton (1912) as professor of jurisprudence and politics. I had
the privilege of his advice as consultant in the Library of Congress in 1939.

[10]It seems worth while to say this mainly because a recent writer has said that
"like Pomeroy, those people who have dealt with [the territories of] the trans-
Mississippi West have tended to base their studies on the unwarranted assumption
that the government of their areas, primarily after 1860, differed fundamentally
from that of the earlier, more eastern territories." This is an idea that I had not
intended to convey. I should particularly regret having suggested it because it
has seemed to me that one of the fruits of studying territorial government should
be achieving a larger setting for state and regional history: realizing, for instance,
that the organic acts, which some local historians quote, were not custom made but
parts of an almost automatically applied system that had become essentially
standardized within the first half century after the Northwest Ordinance.

been at most earlier times. Though they would have ranked high on national scales of education, they were so transient as residents, and their activities as miners, cattlemen, and trespassers on Indian lands led to so much trouble, that territorial government had to be somewhat less an anteroom to statehood, somewhat more a minimal guarantee for law and order than it had been. Their distance from the East was at once their misfortune and their good fortune: it modified the quantity and sources of migration to varying effects; it made closer control both desirable and impossible. Each President of the United States during 1861-90, moreover, distributed patronage for nine or ten territories, rather than the one to seven of his predecessors.

I was interested in both the spectacle of administration as a phase of national politics, an index to the morals, motives, and methods of bureaucrats and of politicians in Congress, the White House, and the departments, and also what seemed to be a significant channel for the transmission of political ideas and practices from East to West. Having established the more or less uniform administrative framework, I hoped to go on to look at more variables within territories, especially the development of politics and of what today we call political culture. In the materials that I used, I saw opportunities to follow various special themes. Correspondence over chronic shortages of law books and elementary legal information in the territories suggested a look at the development of law libraries and of the legal profession. I took large batches of notes on the origins of political parties in California and even on French journalism in San Francisco, planning an account of the political assimilation of a state that was never a territory—only to find that the coeditor of a series who encouraged me to go ahead had forgotten to tell me that someone else was working on a similar topic. Teaching naval history to midshipmen during the war and hoping to go overseas myself, I began to study government in American insular possessions.[11] Little came of

[11]William H. Ellison, *A Self-governing Dominion: California, 1849-1860*, Chronicles of California (Berkeley: University of California Press, 1950). Cf. Earl Pomeroy, "California, 1846-1860: Politics of a Representative Frontier State," *California Historical Society Quarterly*, XXXII (1953), 291-302.

The overseas possessions of the United States, as of other countries, are significant opportunities in themselves and as parts of the history of administration; after 1898, as Howard Lamar has pointed out, our relations with the Spanish islands seemed to affect attitudes toward territories that later became states. I suspect that one soon depletes the profits of emphasizing the ideas of colonial and especially imperial domination in relations with the continental territories, however similar constitutionally they may be to overseas possessions, however striking the spectacle of republican imperialism has been at various times, including the present. For illuminating the history of the American West, the greater opportunity in studying other developing areas, colonial and noncolonial, may be in noting aspects of in-those false starts; I turned to other relationships between East and West.

I made some errors in the book itself that I am glad to be able to correct. The Press has made several corrections within the text. In addition, on page 53, I say that New Mexico had four judges; the correct number (by the acts cited) is five.[12] And on page 118, in the list of judges for Utah, I should have included, after the name of Chief Justice McKean, that of William H. Mitchell of Michigan, nominated January 8, 1873, confirmation withdrawn.[13]

Fourteen years ago Carter referred to the territorial period, by contrast with pre-Revolutionary colonial and later national history, as "the 'dark age' in American historiography."[14] He probably would not speak of it so now, especially since Howard R. Lamar's *Dakota Territory, 1861-1889: A Study of Frontier Politics* (1956) and *The Far Southwest, 1846-1912: A Territorial History* (1966).[15] Lamar has shown how, in years when the thinness of Far Western population was argument for not admitting more states, territorial offices constituted more patronage for Congress and President than before, and expenditures by the national government contributed importantly to Western economies and to the interest of Western politics. In his *Great Basin Kingdom: An Economic History of the Latter-day Saints, 1830-1900* (1958),[16] the most outstanding single volume in a remarkable efflorescence of scholarship on the history and society of Utah, Leonard J. Arrington has developed the theme of Utah's economic dependence on the national government. In other studies he has shown how, as Lamar suggested for Dakota, the general pattern of dependence has continued into recent times, the American Zion as well as modern Israel drawing on remittances and investments from the gentile world. The quality of some of the new state histories represents and draws on recent studies of territorial politics. Lewis

dividual human behavior in conditions of change and stress analogous to those of the frontier. Cf. Earl Pomeroy, "The West and New Nations in Other Continents," in *Reflections of Western Historians,* ed. by John A. Carroll and James R. Kluger (Tucson: University of Arizona Press, 1969) , pp. 237-61.

[12]Noted by Paul L. Beckett, *From Wilderness to Enabling Act: The Evolution of a State of Washington* (Pullman: Washington State University Press, 1968), p. 9.

[13]Mr. William L. Knecht of Berkeley, California, has called this omission to my attention. I may have missed others. Clarence Carter planned a complete list of territorial officials for the final form of *The Territorial Papers,* Volume I, which he issued in preliminary form ("incomplete and provisional") in 1934. On law in the territorial West, see William B. Hamilton (ed.) , *Anglo-American Law on the Frontier: Thomas Rodney & His Territorial Cases* (Durham, N.C.: Duke University Press, 1953) , and Clarence E. Carter, "The Transit of Law to the Frontier: A Review Article," *Journal of Mississippi History,* XVI (1954) , 183-200.

[14]*Mississippi Valley Historical Review,* XLII, 522.

[15]Both published by Yale University Press.

[16]Harvard University Press.

Gould's *Wyoming: A Political History, 1868-1896* (1968)[17] sets an especially high standard.

If I were writing on this subject now, I would do it at greater length than when I wrote the original version as a doctoral thesis in 1939 and then compressed the account to meet the needs of wartime publication in 1942-44. I would hope to relate territorial politics to the town-site speculators with Howard Lamar; the Army with Paul Prucha and Turrentine Jackson;[18] the disposition of the public lands with James C. Malin, Louise Peffer, Paul Gates, and Allan Bogue; internal improvements and railroads with Harry Scheiber and Wallace Farnham; the origins of legislation for the territories with Robert Berkhofer; the intricacies of party factionalism with Robert Johannsen and James Hendrickson; cattlemen with Gene Gressley and Lewis Gould; miners with Rodman Paul and Clark Spence; educators with David Tyack. They and others have explored themes that lead into new dimensions of territorial politics, and that thus pertain to territorial administration.

Government in even the most obvious sense extended much beyond territorial administration, strictly speaking, though no other territories had governments so complex as those of Utah, which according to Governor James Duane Doty (1865) had four: the church, the State of Deseret, the Army, and the federal (territorial) officials;[19] but the conditions of politics were often no less complex than in older economies. I agree with Jack Eblen that writers on territorial government should take more account of local and state government. I would want to consider the emergence of politics on the frontier, particularly in relation to the ties of provincialism as Josiah Royce defined them, both on the plane of adjustment to the physical setting that Henry Nash Smith and Roderick Nash have explored and on the plane of developing social commitments. Nevertheless I think that the system of territorial administration—the links between territorial and national government—is a topic separable for the telling as other topics are. I hope that others will continue to follow it further.

Eugene, Oregon   EARL POMEROY
April, 1969

[17]Yale University Press.
[18]W. Turrentine Jackson also published an outstanding series of articles on territorial government in Wyoming and other territories in the 1940's, and in 1947-48 surveyed "Materials for Western History in the Department of the Interior Archives," *Mississippi Valley Historical Review*, XXXV (1948), 61-76. Other significant articles include those by Merle Wells and Ronald Limbaugh on Idaho and Clark Spence on Montana.
[19]Alice E. Smith, *James Duane Doty, Frontier Promoter* (Madison: State Historical Society of Wisconsin, 1954), pp. 375-76.

THE TERRITORIES
AND THE UNITED STATES
1861–1890

Chapter I

INTRODUCTION

THE relations of the continental territories of the United States with the national government have suffered a neglect which may indicate that they are unimportant, or, again, that they are so organic a part of national development that abstraction has seemed unnecessary. Max Farrand's *Legislation of Congress for the Government of the Organized Territories of the United States, 1789–1895* [1] provides a convenient outline of the general framework of territorial government. Most later works on the American dependencies have emphasized the insular possessions,[2] which constitute a distinct problem. In this work an attempt will be made to describe how the territorial and national systems of government functioned at their several points of contact, and to suggest some of the effects of the national connections on the territories themselves.

The definite phrase "territorial system" is so convenient as perhaps to persuade one to forget how elusive the actual territorial system was. It may be that a coherent territorial system existed as an ideal in the minds of the authors of the Ordinance of 1787 before there were territories. If that ideal was in any way realized, it was not the result of great conscious legislative and executive effort, nor was it the subject of broad contemporary description and analysis.

Before 1862 public lands and slavery dominated national concern with the territories. After 1890 the political body strained to accommodate itself to the new insular dependencies—Hawaii, Puerto Rico, and the Philippines—while four potential states merely marked time before admission.[3] (Samoa and Guam were largely ignored, with respect to government as well as to naval strategy, until after the war with Japan.) After the men to whom territories meant Kansas and Nebraska, and before those to whom they meant Hawaii and Puerto Rico, there came a generation to which territories meant

---

1 Published 1896.

2 E.g., William F. Willoughby, *Territories and Dependencies of the United States, Their Government and Administration.*

3 "The admission of these four States [to be admitted in 1889] practically settles the Territorial question . . . and so will probably put a stop to the discussion . . . as to the need of reform in our methods of making new States." *Providence Journal,* February 25, 1889, quoted in *Public Opinion,* VI (1889), 458.

1

Indian wars and mines, future congressmen and present patronage, but not a great constitutional and administrative problem. There was little desire to exploit the power of absolute control over the territories, a power which the Civil War established but also drained of most of its practical importance. During the fifties both free-state men and slave-state men had been inclined at times to take a narrower view of Congress' power to legislate for the territories—the former denying that Congress could guide territories into statehood on terms favorable to slavery or require full enforcement of the fugitive slave law by territorial authorities, the latter denying that Congress could forbid slavery itself in the territories. The price of national peace set by either side included a narrow construction of national authority. The cost of the war paid for, among other things, affirmation of Congress' power to legislate much as it would in territorial matters, and Congress proceeded to abolish slavery in the territories (1862) during the war and while the author of the Dred Scott decision still sat at the Supreme Court bench. Yet except where polygamy drew its curiosity and outraged its morals, the postwar generation found it convenient to let the territorial machinery operate with fewer innovations, in fact, than in earlier years.

Even admissions of new states dropped off: six had been admitted in the ten years between 1857 and 1867, only one during the twenty-two years following, and that one (Colorado) was, in a sense, a piece of Civil War political business, somewhat delayed. Thus the most distinctive feature of the American territorial system (as contrasted with the British colonial system, which it so closely resembles)—its transitional and progressive character, looking to statehood—was obscured, though never forgotten in the territories. Children born when New Mexico was first brought under American control were to be in their sixties when New Mexico became a state. Alaska, annexed in 1867 and only later to be a territory, stood in an outer political anteroom without the most rudimentary territorial status, governed (when governed at all) more like the Newfoundland fisheries of the seventeenth-century British empire than like a territory; it does not, therefore, come into the present view. The territories were all continental and contiguous. While obviously varied, they were more alike politically than territories had been in earlier times—Montana and New Mexico having more in common, for instance, than Florida and Wisconsin—and they remained under territorial organization and in the same territorial units longer than most earlier territories. The existence of a territorial belt with relative political stability and with certain common social and physiographic characteristics, during most of the period from 1861 to 1890, furnishes a convenient segment of territorial history for study. When it existed, it did not inspire consolidation, or even thorough examination, of existing methods of political control. Territorial control functioned through a few officials of the national government resident in each of the several territories: a governor, a secretary, and three or more justices. Other officials (internal revenue collectors, surveyors, United States attorneys, and the like) came from Washington to administer services in states as well as in territories. These men figured in the history of the individual territories, but not directly in the history of the territorial system. In earlier years there had been more confusion among the two sets of functions: governors had been assigned to duties affecting public lands, Indian and military affairs, while military men in particular had sometimes usurped civil functions. The confusion was chiefly verbal by the sixties. Westerners were accustomed to call all officers from the East "federal officers," to distinguish them from the "territorial officers" chosen locally. But while postal and land office officials, for example, might have relations with local agencies in territories as well as in states, the relations of territorial governor, secretary, and judges constituted the principal connections of national with territorial government.

The principal framework for a territorial government was an "organic act" made along the lines of the Ordinance of July 13, 1787. In the organic act Congress sketched briefly the structure and functions of the executive, legislative, and judicial departments, adding some general—and often superfluous—restrictions. The principal departures from the forms of the Ordinance of 1787 comprised elimination of the first stage of government (by which governor and judges constituted the legislature) and, beginning in 1816, election (rather than appointment) of the upper house of the legislature. Even these extensions of popular government left the government of the Territory of Wisconsin in 1836, say, in its main structural features more like the government of the Colony of Massachusetts Bay under the charter of 1691 than like the government of the State of Wisconsin in 1946, or, for that matter, the Commonwealth of the Philippines under the Tydings-McDuffie Act of 1934. (One notable difference in operation was that the Massachusetts colonial legislature could withhold the governor's salary, while the Wisconsin territorial legislature could not.) After the Wisconsin Act of 1836, provisions became standardized; [4] aside from statements of boundaries, variations were half-accidental as often as they were designed to meet new conditions. The organic act was as brief as the federal constitution or as a British colonial charter, whose purposes it served for the

[4] Clinton *et al. v.* Englebrecht, 13 Wallace 444 (1872); Farrand, *op. cit.,* pp. 15–16, 38–39.

TERRITORIES AND THE U.S.

4

territorial unit; it was never so sufficient or elastic a fundamental law, however liberal its principle of home rule, however generous the promise of statehood implicit in the territorial status. The very transitional and temporary character of the American colonial system, which is its best claim to liberalism and novelty, permitted legislative improvisations which might not have been tolerated in a permanent setup. The organic act designated a new political unit and applied a general formula; [5] details and new problems were attacked in a great mass of supplementary general and special legislation, executive and administrative action, not so well known and not so easily followed as the simple organic acts and enabling and admission acts.

The beginning was an experiment [wrote the Governor of Idaho in 1879]; and in creating and administering the hybrid government thus instituted, a mixture of Congressional enactments and crude local legislation, it is but a lame experiment still. There is no compacted and consistent body of national law concerning the Territories. Acts have been passed, sections amended, overlapped, and repealed, and special features introduced to fit special cases. . . . Common people . . . cannot understand them; lawyers are paid for disagreeing on their meaning; and judges, when failing from its obscurity to ascertain what the law is, are compelled to decide what it ought to be.[6]

Under the Constitution, Congress retained supreme power over the territories, however confused and ineffective its exercise of it. It organized new territories and admitted new states, developing (after 1820) a striking degree of detail in the progress of admission. The total volume of congressional legislation increased rather than diminished over the years. By other acts Congress made appropriations for certain salaries and overhead expenses charged to the national government in the organic acts (eventually formularized in amount) as well as for occasional extraordinary purposes. The Senate examined presidential nominations for territorial offices, thereby controlling policy, as well as patronage, in its confirmations and rejections. In practice, however, Congress renounced, by delegation and by default, the direct administration of continuing affairs which under the Articles of Confederation might have gone to congressional committees. The adoption of the Constitution scattered the business

[5] The brevity of the organic act has led to oversimplification in studies of actual territorial government. Thus Willoughby justifies the small space he devotes to the continental territories: "the form of government . . . as laid down in their organic acts is a simple one and permits of statement in brief compass." Willoughby, *op. cit.*, pp. viii–ix.

[6] Mason Brayman to Carl Schurz, October 8, 1879, *Annual Report of the Secretary of the Interior . . . 1879*, II, 425.

of territorial control among several departments and agencies; with the passage of years and the creation of new departments, there was more rather than less scattering.

When the Congress of the Constitution confirmed the Ordinance of 1787, the appointment of territorial officers fell to the president. Territorial governors were to address their reports to the president: this was still the procedure long after the White House had ceased to be more than a forwarding office in such matters. The ordinary supervision of territorial affairs fell to the office of the secretary of state, because Thomas Jefferson claimed it for his department and because at the time there was no more logical place for it. Here appointments and removals of governors and secretaries were studied and submitted for presidential action; here leaves of absence were granted or refused in the name of the president; here instructions, advice, and reprimands were sent out on a variety of subjects.

These were important matters, but not all of territorial administration, and always overshadowed by the department's diplomatic business. Never mainly a department of territories, the Department of State never became the sole agency of territorial control. Territorial judges, who acted part of the time much as district judges of the United States, were appointed and supervised much as federal judges, eventually under the Department of Justice. The Treasury derived influence over territorial governments and officials through its responsibility for the payment of salaries and expense accounts; its discretion increased when it had to prorate salaries according to rightful absences of officers from their posts, examine the quality of legislative printing, and supervise the care of public buildings. The congressional committees on territories and the territorial delegates to Congress formed still other links between the national government and the territories. The operation of all these agencies in the disposition of territorial business suggests something of the place the territories held in national politics, and something of the effects of the national connection on future partners in American federalism.

Chapter II

THE DEPARTMENT OF STATE

THE sphere of the Department of State in territorial affairs had no precise legal definition or basis. The committee which was to prepare the Ordinance of 1787 told the secretary for foreign affairs that the matter of temporary government for new states, "altho' not immediately within your province we consider as intimately connected with it."[1] In 1793 Secretary Jefferson instructed Governor St. Clair of Northwest Territory that, aside from military matters,

> every thing else falls into the department of State, to the head of which it should be addressed—to him the general report [of the governor] . . . is referred, and if there are matters in it proper for the other departments he reports them to the President, who sends the extracts to the proper department.[2]

It was an undefined jurisdiction which the department received, and an undefined jurisdiction which it passed on to the Department of the Interior in 1873.[3] The clerk who prepared a memorandum on the functions of the Department of the Interior in 1900 could say only that

> the connection [of the Department of State] with Territorial matters [in 1873] . . . consisted principally of issuing and recording the commissions for appointment of the Governors and Secretaries, recording their subsequent changes of status, and receiving their annual reports.[4]

[1] "Shall it be upon colonial principles, under a governor, council and judges . . . and they [then] admitted to a vote in Congress with the common rights of the other States, or shall they be left to themselves until that event? In the former instance how the correspondence or superintendence of such colony or colonies, shall be systematically preserved and presented to the view of Congress?" James Monroe to John Jay, April 20, 1786, Henry P. Johnston, ed., *The Correspondence and Public Papers of John Jay*, III, 191.

[2] September 13, 1793, Clarence E. Carter, ed., *The Territorial Papers of the United States*, II, 460.

[3] The law of March 1, 1873, referred to functions handled by "law or by custom." *Statutes at Large*, XVII, 484.

[4] Extract from Revised Statutes, Duties of the Secretary of the Interior in relation to the Territories, copy, enclosed in Register of Appointments (Department of Interior).

In a liberal sense, the appointment of governors and secretaries did constitute the most essential concern of the Department of State with the territories. Besides recording appointments made, the department received applications and recommendations. These were referred, not to the clerk in charge of what was sometimes called, informally, the "territorial desk," but to the clerk in charge of appointments for the whole department. He filed such papers by name of applicant, not by office. This lack of differentiation in filing permitted generally phrased applications and a considerable interchange of applicants for the foreign and the domestic services. Thus a candidate who was appointed governor of New Mexico had been recommended for minister to Brazil.[5]

Ordinarily, approval by the secretary of state was of considerable weight in determining appointments, if one may judge by the tone and direction of applications, but the president continued to appoint in fact as in form. Although there is no record of application papers referred to the president, there are occasional notes from the White House directing nomination of persons officially unknown to the department. Those who could reach the president did so. The secretary examined routine applications, presumably suggested appointments, and occasionally even made inquiries in search of candidates.[6]

While territorial appointments were handled at the general departmental appointments desk, all other territorial relations with the department were confined to a single division. In 1861 there was no official listing of separate bureaus within the department, but in practice the bureau arrangements established by Secretary Forsyth in 1836 obtained until 1870.[7] Hence, although the official registers recognized no such designation, there were informal references to the "Territorial Bureau."[8] In reorganizing the department in 1870, Secretary Fish formally established the Domestic Records Bureau, where a single clerk had charge of correspondence with territorial officers as well as of other miscellaneous correspondence not concerning the diplomatic and consular services.[9] The designation became "Territorial and Domestic Records Bureau" in 1872.[10]

---

[5] William A. Pile, appointed 1869. Pile resigned to become minister to Venezuela. Appointments File.

[6] E.g., Hamilton Fish to Elisha P. Ferry, October 11, 1872, Domestic Letters, XCVI, 36.

[7] Gaillard Hunt, *The Department of State of the United States*, pp. 211–18, 221–22.

[8] Endorsement, December 21, 1868, with Herman H. Heath to William H. Seward, November 26, 1868, Territorial Papers (hereafter cited as TP), New Mexico, III, 310.

[9] *Register of the Department of State . . . 1871*, pp. 6, 8; Hunt, *op. cit.*, p. 224.

[10] *Ibid.*, p. 226.

The departmental reorganization of 1870 recognized a clerk of the fourth class, Edward Haywood,[11] as the government employee most concerned with the business of territorial control in Washington. But Haywood, like his predecessors, was in no sense an administrator. He had no extra-departmental relations. He prepared memoranda on territorial business, often long and detailed, but he did not have the responsibility of acting on them. He wrote letters but none over his own signature. His subordinate station withheld authority, as his concern with other business [12] and his lack of direct experience with western affairs limited judgment.

Responsibility pertained to officers whose duties were less specialized. The clerk of Domestic Records, in 1870, was "under the superintendence of the Assistant Secretary." [13] The assistant secretary or the secretary endorsed and signed territorial correspondence; occasionally the chief clerk gave instructions.[14] Such officers lacked Haywood's relative familiarity with territorial affairs; they exercised the authority which he lacked, but themselves were occupied chiefly with other matters.

Charges against officials, though relevant to appointments, went in the main to the territorial desk.[15] The great and increasing bulk of such papers, and the patent inconsequence of many charges, limited the ordinary reception to the filing process. When the department did take action, it most often simply referred charges to the officer in question and asked for a reply.[16] Except when to do so was very important or acidentally convenient, such action did not require a personal interview. In the period from 1861 to 1873, there were no investigations in the territories by agents of the department, although the Treasury Department [17] and later the Department of the Interior,[18] whose agents were nearer at hand, did make such direct

[11] Appointed from New York. *Register . . . 1871,* pp. 6, 8.

[12] Similarly other clerks handled territorial correspondence occasionally, so that not even the residue from the very important exception of appointments was exclusively his.

[13] *Register . . . 1871,* p. 8.

[14] E.g., endorsement by Haywood, December 13 [1870] on Henry Wetter to Fish, December 3, 1870, TP, New Mexico, III, 422.

[15] The division was not quite logical. Charges included in recommendations for successors went almost invariably to the appointment office of the department. Charges brought by a governor or secretary, independently or in an informal report on territorial affairs, went to the territorial desk, but papers relating to one man, and covering a single period, might be divided between the two desks.

[16] E.g., Seward to William F. M. Arny, February 25, 1864, Domestic Letters, LX, 301.

[17] *Infra,* p. 34; Hugh McCulloch to James Tufts, January 17, 1868, Gs53 series (Treasury Department).

[18] *Infra,* pp. 19–20.

inquiries. Local proceedings by legislative committees [19] or by grand juries [20] were more frequent, if often ineffective. Administering leaves of absence accounted for much time at the territorial desk. By the Act of 1852, salaries were not to be paid to officers of territories in years when unauthorized absences occurred, unless good cause should be shown to the president.[21] The routine work of sanctioning leaves fell to the departments.[22] In pursuance of the law's purpose, the Department of State added some requirements in its administration. It was not customary to grant leaves to a secretary without approval of the governor.[23] Secretary Fish further required that both secretary and governor should not be absent concurrently, nor during a legislative session.[24] Seward, endeavoring to limit absences, had instituted a policy of inquiring closely into the purposes of leaves.[25]

Despite statutory and departmental precautions, territorial absenteeism reached a harmful and notorious degree. There is evidence of this in the periodical denunciations in departmental letters and circulars and in occasional discussions in Congress [26] as well as in the more pungent comments of Westerners. Leaves were granted for purposes as unrelated to territorial welfare as service in the army,[27] "good service to the party in Illinois," [28] attendance at a railroad promotion meeting,[29] or simply "for the winter." [30] Absences without permission

[19] Santa-Fé *Gazette*, January 18, 1882; (Denver) *Rocky Mountain News*, March 19, 1863.

[20] Copy, P. W. C. Rowell to Amos T. Akerman, November 1, 1871, TP, Arizona, 141–42; copy, Rowell to Akerman, November 1, 1871, enclosed in Akerman to Fish, November 23, 1871, TP, Arizona, pp. 145–47.

[21] Act of June 15, 1852, *Statutes at Large*, X, 10; cf. Act of March 3, 1851, *ibid.*, IX, 611; Act of May 1, 1876, *ibid.*, XIX, 41; *Official Opinions of the Attorneys General*, VI, 57.

[22] Executive Order, March 31, 1871, in James D. Richardson, *A Compilation of the Messages and Papers of the Presidents, 1789–1897*, VII, 141.

[23] Seward to Richard C. McCormick, September 19, 1864, Domestic Letters, LXVI, 186.

[24] J. F. Chaves to Fish, December 1, 1870, TP, New Mexico, III, 421; Fish to John A. Burbank, June 1, 1871, Domestic Letters, LXXXIX, 461.

[25] Endorsement on John Hutchinson to Abraham Lincoln, September 8, 1863, TP, Dakota, I, 667.

[26] *Congressional Globe* (39 Cong., 2 Sess., January 28, 1867), 789–90; *ibid.* (40 Cong., 1 Sess., April 10, 1867), 826, 844; *Senate Executive Documents* (40 Cong., Spec. Sess.), No. 6.

[27] In Nebraska to both governor and secretary. Alvin Saunders to Seward, July 24, 1861; Algernon S. Paddock to Seward, October 9, 1861, TP, Nebraska, pp. 143, 145.

[28] J. H. Platt to Fish, October 13, 1870, TP, Wyoming, p. 28.

[29] William M. Stewart to Fish, March 20, 1871, TP, Arizona, p. 134.

[30] Samuel H. Elbert to Seward, November 19, 1862, TP, Colorado, I, 88–90. In asking an extension, Elbert wrote that there was "nothing of importance" in Colorado. Elbert to Seward, February 8, 1863, *ibid.*, I, 98.

were not uncommon, generally being attributed to the slowness of communications in emergencies.[31] A single absence might approach five months.[32] Yet the department denied many applications and hedged in others with strict conditions.[33] The correspondence on leaves of absence forms a large portion of the Territorial Papers; its bulk and its detail suggest the high degree of supervision that might be undertaken in territorial relations, while the continuance of abuses illustrates the limitations of long distance enforcement of the simplest of regulations.

Regular reports of territorial governors, by the Act of 1789, were to go to the president,[34] and in 1861 the annual reports and the records of executive proceedings were still addressed to the White House. There is occasional evidence that the president took note of the less formal letters which came as well; [35] and the department brought some papers to his attention;[36] but he forwarded the regular reports and proceedings to the Department of State. In 1867, Seward eliminated this indirection, ordering that all territorial correspondence be directed to the department rather than to the White House.[37]

The executive proceedings were in no way suited for presidential examination. Extraneous material, such as the text of the organic act or the laborious detail of forms of commissions, sometimes gave them tremendous bulk.[38] At some other times they consisted merely of short lists of commissions or lists of legislative acts.[39] There is no evidence that any officer in Washington read them in this period, and little indication that reading would have been helpful for the type of control exercised.

The annual reports were less stereotyped and seemingly received some attention.[40] More informative, probably, were the informal executive communications which came irregularly and without statu-

[31] E.g., John Evans to Seward, August 18, 1862, TP, Colorado, I, 80–81.

[32] Memorandum with J. A. Hand to Fish, May 26, 1870, TP, Dakota, I, 226.

[33] E.g., Fish to Burbank, June 1, 1871, January 16, 1872, Domestic Letters, LXXXIX, 461; XCII, 223–24.

[34] Act of August 7, 1789, *Statutes,* I, 52–53.

[35] Seward to James W. Nye, August 5, 1861, Domestic Letters, LIV, 410–11.

[36] Seward to S. S. Harding, September 20, 1862, *ibid.,* LVIII, 239.

[37] Seward to S. R. Howlett, April 2, 1867, *ibid.,* LXXV, 535. The Department of the Interior returned to the letter of the law. Schurz to George H. Hand, February 27, 1878, Miscellaneous Letter Book (Department of the Interior), VII, 434.

[38] E.g., the Nevada executive proceedings dated December 9, 1861, covered 151 pages. TP, Nevada, I, 32.

[39] McCormick to President, December 31, 1865, TP, Arizona, pp. 8–16; Arny to Andrew Johnson, October 16, 1865, TP, New Mexico, III, 13–29.

[40] Some extracts were made for the use of other agencies. Endorsement (*ca.* January 19, 1866) on Thomas F. Meagher to Seward, December 11, 1865, TP, Montana, I, 4.

tory requirement. Herein a governor might be inspired to comment on election results, explain his vetoes, or summarize legislation,[41] privately and at intervals closer to the events than those prescribed for annual reports. In special circumstances these letters were referred to the president,[42] and the president occasionally encouraged direct communication from a territorial officer, as when Grant encouraged Governor Woods of Utah "to keep him informed of whatever transpires."[43] Other irregularly occurring communications included legislative memorials and resolutions, and letters commendatory of administration policies.[44]

In the face of this influx of letters from the territories, instructions on the general conduct of office were so infrequent as to be exceptional. The department did not expect officers to come to Washington for consultation upon their appointment, nor did it send any general written instructions. Governor William A. Pile of New Mexico, who requested such advice, was told that "no special instructions are necessary in regard to your official duties."[45] An officer was expected to refer to the law rather than to a departmental superior.[46] To discover the functions of his office, he might have to make use of a private library, as the department did not furnish the published laws.[47] An Idaho officer complained that "not one of the laws . . . which you cited . . . is to be found in this place."[48]

In similar spirit the department frequently refused to give advice or instructions on particular problems.[49] Even comments on reports of officers' conduct tended to be cautious and non-committal.[50] In lieu of instructions there might be requests almost as deferential as those to the governor of a state.[51] Occasionally, however, there were

[41] Nye to Seward, December 21, 1861, TP, Nevada, I, 14–29.

[42] As in the case of disturbances in Utah. Endorsement, February 25, 1863, on Harding to Seward, February 3, 1863, TP, Utah, II, 567-72.

[43] Orville E. Babcock to George L. Woods, November 6, 1871, Grant Letter Book (Library of Congress), I, 375.

[44] Legislative communications customarily were forwarded by the governor or secretary, but occasionally were sent directly. E.g., Anastasio Sandoval to Johnson, December 10, 1867, TP, New Mexico, III, 129.

[45] J. C. B. Davis to Pile, June 30, 1869, Domestic Letters, LXXXI, 330.

[46] Report by Haywood, March 4, 1872, to Fish (referring to Wetter), February 23, 1872, TP, New Mexico, IV, 269–70, 250–51.

[47] Vernon H. Vaughan to George S. Boutwell, October 19, 1870, Treasury Miscellaneous Files (Treasury Department), 207-U. After 1874 copies of the *Statutes at Large* were required by law to be sent to the territories. Act of June 20, 1874, *Statutes*, XVIII, 113–14.

[48] Silas D. Cochran to William P. Fessenden, November 29, 1864, Treasury Miscellaneous, 101-I.

[49] Fish to Marsh Giddings, February 3, 1872, Domestic Letters, XCII, 394.

[50] E.g., Seward to William Pickering, March 27, 1863, *ibid.*, LX, 104.

[51] E.g., Seward to Henry Connelly, May 19, 1862, *ibid.*, LVII, 237.

instructions of positive tone. After representations from the territorial delegate, the secretary of Colorado was ordered to divide the public printing "between the two loyal papers"; failing to obey repeated orders, he was removed.[52] An unusual series of orders to the governor of New Mexico in 1869 demanded specific changes in a proclamation outlawing certain Indians, although apparently compliance remained incomplete.[53]

Despite occasional demonstrations of administrative energy, instructions came neither frequently nor on departmental initiative. There was more than lack of administrative impulse, attributable possibly to decentralization and to the press of other affairs: there are evidences of a policy of non-intervention. It should not be surprising that there was often confusion both in the territories and in Washington over departmental jurisdictions, so that even Secretary Fish had the impression that the secretary of the interior had functions which were in fact his.[54] The department was cautious in approaching the jurisdictions of other departments, to the point of referring business elsewhere on any possible pretense. Usually it simply denied the need for supervision. The departmental law officer stated in 1870 that

in construing provisions for the self government of an inchoate state, under our principle of administration, every intentment is to be made in favor of the powers of the local legislature and in restriction (if need be) of the residuary power which Congress might have retained, if it had thought proper.

Characteristically, this memorandum was endorsed, "I have no doubt of the accuracy of the opinion . . . but . . . this should issue through the Dept. of Justice." [55]

While the State Department maintained the principal contacts with territorial governors and secretaries, it referred a considerable portion of territorial business to other offices. Except for business with Congress, the president, and the Treasury Department, the secretary of state served as intermediary.[56]

[52] Copy, Seward to Lewis L. Weld, TP, Colorado, I, 41; memorandum, April 3, 1862, Appointments File.

[53] Action followed representations from the War and Interior departments. John A. Rawlins to Fish, August 31, 1869, TP, New Mexico, III, 344–55; Fish to Pile, September 3, 1869, Domestic Letters, LXXXII, 32; Fish to Pile, September 25, 1869, ibid., LXXXII, 106–7.

[54] Fish to Burbank, November 15, 1869, ibid., LXXXII, 336–37; cf. Hiram P. Bennet to Seward, November 12, 1861, TP, Colorado, I, 33.

[55] Draft by E. Peshine Smith, August 2, 1870, Fish (unsigned) to J. W. Shaffer, TP, Utah, II, 709–11.

[56] A seeming exception is the relationships of governors as superintendents of Indian affairs. Infra, pp. 16–18.

Ordinarily the attorney-general gave opinions on general territorial affairs only at the instance of the Department of State, refusing to consider inquiries submitted directly by territorial officers.[57] Even when an inquiry had gone through channels, the attorney-general— as in the important question of the power of territorial legislatures to grant railroad subsidies—might consider it "improper to express an official opinion . . . as the question is purely a local one."[58] Out of six published opinions on territorial affairs between 1861 and 1873, four referred to the organization of legislatures, two to methods of choosing territorial officers.[59] The Department of State usually transmitted copies of opinions without comment or injunction.[60] Both the attorney-general and the secretary of state apparently were indifferent to such problems on the peripheries of their major functions.

Disorders—whether from civil resistance to authority or from Indian attacks—not infrequently required more extensive military action than the territorial authorities could handle. The secretary of state referred reports of such circumstances to the secretary of war, who forwarded the information to the military commanders on the scene.[61] When an emergency demanded coördination of authority and more speed in action, the military and civil authorities in the territories communicated directly, rather than through the departments.[62] The small number of regular troops available generally limited the War Department's concerns with civil affairs; territorial militiamen and volunteers were enough to handle ordinary needs. Nor did the War Department have funds for military emergencies, which were an occasional financial embarrassment to territorial governments.[63]

Financial business, strictly speaking, was outside the concern of the Department of State. Salaries and accounts issued directly through the Treasury, which developed distinct administrative re-

[57] Copy, John M. Binckley to McCormick, April 8, 1866, enclosed in Binckley to Seward, April 8, 1866, TP, Arizona, 104–7.
[58] Fish to Benjamin F. Potts, March 1, 1873, Domestic Letters, XCVIII, 39–40. Cf. (relative to Dakota) Akerman to Fish, April 11, 1871, TP, Dakota, I, 244.
[59] Five occurred after August 16, 1870. *Digest of the Official Opinions of the Attorneys General of the United States . . . 1789 to 1881*, pp. 466–67.
[60] E.g., Fish to George A. Batchelder, November 19, 1873, Domestic Letters, LXXXVII, 92.
[61] Seward to Connelly, February 18, 1862, Domestic Letters, LVI, 379; Edwin M. Stanton to Seward, September 23, 1862, TP, Utah, II, 557.
[62] Santa Fé *Weekly Gazette*, March 5, 1864. Relations were close in New Mexico and Arizona, where the presence and coöperation of the military were necessary for civil order.
[63] E.g., Meagher to Ulysses S. Grant, April 9, 1867, Johnson Papers. Congress made reimbursement in several instances.

lationships. As the acting secretary of state wrote in 1873, no territorial officer made

requisition upon this Department, for funds for any purpose whatsoever. . . . This Department has never claimed any jurisdiction over appropriations made for the benefit of the Territories, except to require a satisfactory explanation of charges brought against their alleged misapplication by the officers commissioned by this Department.[64]

When such charges of misapplying government moneys arose, the Treasury apparently regarded them as the joint concern of the two departments.[65] Interdepartmental correspondence related also to leaves of absence and appointments, for the Treasury needed precise dates of service.[66] Convenience occasionally led the Department of State to act as intermediary for officers in need of funds not due by law, making recommendations to the Treasury or to Congress.[67]

Communications with Congress were chiefly suggestions for legislation, especially appropriations, relayed from governors and secretaries. There was no close or continuous connection with the Capitol. Content with a routine and unenergetic administration of the law, the Department of State had little interest in changing it.

In the last years of the department's supervision of territorial affairs, there was little of the active interest in western matters which permeated the policies of Jefferson, Monroe, J. Q. Adams, Clay, and Cass. Seward and Fish entered office with no acquaintance with territorial and western problems, at a time when diplomacy, having served the needs of the frontier, had passed on to seek its clientele on a more national scale. They served without sufficient leisure to attend to the peripheral functions of the department. Appointed for their accomplishments in New York politics, they were occupied with the heaviest of diplomatic burdens—a civil war and its aftermath. Seward's background suggests that without the war he might have developed the territorial system as a patronage machine greater even than it was. The orderly Fish, but for Santo Domingo and the *Alabama,* might have rid the department of territorial affairs before he did. As it was, they administered the system from day to day, reasonably and honestly enough, but sparing only a modicum of attention from business of different and more pressing import.

[64] Davis to Columbus Delano, August 1, 1873, Domestic Letters, CIII, 136–37.

[65] Boutwell to Fish, August 7, 1871, TP, Washington, II, 743–47.

[66] The Department of State usually (but not always) sent lists of appointments and leaves covering stated intervals, e.g., Frederick W. Seward to W. Medill, April 6, 1861, Domestic Letters, LIII, 543.

[67] F. W. Seward to R. W. Tayler, October 15, 1867, Domestic Letters, LXXVII, 233; W. H. Seward to Heath, September 2, 1867, *ibid.,* LXXVII, 52.

Chapter III

THE DEPARTMENT OF THE INTERIOR

WITHIN the year in which Secretary Fish designated the first territorial bureau, the administration took the first steps toward removing territorial affairs from the Department of State. President Grant in 1870 and again in 1872 recommended transfer to the Department of the Interior.[1] The idea of change probably was Fish's rather than Grant's: the secretary offered the first drafts of the reorganization bill [2] and personally urged its passage. "It will give relief to this Dept.," he told Delegate McCormick of Arizona, "and put the Territorial business where it properly belongs." [3] As signed on March 1, 1873, it provided: "That the Secretary of the Interior shall hereafter exercise all the powers and perform all the duties in relation to the Territories . . . that are now by law or by custom exercised and performed by the Secretary of State." [4] Before the end of the month the necessary papers had been transferred,[5] and the territories were under the new régime.[6]

From Secretary Fish's point of view, the transfer of territorial affairs was desirable to rid the diplomatic department of a domestic concern. It followed naturally on the departmental reorganization of 1870. Fish's sponsorship of the transfer suggests that if he was an imperialist in his Caribbean policy, at least he had no desire to administer empire. At the establishment of the republic, when the problems of territories were in large part diplomatic, when the back-

[1] *House Journal* (41 Cong., 3 Sess.), p. 17; *ibid.* (42 Cong., 3 Sess.), p. 15.

[2] As early as March 13, 1872. *Cong. Globe* (42 Cong., 3 Sess.), 1897.

[3] Fish to McCormick, March 1, 1873, Fish Letter Book (Library of Congress), VII, 325; cf. Fish to McCormick, February 17, 1873, *ibid.*, VII, 285.

[4] *Statutes*, XVII, 484.

[5] Papers transmitted included "recommendations . . . for Territorial appointments, also papers of remonstrances against appointments and complaints on charges against Governors and Secretaries . . . received since the 1st of September 1872." Fish to Delano, March 13, 1873, Interior Appointment Papers, File 120. All other correspondence remained in the Department of State. The simplicity of the move recalls the undifferentiated nature of the department with regard to territories: there was no transfer of personnel as occurs ordinarily in shifting a function worthy of a separate administrative division.

[6] Although the Act was in effect from date of passage, notice was not sent to the territorial officials until March 20. Fish to governors and secretaries, March 20, 1873, Domestic Letters, XCVIII, 191. Understandably, letters continued to come to the Department of State for some time.

grounds of some territories were foreign, there was a logic in the territorial jurisdiction of the Department of State. In the era of twentieth-century imperialism there was again more logic in such a connection than there was in the half-century between the Mexican War and the Spanish American War.

The Department of the Interior was suited to receive territorial business as much because it was a department of domestic residua as because it already had related functions. Despite impressions to the contrary, the secretary of the interior had had a negligible part in territorial control proper, limited to casual supervision over a few public buildings.[7]

The secretary's most significant connection with territorial officers before 1873 (although it was not with the territorial system in any strict sense) grew out of his supervision of those governors who were ex-officio superintendents of Indian affairs. The functions of governor and superintendent had been united under the Articles,[8] and the combination was continued under the Constitution with Indian affairs under the War Department until the Department of the Interior was established in 1849.

During the sixties there was increased dissatisfaction with the incidence of two distinct responsibilities in a single officer. A governor complained that supervision of the Indian agencies required him

to be constantly in the saddle and performing journeys of two or three hundred miles at a stretch, whilst his administration of the territory . . . equally demands his presence at the Capital. . . . [To attempt to combine the two functions] is futile, or rather involves the sacrifice of one class of duties to the other.[9]

Often the governor-superintendent was too conscious of the dignity of his post and of his connection with the Department of State as governor to be sufficiently attentive to his responsibilities to the Department of the Interior as superintendent. Sometimes it was "next to impossible to get any report." The typical governor of a territory, moreover, was an eastern politician who had no intention of leaving political ambitions behind him; he was "a candidate for Congress

[7] *Infra,* pp. 42–43. Advocating transfer, Senator (former Governor) Nye of Nevada told the Senate that "the entire territorial accounts" had been formerly in the Department of the Interior. *Cong. Globe* (42 Cong., 3 Sess.), p. 1133. Cf. Fish to Burbank, November 15, 1869, Domestic Letters, LXXXII, 336–37.

[8] After August 14, 1788, by Act of October 3, 1787. *Journals of the Continental Congress,* XXXIII, 601; Charles Thomson to Winthrop Sargent, March 11, 1789, in Carter, *op. cit.,* II, 189–90.

[9] T. F. Meagher to Johnson, July 13, 1866, Johnson Papers. Governor McCook of Colorado was "relieved of the duties of the Indian superintendency at his own request . . . as . . . it interfered with his other duties as an executive officer. . . ." *Rocky Mountain News,* February 22, 1871.

from the day" he went west.[10] Simple neglect of duties, in consequence, might well be a lesser evil; obviously the welfare of the Indians and consequently the safety of the settlers were not secure with an officer dependent for favors on a frontier constituency, which might vote him one office or petition him out of another. The secretary of the interior, at one time, feared that the consequence of such neglect in Montana would be an Indian war.[11] A governor of Idaho, kept in office by the deadlock between President Johnson and Congress, was accused not merely of complete neglect and incompetence as superintendent, but of fraud; pending his removal, the Department of the Interior refused to put further Indian funds into his hands.[12] Indian affairs in such circumstances, as the commissioner complained, were truly critical.[13] The white settler had methods of self-protection against dishonest and incompetent officers; the Indian had none short of the warpath.

Combination of the two functions, of governor and superintendent continued, if for any reason, because such a combination seemed economical and because there was need for harmony between the Indian administration and the territorial authorities. The organization of Montana in 1864 was defended as the cheapest way of handling Indian affairs.[14] The argument that governors were of higher character than professional Indian managers [15] contained, regrettably from the Indians' point of view, an element of truth, even though it did not touch the main administrative problem. In addition, in territories where the governorship was separated from the Indian superintendency, questions of jurisdiction were troublesome, if perhaps inevitable.[16]

[10] *Cong. Globe* (40 Cong., 2 Sess.), p. 2800.

[11] James Harlan to Seward, April 11, 1866, TP, Montana, I, 55–56; cf. D. W. Cooley to Harlan, April 10, 1866, enclosed in Harlan to Seward, April 11, 1866, TP, Montana, I, 57.

[12] *The Diary of Gideon Welles*, III, 186; Edward D. Holbrook to Johnson, May 1, 1867, TP, Idaho, I, 348–49. The previous governor apparently also had mishandled Indian funds. John Hailey, *The History of Idaho*, 166–67.

[13] "It is of momentous importance that an official be appointed who can be recognized by this Department." Charles E. Mix to Holbrook, August 8, 1867, TP, Idaho, II, 111.

[14] *Infra*, p. 96. It was argued that the governors' civil duties were light, and that they might devote almost their whole time to Indian affairs. *Cong. Globe* (40 Cong., 2 Sess.), pp. 2800–01.

[15] *Loc. cit.*

[16] "Executive Minutes of Governor John W. Geary," Kansas State Historical Society *Transactions*, IV (1890), 641. In resigning as governor of Arizona, John C. Frémont complained that "as the Governor . . . has neither force nor money in the settlement of Indian difficulties, my experience in Indian affairs could not be put to any practical use." To Chester A. Arthur, October 11, 1881, Interior Appointment File 163.

The governors ceased to be superintendents between 1857, when Congress authorized the president to discontinue superintendencies,[17] and 1871, when he had discontinued the last remaining ones.[18] In the interim, as before, the secretary of state had no direct control over Indian affairs, and the secretary of the interior had no hand in the territorial system.[19] Thus transfer of territorial affairs to the Department of the Interior in 1873 was less clearly a step toward concentration of control than it would have been as late as 1870, when some governors were still superintendents ex-officio. With independent agents in all the territories who reported to the commissioner of Indian affairs, the possibility of including Indian administration in the territorial system was no greater than it had been before.

Assignment to the new jurisdiction effected, in fact, a slight decentralization. The appointment division of the Department of the Interior handled a much wider range of business than the State Department's territorial desk had done, including resignations, removals, charges, official bonds, and leaves of absence, as well as letters of application and recommendation.[20] Thus all matters relating to tenure of office were given over to a departmental division decidedly less specialized than the old territorial bureau. Doubtless there was some logic in treating charges and leaves of absence along with appointments, but the new alignment subtracted from the range of affairs formerly treated at the old territorial desk, together with reports and general correspondence of territorial officers. Superior filing methods, however, did make material in the appointment division of the Department of the Interior more accessible than it had been in the appointment office of the Department of State.[21]

[17] Act of March 3, 1857, *Statutes*, XI, 185.

[18] The author has not been able to find the exact date of the final elimination of dual functions. Superintendents were named for New Mexico, Washington, Oregon, and Utah in 1857, for Arizona in 1863, for Idaho and Montana in 1869; the combined superintendencies of Wyoming, Dakota, and Colorado were discontinued after the annual reports of 1870. *Ibid.; Annual Report of the Secretary of the Interior . . . 1869*, pp. 719, 731; *ibid., 1870*, pp. 626–32, 638–42, 666–74; Delano to Fish, December 16, 1870, TP, Colorado, I, 344–45.

[19] Curiously, Governor Doty of Utah expected the superintendent to take over the executive office after his own death. O. H. Irish to W. P. Dale, June 15, 1865, enclosed in Harlan to Seward, July 22, 1865, TP, Utah, II, 624–25. Doty, appointed superintendent in 1861, had retained office upon assuming the governorship in 1863. Doty to Seward, June 20, 1863, TP, Utah, II, 597.

[20] Memorandum by J. Stiles, the Appointment Division, May 13, 1876, in letter press book of Interior Appointment Division, 1874–81, pp. 110–15.

[21] Papers were filed by offices rather than in one alphabetical series. Jacket endorsements after 1879 were quite complete, including lists of relevant correspondence, with occasional summaries of contents, and dates of leaves and appointments. From 1885 typewritten abstracts were made of recommendations and

Administration of appointments themselves was not essentially different after 1873. There are written evidences, however, of more systematic scrutiny of candidates' qualifications, but such use of memoranda is to be expected in a period and a department with vastly larger volumes of business, irrespective of the care given to the business in hand.

Charges against officers were occasions of considerable departmental activity. Instead of relying wholly on comparisons of the written charges of the accuser with the written rebuttals of the accused, the Department of the Interior at times made independent inquiries. The simplest method was to ask a report of a third party, an officer on the scene in the territorial service or in some other branch of the department.[22] Resident officers, lacking special powers and suspect of personal motivation, found difficulties in investigating their colleagues,[23] but a special agent sent to New Mexico in circumstances of international implication was able to command little more respect. The accused, Governor Samuel B. Axtell, claimed that "the Interior Departments [had] no control over him—and that he [would] not be investigated," [24] and that "the Governor [was] not a Federal but a Territorial officer," with inviolable tenure.[25] Easy and dilatory administration from Washington thus gave rise to a claim of independent prerogative, which the department could, and on occasion did, when the issue was sharply drawn, deny by its power of removal but which it did not extinguish by continuous policy.

Relative to the mass of accusation and rumor, investigations were exceptional, but perhaps no more frequent than the character of the written evidence merited. The department seems to have worked out no regular technique for handling the charges, directed against

charges, with occasional analyses or suggestions added. A less desirable practice was that of allowing candidates to withdraw their appointment papers, often after failing to be appointed or just previous to a new administration. Some items of interest to the historian and not irrelevant to the needs of administration doubtless were lost because of this practice.

22 Carl Schurz to Potts, November 14, 1878, Interior Letters of Appointment, XXV (Pt. 1), 74; memorandum by Rutherford B. Hayes, n.d. (ca. October 20, 1877), with Oliver A. Patton to Hayes, May 27, 1877, Appointment File 138; W. P. Dewey to Delano, November 25, 1873, ibid. 139.
23 Samuel C. Wingard to George H. Williams, July 31, 1874, enclosed in Williams to Delano, August 17, 1874, Appointment File 142.
24 Frank W. Angel to Schurz, August 24, 1878, ibid. 137. Official corruption was involved in the death of a British subject. M. R. Leverson to Hayes, March 16, 1878, ibid.
25 Newspaper clipping, n.p., n.d., in Angel to Schurz, October 3, 1878, testimony, 4, ibid. Like Angel, a Treasury agent sent at the request of the secretary of the interior to investigate the secretary's office in Montana found that resident federal officers impeded his efforts. Copy, H. A. Moore to William Windom, September 18, 1889, enclosed in Windom to John W. Noble, September 24, 1889, ibid. 354.

nearly all officials, which arrived in large numbers. To accept written charges without question was manifestly unfair; too often they were malicious and "supported only by hearsay evidence and general statements." [26] A special investigator was likely to undermine confidence in an innocent officer or, in any case, to stimulate intrigue. Distances and the lack of mileage funds made it impossible to summon officers to Washington for personal interview, which in at least one case the department desired to arrange.[27] In the ordinary case there was no investigation of any kind, and displacement followed on the informal but accumulated petitioning of local political enemies and eastern place-seekers.

Leaves of absence, as before 1873, were subjects of a considerable body of correspondence. The department prescribed procedure in some detail, normally allowing leaves for sixty-day intervals.[28] Secretary Delano gave warning that absence without permission would be equivalent to a tender of resignation,[29] but administration of the law does not seem to have become more effective. There were apparently fewer cases of unauthorized absence, perhaps owing to the wider use of the telegraph. When permission came almost without explanation or question, it was as easy to telegraph ahead as to break the rules.[30] Permission was often a political favor, following on a congressman's endorsement.[31] The department accepted fairly perfunctory explanations except when there were definite reasons for an officer's presence in the territory; at times it would appear that the burden of proof rested on the department rather than on the officer.

The residue of territorial business in the Department of the Interior ordinarily, though not invariably, passed through the Patents

[26] Referring to charges against Governor Elisha P. Ferry of Washington. A. Bell to Schurz, May 23, 1878, *ibid.*, 138.

[27] The case of the secretaryship of Montana, *supra*, Note 25. Noble to A. C. Matthews, June 13, 1889, Miscellaneous Letter Book, XXX, 67–68.

[28] Henry M. Teller to W. B. Allison, December 20, 1882, "Appointment Letter Book," XXXII (Pt. 3), 87–88.

[29] December 19, 1873. Moses K. Armstrong, *The Early Empire Builders of the Great West*, p. 270. Cf. circulars of November 25, 1878 and June 11, 1883, Schurz to secretaries of Territories, "Orders and Circulars" (Department of the Interior), pp. 25–26; Teller to each Governor and Secretary, *ibid.*, pp. 93–94.

[30] Even telegraphed notice that written explanation would follow was sufficient on occasion. William G. Ritch to Samuel J. Kirkwood, March 10, 1881, Appointment File 171. Teller and Lamar permitted leaves for short periods fixed by the officers and reported as taken. Teller to John W. Hoyt, May 29, 1882, Appointment Letter Book, XXXI (Pt. 2), 173; Lucius Q. C. Lamar to C. M. Zulick, February 7, 1887, *ibid.*, XLI (Pt. 1), 145.

[31] Often abrupt, without explanation. E.g., W. B. Allison to Teller, September 24, 1883, Appointment File 166.

and Miscellaneous Division. It included substantially the business of the territorial bureau of the Department of State, less leaves of absence and charges against officers, plus the special machinery applied to Utah, and a limited supervision of public buildings.[32] The division was occupied with a variety of other affairs,[33] and did not develop a specialized branch for handling territorial relations. A considerable volume of general business went to the Appointments Division, without apparent logic.[34]

The outworn routine of formal reports went on much as before 1873, probably attracting little more attention in official circles. The required copies of executive proceedings were addressed to the president, according to the letter of the law; [35] he customarily referred them to the secretary of the interior. Probably no one read them either at the White House or at the department; the territorial secretaries failed to write them for periods as long as two years,[36] and occasionally the White House failed to forward them.[37] Archival practice was lax, nor was it to be expected that it could be above criticism. The law required the secretary of a territory to send the copies of executive proceedings, but his office had grown apart from the governor's, and territorial business had reached a point where transcription itself was a large burden.[38] The department insisted on "full and literal compliance with the law" when the question was raised: Secretary Lamar held that " 'official correspondence' . . . would include all official letters received as well as all official letters

[32] The Cockrell Committee's report (1888) gives a convenient outline. *Senate Reports* (50 Cong., 1 Sess.), No. 507 (Pt. 3), pp. 31, 32.

[33] *Ibid.*, 31–34.

[34] Note the large number of references in this chapter to the Appointment Files.

[35] *Supra*, p. 10, note 37.

[36] W. L. Joslyn to Hiram M. Van Arman, April 28, 1884, Miscellaneous Letter Book, XXI, 94–95.

[37] The Montana executive proceedings for the six months ending December 31, 1880, for instance, remained in the presidential file. Hayes Papers (Hayes Memorial Library, Fremont, Ohio).

[38] Secretary Murphy of Arizona said that the law had been "considered obsolete in that the offices of Governor and Secretary are entirely distinct and the Secretary has no hand in nor authority over the Correspondence of the Governor nor the possession thereof."
He continued, "I believe that the Statutes originally contemplated that the Secretary of a Territory should also act as Secretary of the Governor but such practice . . . has long since ceased and the offices are separately conducted—The Governor having a Private Secretary to do his work; besides no provision exists for the transcribing. . . . I am informed that my predecessor asked the copies to be furnished by the Governor . . . and the Governor gave him a meagre part of the correspondence." Nathan O. Murphy to G. Chandler, February 16, 1891, Miscellaneous File 253.

sent." [39] In practice compliance tended to be scanty and irregular. Governor Hoyt of Wyoming wrote that the law was "practically inoperative." "With this provision," he complained, "there appears never to have been a compliance on the part of any Secretary of this Territory . . . [or] in the other Territories. . . . [In] this office copies of all the official correspondence . . . have [not] even been preserved." [40]

Copies of territorial laws arrived only irregularly before 1876, whenever secretaries chose to include them in the executive proceedings or to send printed copies for particular purposes. In 1876 Secretary Chandler asked for full copies of all laws passed since territorial organization, with copies of future laws as they should appear.[41] Even then secretaries were not always prompt in sending the copies,[42] and there is no evidence that the department gave them even routine examination as they did appear. Usually the copies went immediately to the Law Library.[43]

Annual reports became fuller, covering a wide range of descriptive material, but also more formularized, after 1878. Hitherto prospective settlers had had no uniform and official source of information on all the territories: they used instead railroad advertisements, tracts of local immigration bureaus and societies, and writings of territorial officers. A letter which Governor John L. Pennington wrote minimizing the effects of the Dakota grasshopper plague was widely circulated and was said to be "the means of dispelling much of the false impression of general devastation." [44] Officers were expected to write favorably of the territories for publication and frequently did so. Contrary sentiments might be grounds for a campaign for removal. The secretary of state, having no direct concern with land sales or natural resources, had not asked for economic data; Secretary Seward told the governor of Colorado that while an account of resources would be very useful for ministers and consuls, no funds were available for preparation and publication.[45] Secretary of the Interior Schurz, however, in 1878 asked the governors for statements including accounts of natural resources, soil, climate and population, educational and other institutions, the legislative assembly, and

[39] Lamar to Gilbert A. Pierce, April 1, 1886, Miscellaneous Letter Book, XXV, 11–12.
[40] Hoyt to Hayes, July 24, 1878, Miscellaneous File 221.
[41] Zachariah Chandler to Ritch and others, February 25, 1876, Miscellaneous Letter Book, IX, 238–39.
[42] Teller to Benjamin Harrison, April 19, 1884, ibid., XX, 75.
[43] E.g., endorsement, May 16, 1882, on Elliott S. N. Morgan to Arthur, May 4, 1882 (received May 16), Miscellaneous File 221.
[44] Yankton Press and Dakotian, August 20, 1874.
[45] Seward to John Evans, October 21, 1862, Domestic Letters, LVII, 379.

Indian tribes.[46] Publication of the annual reports of governors, as thus specified, met with public favor, and the department continued the practice.[47] Later instructions to the governors stressed information for "those who contemplate establishing homes" and specified the desired treatment of particular phases of economic opportunity.[48]

Annual reports after publication began in 1878 were increasingly nonpolitical. The governor became the director of an annual census.[49] At times he borrowed material verbatim from territorial immigration pamphlets;[50] more often his report itself became a prospectus for settlers. Governor Warren of Wyoming wrote that "the printed copies of the Annual Reports . . . have constituted the only available means . . . of furnishing . . . reliable information, sought for by those who intend making Wyoming their future home, or making it a point for the investment of capital."[51] The Government Printing Office sent thousands of copies to the territories for distribution over the country. "They are in great demand," said the Dayton (Washington) *Columbia Chronicle,* "as they are official . . . and are thereby much more to be depended upon by the intending immigrant, than are railroad advertisements or Immigration documents."[52] The Northern Pacific Railroad published a special edition of a report of Governor Squire of Washington;[53] territorial legislatures paid for editions larger than allowed by the department.[54]

As the annual report became a report to the public on economic resources, material of a confidential or controversial nature tended to turn into less formal channels. The published report was largely

[46] Also "suggestions . . . looking to an improvement in Territorial management, the promotion of the public welfare, or to an increase of immigration to the Territory." Schurz to Samuel B. Axtell, August 9, 1878, Miscellaneous Letter Book, XII, 357–58.

[47] Bell to Frémont, August 28, 1879, *ibid.,* XIV, 53.

[48] Bell to William A. Newell, September 19, 1881, *ibid.,* XVII, 23–25. From 1887 fifteen topics were specified. Lamar to A. P. Swineford, August 11, 1887, *ibid.,* XXVI, 483–84.

[49] Governor Squire of Washington used seven elaborate questionnaire blanks. Watson C. Squire to Teller, October 6, 1884, Miscellaneous File 216.

[50] Cf. *Report of the Acting Governor of Arizona* (Washington, 1881), pp. 10–20, with Patrick Hamilton, comp., *The Resources of Arizona: . . . A Manual of Reliable Information . . .* Under authority of the Legislature (Prescott, 1881), pp. 81–94.

[51] Francis E. Warren to Lamar, n.d. (received December 14, 1885), Miscellaneous File 221. Cf. W. G. Morris to Thomas H. Brents, January 27, 1880, Appointment File 168.

[52] January 14, 1884.

[53] Watson C. Squire, Dictation [*ca.* 1890], pp. 18–19.

[54] E.g., Warren to Lamar, August 13, 1886, Miscellaneous File 221.

formularized and non-current.[55] The governor described political problems more freely by writing informal letters at irregular intervals, as the events demanded. Improved communications made it possible to keep in close touch with the department during the course of unusual happenings; [56] as the telegraph and long-range post developed, recapitulation suffered the same decline in official as in private correspondence.

Knowledge of events in the territories became more detailed and immediate, but there was little advance toward closer general control over territorial government. The department might keep in close touch with governors in emergencies; it gave out instructions infrequently and at times with reluctance. As under the Department of State, there were no general instructions on the duties of office.[57] The usual reply to requests for advice was reference to the *Revised Statutes*. When an officer acted within his statutory powers, the department usually refrained quite positively from interfering in his decisions.[58]

Officers were accustomed to freedom from guidance, and sometimes resented what guidance there was. Governor Edward G. Ross of New Mexico, whose appointment was a tardy reward for his vote in President Johnson's impeachment trial, was a nonconformist still after his years of political exile. He regarded Secretary Vilas' disagreement with his views in a matter of assigning office space as "a public rebuke," "discouragement to active friends of the administration," and an act to "redound to the advantage of its enemies." [59] The governor of Washington, William A. Newell, signed a bill to give postage money to legislators despite specific advance notice (which appears to have been unique) that it was illegal.[60]

[55] Governor Warren of Wyoming referred to the current part of his report as covering 13 out of more than 175 pages. Warren to Lamar, n.d. (received December 4, 1885), *ibid.*

[56] Governor Wallace sent an especially large and full series of telegraphic despatches relative to civil disorders in New Mexico, including a telegram of 1605 words. Lew Wallace to Schurz, October 5, 1878, Appointment File 140; Miscellaneous File 275, *passim.*

[57] Upon the removal of Governor Axtell of New Mexico, Schurz asked that General Wallace, his successor, come to Washington first to receive information "so as to be well posted and to avoid mistakes in the beginning." Schurz to Hayes, August 31, 1878, Hayes Papers.

[58] Thus when the attorney-general upheld the powers of the governor of Dakota, Secretary Delano wrote, "My past correspondence with you is not to be considered as indicating your official duty in future. That must be dictated by your own Judement [sic]." Oscar A. Whitney to Delano, January 10, 1874, Appointment File 139.

[59] William F. Vilas to Ross, August 15, 1888, Miscellaneous Letter Book, XXVIII, 482–83. Cf. Giddings to Delano, August 23, 1873, Miscellaneous File 275.

[60] Kirkwood to Newell, October 17, 1881, Miscellaneous Letter Book, XVII, 76; Nicholas H. Owings to Teller, February 7, 1884, Appointment File 168.

The department could exercise a stronger authority, and did so in occasional emergencies. It demanded an immediate investigation and report relative to border riots in Washington Territory in 1884,[61] and gave vigorous counsel and support during the anti-Chinese riots in Washington in 1885 [62] and the "White Caps" disorders in New Mexico in 1890. Yet the general principle was that territorial authorities should be left to work out practical details and to make all possible use of local resources. Governor Prince of New Mexico was told: "You will be supported, but you must go to the full length of your ability and territorial force first." [63]

Seldom offering advice, the department was even less frequently a channel for advice from the attorney-general. Only seven opinions relating to territorial matters are included in the printed digests.[64] Ordinarily the attorney-general avoided intra-territorial questions entirely, as questions "of purely local concern, in which the General Government is not interested and over which its Departments have no jurisdiction or control." [65]

Relations with the War Department with respect to the territories were sporadic, depending chiefly on emergencies requiring use of troops. Territorial laws could be considered as laws of the United States in that the president might call out the Army to assure their enforcement.[66] At times the War Department made loans of supplies not otherwise available to territorial authorities.[67] Direct cooperation of territorial officers and commanders in the field continued.[68]

Financial matters occasioned some departmental correspondence with the Treasury Department, though the Department of the Interior in general lacked responsibility and avoided intervention. The Interior had no information on the expenditure of territorial funds,[69]

---

[61] Teller to Newell, May 9, 1884, Miscellaneous Letter Book, XXI, 122.

[62] Lamar to Squire, November 5, 1885, and *passim*. Miscellaneous File 216.

[63] Noble to L. B. Prince, August 18, 1890, Miscellaneous Letter Book, XXXII, 275; Noble to Prince, August 19, 1890, *ibid.*, 277; and *passim*.

[64] As before 1873, most of these related to the powers of territorial legislatures. *Official Opinions of the Attorneys-General*, XIV (October 8, 1874), 462; XVI (August 2, 1878), 114; XVI (May 13, 1880), 678; XVIII (February 8, 1887), 540–42; XIX (March 16, 1887), 260–61; XIX (May 29, 1889), 319–24; XIX (June 19, 1889), 335–41; XIX (April 8, 1890), 530–33.

[65] Relative to the power of a governor to canvass a vote. George H. Williams to B. R. Cowen, October 8, 1874, Miscellaneous File 206.

[66] *Congressional Record* (47 Cong., 1 Sess.), pp. 3457–58.

[67] Functions such as road-building, while sometimes recommended by officers and delegates, were carried on quite independently of the civil territorial administration.

[68] It frequently led to testimony by the military relative to reappointments. E.g., O. O. Howard to Schurz, January 27, 1880, Appointment File 168 (under Ferry).

[69] Schurz to George Ainslie, January 20, 1880, Miscellaneous Letter Book, XIV 271–72.

and no funds of its own available for travel expenses, postage,[70] or telegraphic charges [71] involved in its relations with officials. Cases of official corruption, where malfeasance in handling funds might justify removal, gave rise to some interdepartmental correspondence and coöperative action. Likewise the Treasury had to inquire for dates of appointments and leaves.[72] The Interior's supervision over public buildings occasioned a nice and cautious demarcation of jurisdiction rather than coöperation or conflict.[73] Altogether such relations were chiefly incidental and disconnected with established policies.

The department's communications with Congress consisted chiefly of recommendations for legislation suggested by territorial officials. Ordinarily the department made no inquiry on the receipt of such suggestions and no comment in forwarding them to Congress, but occasionally it did both.[74] On the whole it made no continuous attempt to guide congressional legislation for the territories. Beginning in 1886, it required "that the copies of the session laws of all the territories be transmitted to Congress through this Department." [75] This new mode of transmission did not indicate a desire to control all territorial relations. Rather it was the means of ascertaining, simply for the information of the public, what territorial laws had been approved by Congress.[76]

Aside from appointments, there was little reference to the president in the course of ordinary territorial affairs. After 1874 Congress required presidential approval for the calling of extraordinary legislative sessions in Washington, Idaho, and Montana,[77] but such approval was a formality. Despite the wording of the law the secretary of the interior administered leaves of absence by custom. The president took interest in occasional episodes in territorial politics, but

70 Cowen to Ritch, September 16, 1874, *ibid.*, VIII, 310.

71 Teller to Gilbert A. Pierce, February 3, 1885, *ibid.*, XXII, 435.

72 As before 1873, notification was not always automatic. The first intimation of an appointment might come as a request for salary. W. Lawrence to Schurz, November 18, 1880, Appointment File 168 (under Newell).

73 *Infra*, p. 42.

74 Cowen to James G. Blaine, January 13, 1875, Miscellaneous Letter Book, VIII, 417–18; Bell to Wallace, September 24, 1879, *ibid.*, XIV, 88–89.

75 Lamar to secretary of Arizona and others, January 30, 1886, *ibid.*, XXIV, 380–81.

76 A New York investment firm, inquiring whether a territorial bond issue had been submitted to Congress, had been told that it was "not officially known to this Department." Lamar to Kountze Brothers, March 18, 1885, *ibid.*, XXIII, 98.

77 Act of June 22, 1874, *Statutes*, XVIII, 135. The secretary of the interior submitted the matter to the president with a recommendation. E.g., Kirkwood to Hoyt, April 13, 1882, Appointment Letters, XXXI, 415.

expressed his opinions through departmental channels; [78] generally he left decisions to the secretary. Cleveland apparently began the regular practice of asking departmental advice on bills affecting the territories.[79]

The secretary of the interior, after 1873, was concerned with territorial control above all other responsible officers in Washington. He had more authority over territorial officers than the secretary of state had exercised before him. His other administrative concerns had at least geographical extent in common with the territorial jurisdictions. Yet no secretary attempted to consolidate his territorial responsibilities in a large and systematic way, or to exercise strong and continuous control through the existing administrative structure.

The men who served as secretaries from 1873 to 1890 can be classed, so far as the West was concerned, chiefly as machine politicians or as conservationists. Neither type of man shared completely the western point of view. Men like Columbus Delano and Zachariah Chandler showed interest in the territories as a field for patronage. Schurz and Lamar, both conservationists, approached the West more as an administrative than as a political and constitutional problem. Carl Schurz, who had not sought the secretaryship, probably was more actively concerned with the territories [80] than any other secretary, but the territories were subordinate in his attention to other phases of the departmental duties. Lamar in his sincere desire to establish home rule discovered that the reform of appointing resident officers was not quite compatible with the reform of conservation.[81] Of the eleven secretaries during this period, only one, Henry Moore Teller, had lived under territorial organization, and though Teller could criticize the system,[82] he did not attempt to change it. Since the system pretended to do so little, perhaps it was not of much importance that he made no such attempt.

[78] E.g., Schurz to Wallace, November 23, 1878, Miscellaneous Letter Book, XIII, 29.

[79] E.g., Lamar to Grover Cleveland, ibid., XXV, 282.

[80] "As to the territories, Mr. Hayes's Secretary of the Interior was to all intents and purposes President of the United States," A. H. Swan to Arthur, n.d. (received April 11, 1882), Appointment File 169.

[81] Infra, pp. 77–78. William Andrew Jackson Sparks was not the first reformer in the department to draw frontier criticism. Schurz's prosecutions for removal of timber from public lands were highly unpopular. Elmer Ellis, Henry Moore Teller, 97–98.

[82] As senator. Cong. Rec. (49 Cong., 1 Sess.), p. 3258.

Chapter IV

TERRITORIAL FINANCES

THE national subsidy to territorial government far exceeded the amount which Great Britain had paid (not counting wars of colonial origin) for the government of the thirteen colonies. It covered, in the main, all expenses of offices and organs established directly under the organic acts. These expenses included salaries of officers appointed by the president, the constituent expenses of legislatures,[1] and expenses of supreme and district courts and of the executive offices. They did not include expenses of local political units, or costs incidental to territorial legislation. The total sums appropriated by Congress varied in practice only slightly from year to year, although legally they were as subject to change as any other appropriation.

Estimates for appropriations were made up in first form by the territorial secretaries, revised and approved by the first comptroller of the treasury, and forwarded to the appropriation committees of Congress by the secretary of the treasury.[2] The treasury required that estimates "be made in detail, with such explanations as will enable Congress to intelligently decide upon the propriety of granting them." [3] In practice the territorial secretary's estimates varied greatly in length and detail, from a single figure to a very lengthy itemization; his influence over appropriations was slight. Salaries of governors, secretaries, and judges did not form a regular part of estimates, for they were fixed by law and sometimes omitted for that reason.[4] Judicial expenses were computed together with expenses for United States courts.[5] The territorial secretary's concern was chiefly with

[1] Payment of legislators by the United States began with Orleans in 1804–5 but did not become regular until Florida was organized in 1822. Farrand, *Legislation of Congress*, pp. 22, 51, note 29.

[2] The law establishing procedure did not mention the comptroller. Act of August 29, 1842, *Statutes*, V, 541. The occasion was a series of difficulties in Wisconsin and Florida. Charles Henry Meyerholz, "Federal Supervision over the Territories of the United States," *Beitrage zur Kultur- und Universalgeschichte* (Leipzig), VI (1908), 212.

[3] W. A. Richardson to Herman Glafcke, September 20, 1870, Treasury GS7–98.

[4] E.g., Cochran to Fessenden, November 29, 1864, Treasury Miscellaneous File 101-I.

[5] *Infra*, p. 52.

28

legislative compensation and mileage and with the contingent expenses of the governor; [6] even within these limits, there was little probability that his recommendations would stand. The first comptroller was free to increase or delete items; more usually he lowered them. In revision he usually followed the standard rates established by Congress for items such as printing and mileage and the per diem of legislators; [7] but in the 1880's he recommended increases of such rates or entirely new items as the need occurred, as for the printing of a territorial code.[8] When the secretary was delinquent, the comptroller submitted his own figures.[9] In all cases, he added the estimates for salaries, with which the territorial secretary had no direct concern.

Disbursements followed roughly similar channels. Governors, secretaries, and judges received their salaries from Washington, without the interposition of a disbursing officer. To compute the exact amounts due, the first comptroller required reports on leaves of absence from the officers themselves,[10] in addition to the information he received from the secretary of state or secretary of the interior. Legislative funds went through the hands of the territorial secretaries, who had to give bond and follow the usual regulations governing disbursing agents. Similarly, governors were accountable for the contingent expenses of their offices. No funds could be paid out in the absence of the proper bonded officer, a necessary and usual requirement which did not prevent fraud and was the occasion of some inconvenience.[11]

Funds for contingent and legislative accounts were transferred usually by treasury warrant following requisition of the disbursing officer. When appropriations or drafts were delayed, as happened

[6] Contingent expenses included only those incurred by the governor; the incidental expenses of the secretary's office were considered part of legislative expenses. Richardson to Glafcke, September 20, 1870, Treasury GS7–98.

[7] A limit of $2,500 was placed on printing by Act of June 19, 1878, *Statutes*, XX, 193. Previously he had examined specimens of territorial printing and determined rates on the basis of departmental standards. Tayler to John Sherman, January 29, 1878, Treasury Miscellaneous 102-I.

[8] J. Tarbell to McCulloch, December 3, 1884, First Comptroller Correspondence (Treasury Department).

[9] E.g., endorsement on Cochran to Fessenden, November 29, 1864, Treasury Miscellaneous 101-I.

[10] According to Treasury circular of June 24, 1853. Elwood Evans to Tayler, June 4, 1863, Secretary's Letter Book (University of Washington).

[11] Considerable distress followed on the failure of an officer to give bond. A. H. Barret to McCullough [McCulloch], August 31, 1866, TP, Montana, I, 92–93. When Secretary Daniels of Idaho resigned in 1864, Governor Lyons appointed an acting secretary whom the Treasury did not recognize or permit to disburse public moneys. Tayler to Boutwell, March 4, 1872, First Comptroller Correspondence.

occasionally, either vouchers circulated at discount (40–50% in Idaho, 1864) [12] or the secretary contracted debts at high interest rates (up to 30% in Idaho, 1866).[13] To make funds more accessible, the Treasury Department might instruct the collector of internal revenue to cash drafts.[14] Yet the necessity and inconvenience of paying discounts on vouchers continued until as late as 1884 in Arizona.[15]

Supervision over the process of disbursement was slight. Cheques issued by disbursing officers circulated as long as a year before being presented for payment,[16] and an officer might be several years delinquent in sending in his accounts.[17] The government protected itself by the ordinary departmental practice of disallowing amounts paid by an officer "in excess of what it was thought should have been paid, and the amount he had been authorized to pay," and by calling on him and his sureties.[18] Yet in 1885, $124,372.72 was still due from forty governors and secretaries for the period 1860–84, in sums ranging from $114 to $35,550.[19] The latter sum was due from Horace C. Gilson, secretary of Idaho, who departed with the legislative funds in 1866, and, according to a delegate, "seems to have been of a very selfish nature." [20]

There could be a much closer supervision over the requisition of funds before disbursement. The cases which most obviously required action were requisitions beyond total appropriations, beyond the sum of the disbursing agent's bond, or for purposes unauthorized by Congress. From the need to keep disbursements within appropriations, there ensued a concern with the nature of expenditures themselves. In his jurisdiction over disbursements for legislative expenses, for instance, the comptroller might give advice on the legal-

12 Caleb Lyon to Seward, August 10, 1864, TP, Idaho, I, 3–5. For a time legislators in Wyoming received certificates which were discounted at banks well before regular payments could be made. Affidavit, Francis E. Warren, December 22, 1876, Interior Appointment File 142. It was not customary to allow charges for exchange. Durham to Daniel Manning, June 10, 1886, First Comptroller Correspondence.

13 David W. Ballard to Johnson, July 25, 1866, TP, Idaho, I, 54–56.

14 McCulloch to John Cummings, December 28, 1866, Treasury Xa3 series (Treasury Department), 308. On occasion the disbursing officer might be authorized to keep funds on hand. F. Wolcott to Richardson, May 17, 1874, Judiciary Correspondence (Treasury Department).

15 There was no United States depositary in the territory. Van Arman to Lawrence, February 23, 1884, First Comptroller Correspondence.

16 Weekly New Mexican (Santa Fé), April 1, 1873.

17 Copy, Lawrence to C. J. Folger, March 23, 1882 [1883]; Ritch to Teller, April 12, 1883; Lawrence to Teller, May 4, 1883, Interior Appointment File 171.

18 Durham to W. E. Smith, December 23, 1885, First Comptroller Correspondence.

19 Statements by W. P. Titcomb, certified November 24, 1884, February 11, 1885, February 28, 1885. Executive Correspondence, Solicitor (Treasury Department).

20 Hailey, op. cit., III, 167.

ity and wisdom of an extra legislative session,[21] require legislators to take an oath of allegiance to the government,[22] apportion mileage and per diem among contestants,[23] and withhold funds entirely from a legislature improperly organized.[24]

Legislative printing also occasioned close supervision. To keep such expenses within appropriations, the comptroller gave detailed instructions to secretaries upon their appointment [25] and from time to time afterward. He claimed "the right to . . . regulate the price and quantity of the Territorial printing," and to exclude "documents having no necessary connection with the duties of legislation or the dissemination of useful information." [26] He might refuse to allow publication of laws in Spanish,[27] direct that publication of laws be deferred,[28] or limit the per diem of legislators in order to leave funds to cover extraordinary printing expenses.[29] When a territorial secretary proceeded in violation of instructions, the comptroller disallowed the printing contracts.[30]

This careful surveillance over printing was not mere bureaucratic officiousness. No other charge against the national government was so attractive and accessible a temptation to underpaid and ambitious federal officers. Clear cases of printers who paid in money for their contracts were exceptional,[31] but secretaries generally awarded contracts to newspapers expected to advance their party or personal political interests. A delegate from Washington wrote:

> The public printing has always formed the basis for publication of a large, widely circulated and pecuniarily unprofitable party paper . . . , which has largely influenced the politics of the Territory. We cannot hold the Territory if the patronage of the administration is turned against our party.[32]

[21] Nye to Seward, July 20, 1861, TP, Nevada, I, 12–13; *Rocky Mountain News*, May 10, 1862.

[22] McCulloch to Howlett, December 29, 1866, Treasury Xa3, 308.

[23] Copy, Tayler to Hand, February 14, 1877, enclosed in A. G. Porter to Sherman, January 2, 1879, First Comptroller Correspondence.

[24] Copy, Durham to Morgan, October 21, 1885, enclosed in Morgan to Lamar, November 3, 1885, Interior Miscellaneous File 221.

[25] Weld to Seward, March 12, 1862, TP, Colorado, I, 45.

[26] House Proceedings, Colorado Legislature, 2 Sess., July 22, 1862, in *Rocky Mountain News*, July 24, 1862.

[27] Governor's Message in *Rocky Mountain News*, February 10, 1864.

[28] James Mills to Kirkwood, April 12, 1881, Interior Miscellaneous File 206.

[29] Nicholas H. Owings to Tarbell, December 1, 1877, enclosed in Tayler to Sherman, January 8, 1878, First Comptroller Correspondence.

[30] *Senate Reports*, 48 Cong., 1 Sess., no. 355, pp. 2–3.

[31] A clear case involved Secretary John J. Gosper of Arizona, who overcharged the government for printing done by a firm in which he held an interest, splitting the difference. Report, T. Robinson to Sherman, October 17, 1880, First Comptroller Correspondence.

[32] Selucius Garfielde to Fish, August 5, 1871, enclosed in Fish to Delano, September 16, 1875, Interior Appointment File 142.

According to a former secretary of Idaho, "the Secretary holds more power in his hand than the Governor under the Organic Acct [sic] . . . *In wielding the public printing.* He can make and unmake men at pleasure." [33] It was an unusual newspaper that could boast, as did the Helena *Independent,* of "paying expenses, in spite of the fact that it has neither Territorial nor Federal patronage, and went through the *last* campaign without getting a dollar from the candidates." [34] A secretary might even subsidize the press to abuse rival federal officers in his own interest.[35] Of political motives the treasury took little notice, leaving such matters to the Department of State or Department of the Interior, but it watched the line between political and monetary rebates, and held down the amounts of the subsidies in any case.

On the side of the legislature, the treasury had to guard against attempts to divert the printing appropriation to purposes not intended by Congress. The Dakota legislature ordered reports of the committees on agriculture and minerals and railroads in editions of 1,500 to 4,000 copies, hoping thus to advertise the territory at national expense.[36] To escape the cost of printing a code, the Washington legislature simply reënacted all general laws with only verbal changes.[37] During the fifties and sixties at least ten legislatures reached out further over the printing, arrogating to themselves the election of the territorial printer. The Idaho legislature regarded appointment of the printer by the territorial secretary as an "innovation upon the Territorial policy," "an usurpation" on the "right of the Legislative Assembly to appoint or elect its own printer . . . [and to] appropriate money for his compensation out of the money appropriated by Congress." [38] This claim collapsed soon after the treasury indicated that it would support the secretaries' prerogative of appointment and accordingly would pay no funds to the usurpers.[39] The legislatures had no inclination to assume the charges as

[33] William B. Daniels to Seward, November 22, 1865, State Appointments File.

[34] A. M. Woolfolk to Martin Maginnis, January 12, 1885, Maginnis Papers (Montana State Historical Society).

[35] Santa Fé *Weekly Gazette,* November 18, December 9, 1865.

[36] 1867–69. Herbert S. Schell, "Official Immigration Activities of Dakota Territory," *North Dakota Historical Quarterly,* VII (1932), 6.

[37] This attempt failed through Governor Flanders' vetoes. Arthur S. Beardsley, "Compiling the Territorial Codes of Washington," *Pacific Northwest Quarterly,* XXVIII (1937), 17–19.

[38] *Report of the House Committee on Territorial Affairs, to Whom was Referred Council Bill No. 29,* 3 Sess., n.p., n.d., enclosed in Lyon to McCulloch, January 27, 1866, Treasury Miscellaneous 101-I.

[39] Santa Fé *Gazette,* July 19, 1862, December 27, 1862; *Rocky Mountain News,* September 18, 1861.

the price of autonomy.[40] In later years attempts to transfer the burden of extra printing to the national government fell off, and the territories paid for such work as large editions of the governors' reports.[41]

The treasury's relations with territorial officers in their capacity as disbursing agents were often the source of a larger supervision over their conduct of territorial affairs; in this way the treasury shared some of the general concerns of the state and interior departments. So routine a matter as the territorial printing could be the occasion of advice to the governor on relevant pending legislation, or, beyond that, of practical nullification of territorial law.[42] When a disbursing officer was suspected of financial misconduct, it was natural that the treasury should share the task of personnel supervision with the other departments: the line between investigating an officer's accounts and deciding him culpable enough for dismissal was never quite clear, and the secretaries of state and of the interior had no great disposition to guard their own jurisdictions. Territorial officers very easily came to address the secretary of the treasury on subjects of a broad jurisdiction, ignoring the narrow source of his powers. Statement of the dates of leaves of absence became explanation of reasons for the leaves.[43] Submission of printing specimens for approval became regular transmission of public documents.[44] Many territorial officers had only vague ideas of how territorial control operated, and many others were prone to write long complaints and appeals which took them beyond whatever ideas of jurisdiction they had.[45]

The possibilities and the diffusion of supervision under the Treasury exceeded, on the whole, its effectiveness within its proper and necessary jurisdiction. No other department was as strict in ordering

[40] House Proceedings, Colorado Territory, 2 Sess., July 22, 1862, in *Rocky Mountain News*, July 24, 1862.

[41] *Supra*, p. 23.

[42] Governor Lyon refused to sign the Idaho territorial printer's bill of 1866, "knowing no better means of settling this question than its reference to the Treasury Department." Copy, Lyon to Council, January 11, 1866, enclosed in Lyon to McCulloch, January 27, 1866, Treasury Miscellaneous 101-I. The New Mexico law of December 14, 1857, apparently was in force until 1862, when the Treasury gave notice that it was void. Santa Fé *Gazette*, July 19, 1862, December 27, 1862.

[43] Evans to Tayler, June 4, 1863, Washington Secretary's Letter Book.

[44] Chase to Elbert, June 11, 1862, Treasury GS: 22.

[45] Territorial officers thrust at least as many concerns on the treasury as it drew to itself. In Utah, 1870, Secretary Black appealed to the treasury to instruct Governor Vernon H. Vaughan, the former secretary, to turn over the office to him. Both the secretary of the treasury and the secretary of state instructed Vaughan. George A. Black to Boutwell, November 19, 1870; Vaughan to Fish, December 7, 1870, TP, Utah, II, 721–22.

details. The number of irregularities in accounts, however, indicates failure to enforce honest and businesslike practice. In 1883 the clerk in charge of the territorial desk in the first comptroller's office protested that

> While annual or special examinations are made in . . . other divisions of the Treasury department . . . , the Territorial service, known as the worst conducted of all the branches of the Department, has been . . . almost entirely overlooked. With one minor exception there has been no examination of the Territorial offices within at least the last fifteen years; and . . . there has been no year when an examination has not been needed. These offices have not been conducted on business principles. Political aspirations of the several incumbents, rapid changes in the personnel, and the slow and uncertain process of instruction in their duties of correspondence, may explain the sources of trouble . . . , and demonstrates the necessity for a more intimate supervision of these offices by the Department. To bring about a uniformity in the conduct of the offices . . . , personal instruction should be given by persons cognizant of their affairs in the Department.

Referring to particularly grievous irregularities in four territories, the clerk suggested that "assistance from the Department would be more economical than a suit, and would be more likely to bring about a more satisfactory conclusion." [46] But this arraignment led to no reform in administration. Secretary Folger noted that if a secretary's accounts "are not sustained, they will not be passed. If he has more public money than his salary and acknowledged dues will set-off, his bond can be sued. It seems to me that . . . we have the club in our own hands." [47] Acting Secretary of the Interior New concurred: "I see no necessity for the sending of a committee to Idaho. . . . I believe a settlement can be *enforced* here without that expense." [48] When a special agent of the treasury investigated the secretary's office in Montana six years later, he found accumulated irregularities such that it was difficult to trace even the amount of embezzlement.[49]

The amounts which Congress appropriated for the national government's share of annual territorial expenses probably varied be-

[46] Government property in New Mexico was not listed in the department, and was in such poor condition that Governor Wallace was obliged to have his office furnished by private gifts. Copy, Robinson to Lawrence, August 7, 1883, enclosed in Lawrence to Teller, September 15, 1883, Interior Appointment File 170; Lawrence to French, August 7, 1883, *ibid.*

[47] Endorsement, September 15, 1883, on Lawrence to Teller, September 15, 1883, *ibid.*

[48] Endorsement, September 6, 1883, on Lawrence to Teller, September 7, 1883, *ibid.*

[49] *Helena Journal*, September 18, 1889; copy, H. A. Moore to Windom, September 18, 1889, enclosed in Windom to Noble, September 24, 1889, Interior Appointment File 354.

tween $25,000 and $35,000 for each territory during most of the period 1861–90.[50] They varied principally with the rates of salaries and item allowances as fixed in appropriation bills, always subject to change regardless of the rates mentioned in the organic acts. There was no collective appropriation for all territorial expenses, as there was no united administration of all territorial disbursements. Salaries as designated in the organic acts were as different as the congressional mind was different at the times of territorial organization. Governors were to receive from $2,500 to $3,000, secretaries from $1,500 to $2,000, justices, including chief justices, from $1,800 to $2,500.[51] In 1867, salaries of justices were set at $3,500 for Montana and Idaho and at $2,500 for the other territories.[52] By acts of 1870 and 1873, the prescribed salaries were to be uniformly $3,500, $2,500, and $3,000 for the three offices.[53] From 1875 to 1880, however, governors actually received $2,600 and secretaries $1,800, and from 1878 to 1880, judges $2,600.[54]

Uncertainties in amounts of salaries were occasional and technical grievances;[55] insufficiency was a constant complaint. Governor

[50] Amounts can be derived partly from figures in the *Annual Report* of the secretary of the treasury. Judicial accounts present special difficulties (*infra*, p. 52), as do values and uses of public buildings.

[51] Territory	Governor	Secretary	Judges
New Mexico	$2,500	$1,800	$1,800
Utah	2,500	1,800	1,800
Washington	3,000	1,500	2,000
Nebraska	2,500	2,000	2,000
Colorado	2,500	1,800	1,800
Nevada	2,500	1,800	1,800
Dakota	2,500	1,800	1,800
Arizona	2,500	1,800	1,800
Idaho	2,500	2,000	2,500
Montana	2,500	2,000	2,500
Wyoming	3,000	1,800	2,500

Salaries for governors include salaries as superintendents of Indian affairs. Acts of September 9, 1850, *Statutes*, IX, 451; *ibid.*, 456–57; March 2, 1853, *ibid.*, X, 177; May 30, 1854, *ibid.*, 282; February 28, 1861, *ibid.*, XII, 175; March 2, 1861, *ibid.*, 213; *ibid.*, 243; February 24, 1863, *ibid.*, 665; March 3, 1863, *ibid.*, 812; May 26, 1864, *ibid.*, XIII, 90; July 25, 1868, *ibid.*, XV, 182.

The Act of July 27, 1854, fixed salaries of judges of Oregon, Washington, Utah, and New Mexico at $2,500, of secretaries of those territories at $2,000, of governors of New Mexico at $3,000. *Ibid.*, X, 311–12. In 1869, Utah judges were to have the same salaries as judges of Idaho and Montana. Act of March 3, 1869, *ibid.*, XV, 313.

[52] Act of March 2, 1867, *ibid.*, XIV, 426–27.

[53] Act of June 17, 1870, *ibid.*, XVI, 152; Act of January 23, 1873, *ibid.*, XVII, 416.

[54] Act of March 3, 1877, *ibid.*, XIX, 308–9; June 19, 1878, *ibid.*, XX, 193–94. From 1880 judges received $3,000. Act of June 15, 1880, *ibid.*, XXI, 225–26.

[55] Officers after 1877, when appropriations fell below the rates of the organic acts or of the Acts of 1870 and 1873, referred indignantly to their "just expecta-

Thomas Moonlight of Wyoming, about to be retired by a new administration, appealed for the sake of his successors that it was "impossible to live here on the salary, however economical one may be. . . . Because others of another faith shall soon take our places makes no difference, the salary is insufficient as appropriated for democrat or republican." Moonlight could not keep a horse on his salary; [56] John C. Frémont, also without a horse as governor of Arizona, could not afford a visit to the Grand Canyon. Out of his salary of $2,600, he paid $90 a month for rent, $40 for a cook.[57] Other office holders increased their incomes by private enterprise, for which the elastic and comparatively light duties of the governorship could be made to make way.[58] Governor Benjamin F. Potts of Montana complained, "the reduction of salary to $2000 makes the position no longer desirable, but as I can attend to my flock of sheep and hold the office—I can make a living out of the two and a little money—" [59] His colleague, Secretary Mills, ran a newspaper.[60] Justice W. W. Peck of Wyoming apparently practised money-lending. He offered to handle loans for ex-President Hayes, noting that "there is no law against usury in the Territory." [61] Lew Wallace, in Santa Fé, found time to write *Ben Hur*. Nearly all tried to retain business connections in the states or to invest in the territories. Governor Thompson of Idaho, attempting to carry on survey and mail contracts in Oregon, could spend little time in Idaho, and had to resign.[62] In such cases low salaries, while fought by territorial spokesmen as well as by office holders, amounted to discrimination against nonresidents. Idaho, wrote Governor Neil, was "almost without a U.S. District Attorney for several years past. . . . Experience has shown that the appointment of persons from without the territory, to the office referred to,

tions" of "the legal salary . . . prescribed in the statutes." Hoyt to Schurz, November 20, 1880, *Report of the Secretary of the Interior . . . 1880*, II, 534. The reductions were upheld in U.S. *v.* Fisher, 109 *U.S.* 143 (1883).

[56] Thomas Moonlight to Vilas, December 14, 1888, Interior Appointment File 239.

[57] I. T. Martin, comp., *Recollections of Elizabeth Benton Frémont*, pp. 154, 158. Miss Frémont recalled that his salary was $2,000; actually it was $2,600.

[58] In applying for the governorship, Chief Justice McKean of Utah explained, "The duties of his office are light compared with mine, and the salary considerably larger. While the governor has an important voice in affairs, he can devote most of his attention to his private interests." James B. McKean to Grant, February 21, 1874, Interior Appointment File 138.

[59] Potts to Maginnis, May 18, 1878, Maginnis Papers.

[60] James Hamilton Mills, "Reminiscences of an Editor," *Contributions to the Historical Society of Montana*, V (1904), 267, 273–88.

[61] Peck to Hayes, December 13, 1882, Hayes Papers.

[62] James H. Hawley, *op. cit.*, I, 179, 212; Boise *Idaho Tri Weekly Statesman*, December 18, 1875, cited in Fred Woodward Blase, "Political History of Idaho Territory, 1863–1890," p. 48.

accomplishes but little, as the compensation is insufficient to support the person appointed, the expense of living in this territory being very great." [63]

To establish a private law practice seemed an attractive alternative to carrying on a business at a distance; yet it invited the charge of impropriety.[64] Moreover, the problem of adjusting income to ordinary expenses was not the only one for men from the states. The expense of coming great distances without transportation allowances made the uncertainty and ordinary brevity of tenure peculiarly burdensome.[65] In the meantime, an Easterner had to abandon or neglect interests in his own state.[66]

Long delays in payments were a complaint less frequent than the complaint of insufficiency, but on occasion as grievous. Congress organized Nevada and Dakota without making appropriations for them, and the treasury could only counsel the officers to "draw upon their private resources" until the next session.

It is hardly to be presumed, on general grounds [wrote the First Comptroller] that Congress should bring into existence a creature, and fail to make provision for its sustenance, yet such is nevertheless the case in the present instance. . . . While, to make provision as far, at least, as the salaries of the several officers, are concerned, would . . . [enable] them to proceed at once to the Territory and set about effecting all the preliminary operations of the new governments, I am unable to indicate a mode by which such provision could lawfully be made.

Territorial resources constituted no remedy, for convening the legislature would be illegal.[67] No salaries were paid in Montana for two years after organization.[68] These and more routine delays were all the more annoying because the amounts held up were so small. The non-resident suffered particularly, having no local business or law practice to follow while waiting for his salary.

The pay Congress set for service in the territories was, at the least, low enough to exclude much of the best talent. Those who knew

[63] John B. Neil to Hayes, January 6, 1881, Hayes Papers.
[64] *Infra,* pp. 38, 101–2.
[65] Governor Pennington of Dakota wrote, "The first mistake I made was in accepting the position . . . , and I am left pecuniarily in a very embarrassing condition." He further commented on "losses . . . in coming here, and the increased embarrassment caused by efforts to help build up here, and how [he] had hoped by another term in office to work out and save some thing for [his] family." John L. Pennington to Hayes, April, 1878, Hayes Papers.
[66] Newell to Hayes, March 27, 1880, *ibid.*
[67] Medill to Chase, April 15, 1861, Treasury A.B. LEO series (Treasury Department), LXXII, 18.
[68] Meagher to Johnson, January 20, 1866, Johnson Papers. An Act of 1887 created an additional judgeship for New Mexico, but provided no salary. Durham to Charles S. Fairchild, August 15, 1888, First Comptroller Correspondence.

western costs of living took office with misgivings; those who took and tried to live on their salaries resigned when they could, for better paid if humbler positions. Congress had forbidden the practice of law to territorial as to district judges; [69] Chief Justice Henry L. Waldo of New Mexico resigned to take the territorial attorney-generalship, which would not interfere with his civil practice.[70] Justice E. P. Oliphant of Washington exchanged the bench for a clerk's stool in the General Land Office.[71] Financial grounds loomed by far the largest in letters of resignation.

The men who retained office in these circumstances were suspect of lacking ability or integrity. In Nevada, "the simple acceptance of a judgeship . . . occasion[ed] suspicion of the honor of the incumbent." A salary of $1,800 was preposterous in view of the earnings of a competent mining lawyer. The Nevada judiciary broke down politically if not morally on the Comstock Lode; [72] elsewhere there was no such general collapse, but there was similar suspicion of corruption. Like machines in the states, the territorial political machine which was worst morally might be best mechanically.

Senator William M. Stewart of Nevada, outstanding example of the rich mining lawyer, expressed the popular attitude toward the poorly paid judge:

Think of a judge receiving a salary of $2500 . . . sent out for . . . four years and liable to be removed by the President at any time, with questions involving millions to decide, in a new country where the expense of living is very great, far exceeding his salary! . . . It is very hard to make people believe . . . that it is possible for him to be willing to sacrifice himself in a country like that. . . . There is universal distrust of him.[73]

A Washington Territory newspaper alluded to corresponding salaries in Canada:

[69] Act of December 18, 1812, *Statutes*, II, 788.

[70] *Weekly New Mexican*, April 6, 1878. Cf. Jason B. Brown to Grant, January 5, 1875, Interior Appointment File 142. Secretary Schurz considered it "improper that the Governor of a Territory should practice as an Attorney." Schurz to Hoyt, September 7, 1877, Interior Appointment Letters, XXIV (Pt. 2), 222–23.

[71] James E. Babb, ed., "Judge E. P. Oliphant," *Washington Historical Quarterly*, XI (1920), 259.

[72] Eliot Lord, *Comstock Mining and Miners*, United States Geological Survey Monographs, p. 164. The charges made against the Nevada judges were not without bias, on the part of William M. Stewart and other interested parties. Professor Austin E. Hutcheson of the University of Nevada points out that when sued for libel in 1865, Stewart retracted charges made against Judge John W. North, who had decided cases against Stewart's clients. Letter, Hutcheson to Pomeroy, August 31, 1945.

[73] *Cong. Rec.* (50 Cong., 1 Sess.), p. 6459. Delegate Cavanaugh of Montana, opposing standardization of judicial salaries at $3,000, attributed the high quality of the Montana judiciary to the salary of $3,500, and urged increase to $5,500. *Cong. Globe* (41 Cong., 2 Sess.), pp. 1336–37.

The three Judges of the Supreme Court of Washington Territory, with the judicial affairs of 100,000 people in their hands, get salaries aggregating $7,800 per annum. The five Judges of British Columbia, having jurisdiction over 30,000 white people, and 20,000 Indians, receive $22,670, with not to exceed half the work done . . . on this side.[74]

It was easy to believe of an officer that it was "no object for him to come . . . simply to be governor, because the salary was so much less than he could make elsewhere." [75] It is difficult to deny, now, that the practice of paying low salaries meant a vastly inferior service.

The national treasury was charged also with allowances for executive, judicial, and legislative expenses. In all cases the amounts were relatively fixed. The governors' contingent funds were originally $1,000 annually for each of the territories except Utah and Washington, where they were $1,500; in 1876 the amount fell to $500.[76] Fees and costs of court procedure were uniform in rates with those in United States courts. The Treasury bore all expenses of supreme and district courts; [77] the territories paid their own attorneys-general and marshals, and for penal custody under territorial law.

Legislators, by the organic acts, were to receive three or four dollars a day, with mileages of three or four dollars per twenty miles going and returning; [78] presiding officers received twice the normal per diem allowances after 1863. In 1873, when Congress raised salaries generally, it raised the per diem of members to six dollars and of the two presiding officers to ten.[79] This increase in rates, however, was coupled with a forty-day limit to sessions, so that no increase in appropriations was necessary.[80] Five years later the per diem of members fell to four dollars, of presiding officers to six; expense was limited further by limitation of councils to twelve members and of houses to twenty-four.[81] The limit for printing expenses was $4,000 a session in 1872,[82] then $2,500 a year in 1878.[83]

By 1878, then, Congress had defined the basic rates for legislative expenses fairly closely. The total amounts necessary could not be

[74] Seattle *Weekly Post-Intelligencer*, March 27, 1882.

[75] Statement attributed to Governor N. G. Ordway, referring to the patronage. George W. Kingsbury, *History of Dakota Territory*, II, 1178.

[76] Additional appropriations in the nature of adjuncts to the contingent funds were for interpreter and translator in the executive offices of New Mexico and Arizona, $500 each. New Mexico had a $1,500 contingent fund from 1867 to 1869.

[77] *Infra*, p. 52.

[78] The lower rate applied to all except Idaho and Montana.

[79] Act of January 23, 1873, *Statutes*, XVII, 416.

[80] *Cong. Globe* (42 Cong., 3 Sess.), p. 413.

[81] Act of June 19, 1878, *Statutes*, XX, 193.

[82] Act of May 8, 1872, *ibid.*, XVII, 73.

[83] Act of June 19, 1878, *ibid.*, XX, 193.

worked out precisely in advance: variations in mileage, for instance, occurred even when the sessions lasted precisely forty days and when thirty-six members attended. It was customary to vote a sum in round numbers, the same for all territories. From $20,000 in 1861, this sum increased for a time to $25,000 in 1874.[84] Deficiency appropriations were frequent.

Such sums were small enough for the mountain and high plains west, and, like salaries, they did not always arrive promptly. Governor Edgerton of Montana paid the expenses of government for more than a year from his personal funds.[85] When Congress reduced rates in 1878–79, territorial spokesmen protested that the reductions were a serious threat to the quality of legislation. The House Committee on Territories declared that they made it impossible to attract the best citizens, leaving a membership "unworthy of trust and unfit for the discharge of . . . duties." [86] According to Mason Brayman, governor of Idaho, "only the rich, or those having no 'visible means of support,' can afford to accept office, too often, in either case, governed by considerations not favorable to safe legislation." [87] Evasion of the law was an alternative only relatively desirable. Congress forbade payment of compensation or salaries above those which it allowed, but as compensation and salaries fell, territorial legislatures tended to take up the slack by their own illegal appropriations.[88] Legislators and appointed officers collaborated in violating the law: the fact that they were poorly paid may have limited their abilities in general; certainly it made them subject to financial temptations in particular.[89] On the other hand, disbursing officers suffered unjust accusations of dishonesty when appropriations were short or delayed.[90]

[84] The increase represented an economy to the treasury: the full amount was payable on alternate years only, while on non-legislative years there were only appropriations of $1,000 to $2,000 for overhead charges and for incidental expenses of the secretaries' offices. There was considerable variation from the standard figure. Between 1863 and 1866 several legislatures received smaller sums, ranging from $4,000 to $18,000. From 1882 Dakota received approximately $40,000 per legislative year, Montana, Utah, and Washington $22,000.

[85] W. F. Sanders, "Sidney Edgerton, The First Governor of Montana," p. 7. When New Mexico changed from biennial to annual sessions, Congress took no note. Edward L. Perkins to Fish, May 21, 1869, TP, New Mexico, III, 333–34; Wetter to Tayler, February 18, 1871, enclosed in W. H. Jones to Boutwell, February 20, 1871, First Comptroller Correspondence.

[86] *House Reports*, 48 Cong., 1 Sess., No. 1322.

[87] Brayman to Schurz, October 8, 1878, *Report of the Secretary of the Interior . . . 1879*, II, 427.

[88] *Infra*, pp. 47–49.

[89] *Infra*, pp. 98–99, 101–2.

[90] Secretary Hand of Dakota was charged with default when Congress failed to appropriate enough for legislative expenses. Hand to Bell, July 18, 1878, Interior Appointment File 139; cf. Owings to Teller, June 10, 1882, *ibid.* 171.

Allowances for expenses of governors were no more adequate than their salaries. Emergencies were particularly disastrous, for the territorial legislative machinery was not designed for immediate action; there was always the problem of stretching appropriations to cover large ordinary expenses. On coming to Idaho, Governor Brayman complained:

I found no Executive rooms—no furniture, and was under the necessity of purchasing.—The two Indian wars . . . have increased the indispensable disbursements of my Department in various ways—clerk hire, printing, telegraphing, organizing militia, handling arms, &c. The contingent fund of my office, $1000 to my predecessors, was, from July 1, 1876, reduced to $500. . . . My necessary disbursements, above the appropriations, I have paid from my private means. . . . I am using borrowed furniture. . . . After paying office rent I have $140 per annum for all expenses.[91]

Court fees in the territories, having been designed for the states, were often fantastically out of proportion to western prices. Jurors and witnesses collected traveling expenses of six cents a mile, but might have to pay stage fare of twenty-five.[92] The House Committee on Territories reported the case of a juror who had traveled four hundred miles to court by working on ranch after ranch. Another was unable to return home.[93] The attorney-general reported:

It is believed that this inadequate compensation causes many of the suits and prosecutions on behalf of the government to fail because of the ill-will of the witnesses. Witnesses frequently avoid a summons, thus defeating justice, or, if served, decline to obey, in order to compel the marshal to arrest them under a bench warrant, preferring to be taken to court as prisoners at the Government's expense, rather than to pay their own expenses without any hope of being reimbursed.[94]

A partial remedy was the creation of additional judgeships, to shorten distances to court.[95]

Aside from such regular contributions to territorial government, Congress from time to time appropriated funds for special purposes. Public buildings were the principal object: these included capitols

[91] Quoted in Porter to Sherman, January 11, 1879, First Comptroller Correspondence. Cf. Brayman to Schurz, October 8, 1879, *Report of the Secretary of the Interior . . . 1879*, II, 426.

[92] According to Delegate Garfielde of Washington, court fees in the far western states were double those in the territories, whereas cost of living in Idaho, Montana, and some other territories was twice as high. *Cong. Globe* (41 Cong., 3 Sess.), pp. 968–69.

[93] *House Reports*, 46 Cong., 2 Sess., No. 1288.

[94] *Annual Report of the Attorney General for 1883*, p. 13.

[95] *Infra*, pp. 52–53.

and penitentiaries only, for hospitals, asylums, and schools were regarded as purely territorial responsibilities.

Appropriations for capitol buildings were highly irregular in time and amount, varying as "the wants, influence, and persistency of those asking for them." [96] Yet they were not always extra favors, but in large part rather substitutes for the rent charges always reckoned in appropriations for contingent and legislative expenses.[97] Congress made appropriations for capitols in Nebraska, New Mexico, Utah, Washington, and Colorado only; [98] construction stopped short of completion in all territories except Washington. The capitol at Olympia, by direction from the Treasury Department, was in the very nominal custody of the territorial secretary; [99] in 1881, after refusal of the treasury and interior to furnish repairs, title passed to the territory. [100]

Public buildings in New Mexico were under fairly continuous supervision. Work on the state house was suspended in 1857,[101] and the territory itself finally appropriated funds for a capitol in 1884.[102] The original custodian of the earlier unfinished structure was a superintendent of construction, appointed by the governor. In 1864, the territorial secretary complained to the secretary of the treasury that public buildings were neglected, and in answer received authority to prevent trespasses.[103] In 1868, Congress made him "ex-officio superintendent of Public buildings and grounds," with (until 1872) an extra salary of $1,000 and "full control and management of the public buildings now erected, in process of erection, or to be hereafter erected . . . under the direction of the Secretary of the Interior." [104] Already the secretary had assumed charge of the Adobe

96 *House Reports* (41 Cong., 2 Sess.), No. 27, p. 2.
97 The House Committee on Territories reported in 1870 that the government was paying annually $6,000 to $10,000 for rent in each of five territories. It recommended construction of capitol buildings at $40,000 each. *Ibid.*, pp. 2, 3; Zulick to Lamar, October 1, 1887, in *Report of the Secretary of the Interior . . . 1887*, I, 760.
98 *House Reports* (41 Cong., 2 Sess.), No. 27, p. 2.
99 Henry Struve to Delano, December 23, 1874, Interior Miscellaneous File 216.
100 *Message of William A. Newell, Governor of Washington Territory . . . 1881*, p. 20; Newell to Windom, July 18, 1881, July 27, 1881, enclosed in Windom to Kirkwood, August 11, 1881, Interior Miscellaneous File 216; Kirkwood to Newell, August 12, 1881, Interior Miscellaneous Letter Book, XVI, 152.
101 Arny to Orville H. Browning, May 15, 1867, in *House Executive Documents* (40 Cong., 2 Sess.), No. 33, p. 11.
102 Samuel A. Losch to Lamar, March 28, 1885, Interior Miscellaneous File 274.
103 Arny to Fessenden, September 24, 1864, Treasury Miscellaneous 145-N; Fessenden to Arny, November 18, 1864, Treasury GS 156.
104 Act of July 27, 1868, *Statutes*, XV, 240; May 8, 1872, *ibid.*, XVII, 127; cf. W. T. Otto to R. B. Mitchell *et al.*, June 13, 1867, in *House Executive Documents*

Palace in Santa Fé,[105] which served as the capitol until 1886 and as official residence of the governor until 1889.[106] United States penitentiaries in the territories were subject to a degree of territorial control. The original custodian was the United States marshal, who might admit territorial prisoners at cost.[107] In 1873, because of the small number of United States prisoners and high cost to the United States, control was to be transferred to the territories of Montana, Idaho, Wyoming, and Colorado,[108] but the arrangement proved impracticable, and the act for transfer was repealed a year later.[109] While control in general remained national, there was a tendency to regard penitentiary buildings as territorial concerns, even as future state property. In several cases legislatures appointed committees to select sites.[110] The Dakota legislature issued bonds for a territorial penitentiary, planning to use penitentiary funds appropriated by Congress. The United States penitentiary at Sioux Falls actually was built as a wing of the territorial structure, under the assumption that "the whole building will undoubtedly soon come under Territorial or State control." [111] Congress donated penitentiary buildings, at or soon after admission, to both Dakotas, Montana,[112] Idaho,[113] Utah,[114] and Washington.[115] These donations were clearly subsidies; the mere building of a federal penitentiary during the territorial period was not necessarily a favor, for the territories did not always find it profitable to keep their own prisoners

(40 Cong., 2 Sess.), No. 33, p. 2. Actually the treasury retained custody of a portion of the Adobe Palace until 1876, renouncing such rights in 1882. Folger to Teller, May 19, 1882, Interior Miscellaneous File 274.

[105] Folger to Teller, May 19, 1882, ibid. 274.

[106] Prince to Noble, April 10, 1889, April 30, 1889, November 19, 1889, ibid. 274.

[107] Act of January 10, 1871, Statutes, XVI, 398.

[108] Act of January 24, 1873, ibid., XVII, 418–19; Cong. Globe (42 Cong., 3 Sess.), pp. 409–10; Potts to Delano, April 1, 1873, Interior Miscellaneous File 206.

[109] Act of June 20, 1874, Statutes, XVIII, 112; clipping, n.p., n.d., Maginnis Scrapbook; W. F. Wheeler to H. H. Bancroft, October 23, 1872 (Bancroft Library).

[110] Including Colorado, Arizona, Washington, and Montana. The Montana committee submitted plans as well. W. Sturgis et al. to Browning, April 18, 1867, enclosed in E. F. Phelps to Browning, April 20, 1867, Interior Miscellaneous File 206; Smith to Browning, November 19, 1867, ibid.

[111] Ordway to Kirkwood, May 5, 1881, ibid., 201; Kingsbury, op. cit., II, 1311. The territorial plan was "to lease the Government wing as soon as it is turned over to the Department of Justice." Copy, W. L. Dow to Teller, November 18, 1884, Interior Miscellaneous File 201.

[112] Act of February 22, 1889, Statutes, XXV, 680–81.

[113] Act of July 3, 1890, ibid., XXVI, 216.

[114] Act of July 16, 1894, ibid., XXVIII, 110.

[115] Act of February 22, 1889, ibid., XXV, 680–81; act of June 4, 1897, ibid., XXX, 56.

in the federal prisons, or even within the territories.[116] Further, since funds for penitentiaries under the Acts of 1867 came from territorial internal revenue receipts, construction did not follow soon after authorization.[117]

The subsidy to the territories in the form of public buildings thus was a minor one, despite the great interest it aroused. The advantage to the territories of Washington and New Mexico, where territorial agencies used the capitol and the Adobe Palace instead of rented buildings, was hardly greater than the savings of the national government where appointed officers used office room provided by certain other territories.[118] Penitentiaries in most cases remained United States property during the territorial period, under United States control. Territories tended to erect public buildings from territorial funds, and to depend less on national aid, so frequently scanty or withheld entirely.

A donation shared more or less equally by all territories was that of legal books for territorial libraries. The Department of the Interior purchased the libraries, generally placing them in custody of some territorial officer.[119] Ownership of such properties was a matter of some dispute. The Treasury Department maintained United States title to supplies purchased through the contingent and legislative funds, claiming proceeds from their sale.[120] Upon the admission of the Dakotas, Washington, and Montana, at the suggestion of the first comptroller,[121] Congress donated to them all "fixtures, furniture, books, papers, and records" purchased for or used by the territorial governments.[122] For practical purposes in estimating the national subsidy to territorial government, one may assume that the territories had title from the original expenditures.[123]

[116] The Act of June 16, 1880 provided that territorial prisoners might be kept in any other territory or state. *Ibid.*, XXI, 277.

[117] *Infra*, p. 45. Act of January 22, 1867, *Statutes*, XIV, 377. For a comprehensive review of expenditures for and administration of penitentiary buildings in the territories, see Noble to Harrison, April 29, 1890, Interior Miscellaneous Letter Book, XXXI, 388–99.

[118] *Infra*, p. 46.

[119] The secretary was usually custodian. In Utah a territorial librarian had custody, under territorial law of 1852. C. H. Hempstead to McKean, April 22, 1871, enclosed in McKean to Delano, April 23, 1871, Interior Miscellaneous File 211.

[120] Mills to Schurz, April 8, 1878, *ibid.*, 206.

[121] A. C. Matthews to Windom, December 11, 1889, First Comptroller Correspondence.

[122] *Cong. Rec.* (51 Cong., 1 Sess.), p. 341; Acts of January 10, 1890, and June 21, 1890, *Statutes*, XXVI, 668, and XXVI, 675.

[123] The recent chairman of the House Committee on Territories believed transfer unnecessary: "It was my understanding that all the books and records that had been purchased by appropriations made by Congress . . . did belong to the Territories." *Cong. Rec.* (51 Cong., 1 Sess.), p. 342.

Congress authorized occasional outlays from the Treasury for extraordinary expenses incurred by territories. Legislatures expected and sometimes received contributions toward large printing bills, as for revisions and codes of laws.[124] Usually Congress gave compensation for volunteer service in Indian wars.[125]

Territories received no grants of public lands. The title of the Morrill Act refers to territories,[126] but the title and a fairly common misconception to the contrary, there was not even a cash provision for education until the Agricultural College Act of 1890.[127] No territory participated in its benefits during the period of this study.[128] Some, it is true, did anticipate benefits from school and university lands reserved against the time of admission. Washington had disposed of nearly half of its university lands by 1864,[129] and leased out school lands for nearly twenty years without authority.[130] Such anticipation was exceptional. Territories were allowed to select but ordinarily not to use lands before admission; [131] land donations, like donations of public buildings, figured very slightly in the general picture of territorial finances.

The national contribution was relatively small and fixed, covering in theory the costs of the highest executive, legislative, and judicial organs. The territorial responsibility in financial matters was large and subject to expansion. It included both the great residuum of governmental functions not covered in congressional appropriations and the system of national taxes, which covered states and territories alike. Amounts of taxes paid into the national Treasury often exceeded the national subsidy, and sometimes were exceeded by the cost of collection. On these grounds Internal Revenue Commissioner Boutwell recommended limiting taxes to the states,[132] though move-

[124] Porter to Sherman, April 24, 1878, First Comptroller Correspondence.

[125] E.g., Acts of March 2, 1861, and March 3, 1875, *Statutes*, XII, 198, and XVIII, 390, 417.

[126] "An Act donating Public Lands to the several States and Territories which may provide Colleges for the Benefit of Agriculture and the Mechanic Arts." Act of July 2, 1862, *ibid.*, XII, 503.

[127] Act of August 30, 1890, *ibid.*, XXVI, 417–19.

[128] On February 13, 1891, Utah was the only territory which had certified its eligibility. G. Chandler to William T. Harris, February 13, 1891, Interior Miscellaneous Letter Book, XXXIII, 427.

[129] When Congress confirmed the sales. Act of March 14, 1864, *Statutes*, XIII, 28; Newell, *Special Message* . . . November 4, 1881, Interior Miscellaneous File 216.

[130] The Act of August 6, 1888 confirmed the practice. *Statutes*, XXV, 358; *Cong. Rec.* (50 Cong., 1 Sess.), p. 6758. The Act of August 9, 1888 authorized leases of Wyoming school and university lands. *Statutes*, XXV, 393.

[131] By authority of the organic acts or subsequent legislation. The Act of February 18, 1881, authorized Dakota, Montana, Arizona, Idaho, and Wyoming to select university lands. *Statutes*, XXI, 326.

[132] Santa Fé *Weekly Gazette*, February 21, 1863. Internal revenue receipts from

ments to grant tax exemption never progressed far. The Santa Fé *Weekly Gazette* expressed a familiar Western view when it argued that frontiersmen "deserve the encouragement of the government. In the end the Government participates in the results of the pioneer's enterprise and the wild Territory which he reduces from the wilderness to the abode of civilization becomes a part of the wealth and power of the nation." [133]

Expenditures by territorial law in general far exceeded the national contribution to territorial government. Territorial and local units maintained the functions ordinarily handled outside the capitol building in a state: education, justice, care of criminals and the sick, and the like. At times territories paid expenses ordinarily charged to the United States, such as rent,[134] furnishings of executive offices,[135] or even parts of the compensation of appointed officers.[136] Amounts fluctuated widely; hence an average is not easily estimated. In the first years of territorial status taxes might be low or nonexistent: it is said that no taxes were levied or paid in Dakota up to 1864 because of the belief that United States appropriations covered all expenses.[137] Later, in most cases, they increased rapidly. By 1880, last census year before the omnibus admissions, territorial and local taxation in eight territories grossed $2,658,761,[138] indebtedness $3,017,501.[139]

During most of the period 1861–90 the national government did little to restrict financial operations of territories after the fashion of restrictions imposed on themselves by states.[140] The exception was Washington, which inherited from Oregon a prohibition on borrowing in the name of the people.[141] The Act of 1886 limited future indebtedness but not taxation.[142] The sphere of territorial taxation

Arizona for 1865–68 totaled $4,837.53, cost of collection $17,853.39. Richardson to Delano, April 3, 1871, Interior Miscellaneous File 252.

[133] Santa Fé *Weekly Gazette*, February 21, 1863; September 7, 1861.

[134] James H. Teller to Durham, June 15, 1886, Executive Correspondence, Solicitor (Treasury Department). The equivalent of rent was paid by all territories owning capitol buildings.

[135] Arthur C. Mellette to Noble, November 3, 1889, Interior Miscellaneous File 200.

[136] *Infra*, pp. 47–49.

[137] Eugene Curie Schneider, "Taxation in Dakota Territory," *South Dakota Historical Collections*, XIII (1926), 405. Governor Sheldon said that as late as 1881 New Mexico had no systematized revenue laws, and that the rich openly failed to pay taxes. Lionel A. Sheldon, Dictation (n.d.; Bancroft Library), p. 14.

[138] *Tenth Census of the United States* (1880): *Valuation, Taxation, and Public Indebtedness*, p. 18.

[139] *Ibid.*, p. 284.

[140] Gilbert A. Pierce to Lamar, October 21, 1885, *Report of the Secretary of the Interior . . . 1885*, II, 937.

[141] Farrand, *op. cit.*, 42–43.

[142] Act of July 30, 1886, *Statutes*, XXIV, 171.

was not materially affected by the territorial status: legislatures and local units alike were free to choose methods and amounts. An important exception was the tax exemption of certain railroad rights of way within the territories, under the Northern Pacific and Atlantic and Pacific railroad charters.[143]

The objects of expenditure likewise were originally unrestricted. In standardizing salaries in 1873, however, Congress prohibited payment of "compensation other than that provided by the laws of the United States" to governors, secretaries, and legislators;[144] judges escaped the prohibition apparently by an oversight in a change of wording.[145] Some restriction was necessary because most legislatures had been supplementing normal salaries and allowances. Thus judges received $4,200 as "increased compensation" in Nevada,[146] $2,000 in Colorado,[147] $2,400 in Idaho,[148] and $1,000 to $1,500 in Wyoming.[149] After the Act of 1873 there was more indirection in payments. Governors of Utah, Wyoming, and Arizona received large expense funds,[150] judges in Washington travel expense accounts;[151] until 1885 most secretaries collected fees for miscellaneous services (the secretary of Dakota thus increasing his income from $1,800 to $5,000).[152] The legislature of Arizona gave to Governor Frémont the office of lottery commissioner, but Secretary Carl Schurz disapproved his acceptance.[153] Yet as late as 1883 the legislature of Washington openly gave the governor $500 for incidental expenses of the executive office.[154]

Territorial spokesmen usually defended such payments by claiming that the normal salaries and allowances were insufficient to main-

[143] Act of July 2, 1864, ibid., XIII, 367; Act of July 27, 1866, ibid., XIV, 294.
[144] Act of January 23, 1873, Statutes, XVII, 416.
[145] Cong. Globe (42 Cong., 3 Sess.), p. 412.
[146] Nevada Laws (2 Sess., 1862), p. 73.
[147] Colorado Revised Statutes (1868), p. 325.
[148] T. Donaldson to Jacob D. Cox, July 29, 1869, Interior Miscellaneous File 204.
[149] Wyoming General Laws (1 Sess., 1869), p. 415.
[150] N. W. Clayton, affidavit, May 16, 1884, Interior Appointment File 171; Peck and A. C. Campbell to Lamar, April 30, 1886, June 30, 1886, ibid. 340; clipping enclosed in Zulick to Lamar, March 19, 1887, Interior Miscellaneous File 262.
[151] House Reports (48 Cong., 1 Sess.), No. 254, p. 1.
[152] Richard F. Pettigrew to Teller, October 16, 1882, Interior Appointment File 170. Departmental instructions of 1876 and 1885 prohibited collection. Chandler to William Sanborn, April 27, 1876, Interior Miscellaneous Letter Book, IX, 314; Teller to Edward Jay Curtis, February 19, 1885, ibid., XXIII, 2–3. The law of June 19, 1878 allowed fees for duties imposed by territorial legislatures. Statutes, XX, 193; cf. John Taffe to Chandler, May 10, 1876, Interior Miscellaneous File 197.
[153] Schurz to Frémont, April 23, 1879, Interior Miscellaneous Letter Book, XIII, 349. Executive Order 9 of January 17, 1873, prohibited acceptance of office under a territorial government by federal officers.
[154] Washington Session Laws (1883), p. 103.

tain competent officers.[155] A chief justice of Nevada innocently regarded payments of $4,200 a year as "a very kind endorsement."[156] But the territorial legislatures endorsed a competency which included response to their demands. The Arizona legislature of 1889, under suspicion of illegality, voted $1,200 for the judges in an attempt to induce them to approve the session.[157] According to a governor of Montana, "The granting of extra compensation of U.S. officers is only used . . . to bribe . . . officers for whenever the officers disagree with the majority of the legislature, the compensation is repealed."[158] It was "not . . . an inducement to get good men to go there and hold office," said Representative D. C. Dyer, "but with a view to controlling them after they got there."[159]

While the object of legislators in granting extra compensation may often have been to achieve influence comparable to that exercised by their colonial ancestors over royal governors, such was not always the result. Intraterritorial rivalries were likely to be stronger than rivalries among legislatures and governors. A member of the House Committee on Territories claimed later that the prohibition of 1873 had been "aimed at certain Territories, in which the removal of capitals was agitated, to prevent the giving of increased salaries to officials in the interest of certain localities."[160] Mastery of the situation might slip from subsidizer to subsidized. When the Montana legislature repealed extra compensation of judges in 1867, one of the judges affected lobbied for congressional disapproval of the laws of that session. Governor Ashley vetoed—unsuccessfully—a bill to repeal extra compensation in 1870.[161] At the first session of the Idaho legislature, the acting governor asked for extra compensation [162] and "carried the measure."[163] The subsidies went to "every officer but the Receiver and Register . . ." as the latter complained: "The Gov gets $2,500 from the Govt and $2,500 from the Territy, The Judges get $3,500 from the Govt and $2,500 from the Territy, The Surveyor Genl $3,000 from the Govt and $8 per day, and so on

155 *Rocky Mountain News,* January 18, 1866.

156 George Turner to B. F. Wade, September 1, 1865. Wade Papers, VII, 2162.

157 W. W. Porter to W. H. H. Miller, May 21, 1889, Department of Justice, Appointment Papers, Arizona. In inquiring into the circumstances of extra payments from counties, the attorney-general mentioned without questioning payments of $600 from the territorial government. Miller to James H. Wright, May 10, 1889, Letters to Judges and Clerks, IV, 6.

158 Potts to Lyman Trumbull, February 17, 1871, Potts Letter Book.

159 *Cong. Globe* (41 Cong., 3 Sess.), p. 971.

160 Taffe to Chandler, May 10, 1876, Interior Miscellaneous File 197.

161 *Cong. Globe* (41 Cong., 3 Sess.), p. 970; Montana *Council Journal* (4 Sess., 1867), pp. 230–31, 233.

162 Idaho *House Journal* (1 Sess.), pp. 9–10.

163 Daniels to William H. Wallace, January 5, 1863 [1864?], Wallace Papers.

through." [164] Nullification by Congress in 1870 was a welcome relief and protection, lessening "the expenses of Territorial government by one-half," according to Hailey,[165] though seven years of payments left the territory deep in debt.[166] From 1865 to 1871 Montana paid extra compensation of nearly $175,000, thus incurring a debt of $104,-000.[167] Imitating the example of the thirteen colonies was expensive, and in such cases a luxury affording little general satisfaction.

Legislatures frequently voted money to their own members as well. In Arizona such payments increased sharply after Congress cut down legislative expense allowances in 1879, reaching $23,955 for a single session in 1885.[168] A "real necessity . . . furnished a pretext for the expenditure of over $78,000 of the taxpayer's money in direct violation of law." [169] It seemed difficult to make up for Congress' niggardliness without risking corruption of men elected in the territories no less than of men appointed from Washington.

On the whole the national government's part in territorial finances was relatively small. The national contribution generally did not exceed a tenth the amount raised by territorial and local taxes. Congress assumed responsibility for a small group of governmental functions, and made appropriations without regard for actual needs in areas radically different from the states, and, until 1873, without much regard for general increases in prices.[170] Inadequate salaries offered to territorial politicians (whether autonomists or town site profiteers) an opportunity to control appointed officers comparable to the opportunity of colonial legislatures which had paid governors' salaries in entirety. Yet there was too much flux in territorial politics and too much surveillance from Washington to permit large and permanent usurpation of control. Distributed as it was, the national subsidy carried a considerable degree of national control, and as-

---

[164] Thos. Donaldson to J. D. Cox, July 29, 1869, Interior Miscellaneous File 204. As he requested, Donaldson was appointed superintendent of the penitentiary. Endorsement, *loc. cit.*

[165] Hailey, *op. cit.*, 164.

[166] Brayman to L. M. Morrill, December 21, 1876, enclosed in Morrill to Chandler, January 11, 1877, Interior Miscellaneous File 204.

[167] Potts to Nye, February 13, 1871, Potts Letter Book; Potts to Garfield, October 21, 1872, *ibid.*

[168] James A. Bayard to Lamar, November 6, 1886, Interior Miscellaneous File 252; cf. (for Dakota) Church to Vilas, October 10, 1886, *Report of the Secretary of the Interior . . . 1888*, III, 753.

[169] Bayard to Lamar, November 26, 1886, Interior Miscellaneous File 252.

[170] The acting comptroller stated in 1871 that "the appropriations for Legislative expenses . . . have been inadequate to meet the increased expense . . . which took place during the rebellion and still continues, the appropriations having been based upon, and made conformable to estimates made prior thereto." Jones to Boutwell, February 11, 1871, First Comptroller Correspondence.

sumed even greater prominence in the public view than it deserved. It was small enough to be a chronic grievance,[171] large enough to be a persistent deterrent to movements for statehood.[172] In the early stages of territorial existence it was all-important as financial aid; in the later, it was significant chiefly for the administrative connections derived from it.

[171] *Infra*, pp. 101–2. Copperheads made a great point of minimizing national financial aid. *Rocky Mountain News*, April 2, 1863. Anti-administration politicians throughout followed a similar line.

[172] E.g., editorial, "Statehood," (Lander, Wyoming) *Wind River Mountaineer*, November 24, 1888. Many believed that the United States paid salaries actually provided by the territories. George L. Shoup, Governor of Idaho, Proclamation, May 11, 1889, Interior Miscellaneous File 204.

Chapter V

TERRITORIAL JUSTICE

THE organization of the judicial system in the territories was simple. Under the organic acts, each territory had three justices appointed by the president for four-year terms. Sitting together, they constituted a supreme court; sitting separately, they acted as district judges. In both capacities they had jurisdiction over cases arising under United States or territorial law; appeals went from the territorial supreme court to the Supreme Court of the United States.[1]

Administrative relations with territorial judges were carried on through the same channels as with federal district judges: the attorney-general received applications and transmitted commissions without differentiation in procedure. The correspondence with territorial judges is bulkier, chiefly on account of leaves of absence and the insecurity of tenure which judges shared with governors and secretaries. In administering leaves, the attorney-general usually exercised more care than did the secretaries of state and of the interior, holding a judge, for instance, to the "condition that his duties were to be performed by one of his Associates."[2] He was no more disposed to render opinions for judges than for governors or secretaries, holding to the requirement that opinions be given only at the request of the president or heads of departments.[3]

United States marshals and commissioners for the territories did not pertain, in any strict sense, to the territorial system: their functions were the same as in the states. Their correspondence reflects the turbulence of territorial politics and the precarious situation of all officers in the territories, but no formal difference in standing.

Chief Justice Marshall had defined territorial courts as legislative courts rather than constitutional or United States courts in the case

[1] Originally in cases where the sum in controversy exceeded $1,000 ($2,000 in Washington). *Revised Statutes,* p. 702; see also *ibid.,* p. 699, and Act of June 29, 1876, *Statutes,* XIX, 62. In 1885 the limit became $5,000. Act of March 3, 1885, *ibid.,* XXIII, 443. The Circuit Court of Appeals was given appellate jurisdiction over territorial courts as over district and circuit courts. Act of March 3, 1891, *ibid.,* XXVI, 830.
[2] Memorandum, n.d., with Schurz to Charles Devens, November 5, 1878, Justice Appointment Papers, New Mexico.
[3] A. H. Garland to J. B. Hays, July 20, 1885, Letters to Judges and Clerks, III, 3.

of American Insurance Company *v.* Canter.[4] The practical significance of the distinction lay in the choice of procedures: when the
same court heard territorial and United States cases, must it follow
either United States or territorial law consistently, or one or the other
according to the individual case in view?[5] The issue was not undis-
puted as late as 1891, when the Supreme Court ruled against a territorial judge's claim of immunity from removal.[6] In practice, presidents removed territorial judges nearly as frequently as governors
and secretaries, despite occasional protests from judges that they
could not "be removed, except by impeachment."[7]

There was less difference over the financial responsibility. The national treasury bore the costs of supreme and district court terms in
entirety:

> In the year 1821 the comptroller decided that, while . . . engaged [in
> trial of cases arising under the Constitution and laws of the United States],
> the expenses should be paid by the United States. . . . In all the Territories
> the expenses of whole terms are charged to the United States, on the ground
> that trial of government cases occur throughout the terms interspersed with
> other business.[8]

Renting separate courtrooms, for instance, would have been impossible or highly impracticable where United States and territorial
cases came up during the same day.[9] The United States marshal requested funds, which the treasury paid out of the regular appropriations for "expenses of the United States courts"[10] at rates uniform
with those established for United States courts.[11] Distinction between
different jurisdictions of one court was of less consequence than differentiation among courts over which a single judge presided, and
judges usually served in county as well as in supreme and district
courts.

The number of judges in a territory significantly affected the

4 1 *Peters* 511.
5 *Cong. Globe* (42 Cong., 2 Sess.), pp. 1732–33; Brigham Henry Roberts, *A Comprehensive History of the Church of Jesus Christ of the Latter-day Saints, Century I*, V, 408, 412; Beardsley, "Territorial Codes," pp. 20–24; *Report of the
Secretary of the Interior . . . 1880*, II, 533.
6 McAllister *v.* United States, 141 *U.S.* 174. There was a noteworthy dissent by
Justice Field (141 *U.S.* 191). Cf. "Removal of Territorial Judges," *American Law
Review*, XXIV (1890), 308–11, and W. D. L[ewis], "Albuquerque National Bank *v.*
Perea," *American Law Register*, XXXII (1893), 262–66.
7 Henry N. Blake to W. H. Clagett, January 21, 1872, Justice Appointment
Papers, Montana.
8 *Decisions of the First Comptroller*, III, 153.
9 Wheeler to C. H. Hill, November 9, 1870, Wheeler Letter Book.
10 *Decisions of the First Comptroller*, III, 152.
11 *Revised Statutes*, 823.

development of the higher and still more of the lower territorial judiciary. No increases above the usual three come until after 1879; during the eighties Dakota reached as many as eight judges,[12] and Washington,[13] Montana,[14] Utah,[15] and New Mexico[16] totals of four each. These additions made it possible to provide, after 1884, that no judge of the territories affected should sit in appeal on cases he had decided in district court. This limitation was a gesture at an old grievance. Where a judge had to review his own decisions, there was necessarily "suspicion of collusion among the judges to sustain the opinions of each other in the courts below." [17] Charges of log-rolling were such that the Supreme Court of Arizona was referred to as the "Supreme Court of Affirmance." [18] "Unless there is some change," wrote a Montana attorney, "it would be better . . . to simply have mining or Justices courts." [19]

Mishandling of appeals was not the only consequence of small panels. Judges were too few to handle their dockets promptly. The legislature of Washington Territory memorialized in 1882 "That the existing state of the Districts and courts of this Territory consequent on an allowance of three Judges only, and the immense territory forming each district, for the holding of the Court, works a grievance to the people tantamount to a denial of justice." [20] Persons in outlying areas suffered hardship from the requirement that cases arising under United States law be heard at only one point in a district. Whereas the first district judge of Montana had his residence at Virginia City, in the most populous county of the district, most of the United States cases arose at Custer City, 433 miles distant.[21] The district court thus was inadequate because it was remote; county courts, held under territorial law in the various county seats, were inadequate because the presiding judge spent so much time in laborious and costly travel. A judge spent four weeks on the road between

[12] Chief justice and three associates, Act of March 3, 1879, *Statutes*, XX, 473; five associates, Act of July 4, 1884, *ibid.*, XXIII, 101; seven associates, Act of August 9, 1888, *ibid.*, XXV, 398.

[13] Act of July 4, 1884, *ibid.*, XXIII, 101. See the attorney-general's recommendation for a general increase. *Annual Report of the Attorney-General . . . 1883*, p. 14.

[14] Act of July 10, 1886, *Statutes*, XXIV, 138.

[15] Act of June 25, 1888, *ibid.*, XXV, 203.

[16] Chief justice and three associates, Act of February 28, 1887, *ibid.*, XXIV, 428; four associates, Act of July 10, 1890, *ibid.*, XXVI, 266.

[17] *House Reports* (50 Cong., 1 Sess.), No. 1341, p. 1.

[18] Richard E. Sloan, *Memories of An Arizona Judge*, p. 79.

[19] Woolfolk to Maginnis, May 4, 1876, Maginnis Papers.

[20] *Washington . . . Session Laws* (9 Sess., 1861–62), p. 162.

[21] *House Reports* (46 Cong., 2 Sess.), No. 470, p. 2.

Virginia City and Miles City to hold two terms of court in 1879.[22] In Johnson County, Wyoming, where personal property was valued at five millions, the district judge could make the five-hundred-mile stage trip only once a year, for a week's session.[23] Such grotesque situations were hardly avoidable when districts in Arizona, for instance, were as large as the state of Ohio. The grievances of the Regulators, rebellious at having to go thirty miles to court, were slight by comparison. Dockets were so crowded in Utah, Dakota, and Washington as late as 1888 that they could not be cleared for many months even if there were no new cases.[24] The volume of business was large even for the number of lawyers at hand, which Congress did not limit. "I came here and opened an office but four (4) days ago," wrote a young lawyer from Lincoln, New Mexico, in 1885, ". . . and have my hands full of business." [25]

The burdens of territorial service would have been heavy for the most energetic and competent of jurists; those appointed were too often unfit for the most routine work. In a given case of dissatisfaction, it may be difficult to say whether personnel or administration was more responsible; citizens of the territories were sure that both were at fault. Delegate Martin Maginnis of Montana told the House:

> While all parts of the territorial system are objectionable, there is no part . . . so hateful as the judicial part of it. It seems to be the prevalent opinion . . . that the causes to be tried . . . are unimportant, and that any one who had the name of lawyer is quite competent to try them. . . . The men who have been appointed as our judges have only too often either been broken-down politicians or men without capacity or integrity. . . . The judges, when appointed, have no independence. They are subject to removal by political influence, and threats of this sort of pressure is often brought against them to determine their judgment in causes before them. When their terms expire they are reappointed or removed by the same sort of political influence that procured the original appointment.[26]

Low salaries did not attract the better judicial talent. Some who came, while perhaps honest and able enough for eastern service, were by temperament and experience unqualified for the peculiar judicial needs of the West. Resourcefulness and a sense of the practical were

[22] *Loc. cit.*

[23] *Ibid.* (48 Cong., 1 Sess.), No. 254, p. 2.

[24] *Ibid.* (50 Cong., 1 Sess.), No. 34, pp. 1–2.

[25] W. S. Ryan to Grover Cleveland, October 4, 1885, Justice Appointment Papers, New Mexico.

[26] *Cong. Rec.* (48 Cong., 1 Sess.), p. 2778. Proponents of statehood for Colorado recognized such grievances in emphasizing that judges would be elected for six- and nine-year terms. "Address of the Constitution-Makers," Colorado Springs *Gazette*, March 18, 1876.

qualities more valuable than legal erudition.[27] Courage was essential in a judge who might have to "invade a community that had been used to the swift and severe justice of the vigilance committee . . . and so act as to practically drive it . . . out of existence in a short period of time." [28] During the Mesilla riots in New Mexico in 1871, Judge Benjamin F. Waters had resigned after one term of court; Judge Daniel B. Johnson, Jr. "stayed three days, made up his mind that it would be dangerous to do any investigating, became demoralized, and returned to his home without any action." [29]

Frequent changes in the territorial judiciary, owing to pressure from those who wanted office and to dissatisfaction of those who received it, held up judicial business and made assured willingness to stay on the bench a primary recommendation. A New Mexican complained in 1866 that with one exception "the Territory has been entirely destitute of her *speculative* and *tricky* Officials—no Judges and no clerks for two years— Some of whom ought to have been in Andersonville Prison, in place of those *honest* men who were there." [30] Appointment of Joab Houghton to New Mexico, the governor urged,

would insure the administration of justice, by, regularly, holding his terms of court. We have been without any term of court in one of our most important districts for two years by the appointment of Judges from the States failed or refused to comply with their obligations in coming to this Territory. . . .[30a]

Those who found their duties distasteful were no more acceptable than those who chose to remain under suspicion of inordinate political ambition or improper financial connection. Indications of most flagrant corruption appeared in Nevada, whose judges allegedly were heavily interested in mines affected by suits in their own courts, and were widely believed to have reversed decisions after receiving new inducements.[31] A twenty-eight-year-old chief justice of New Mexico was disclosed to have been representative of a loan association having heavy mortgage holdings in the territory.[32]

Resistance to unpopular judges was not lacking; remedies were

[27] William J. Trimble, *The Mining Advance into the Inland Empire*, p. 229.
[28] W. F. Sanders, "The Courts of Montana," p. 13.
[29] Silver City *Independent*, quoted in Maurice Garland Fulton and Paul Horgan, eds., *New Mexico's Own Chronicle*, p. 323.
[30] M. B. Duffield to Harlan, January 1, 1866, Department of Justice Files, Interior Department Accounts.
[30a] Henry Connelly to Joseph Holt, February 5, 1865, N.M. Appointment Files, Department of Justice.
[31] Lord, *op. cit.*, pp. 157–65.
[32] *New York World*, October 17, 1885.

usually available, though uncertain in effect. Frontal attacks were exceptional. According to tradition (and the allegations of interested parties), public meetings forced the bench to resign in Nevada in 1864, a month before admission;[33] the attorney-general of the state later said that "Nevada became a State to escape the deadfall of her Territorial courts." [34] That particular tradition is suspect, but almost any territorial judges were suspect when the judges were too few to handle their dockets and too poorly paid to maintain judicial dignity on their ordinary incomes. Judges and courts drew more impatience and hostility than sympathy; the unfair assumption was the usual one. Samuel Bowles wrote in 1865,

One especial motive with the Coloradians for making a State government is to get a judiciary of their own, that shall be both more intelligent and independent than that furnished by the Washington authorities. The men . . . are not apt to be of a very high order either of morals or intellect.[35]

But admission was not always at hand, as the Coloradans found in 1866, and forcing resignations was not for ordinary circumstances. Legislatures might petition for an unpopular judge's removal,[36] or pay him an extra salary to be agreeable. Yet extra compensation was expensive even when it did not involve corruption, while requests for removals of judges as of other officers often were of partisan origin and likely to be discounted. Chief Justice Hiram Knowles of Montana was said to have been attacked and his removal sought to affect the Supreme Court's decision on the location of the territorial capital.[37] Lawyers who signed petitions for removal, on the other hand, risked retaliation in court in the event of failure.[38]

An indirect approach effective while Congress permitted it was "sage-brush districting," or assigning a judge to a district where judicial business was burdensome or almost non-existent. Thus when the Colorado legislature failed to have Justice Charles L. Armour removed in 1862, it "banished [him] to a remote district for the avowed

33 Lord, op. cit., pp. 163–65.
34 Nevada Reports 17, cited in Lord, op. cit., p. 164. Cf. Official Report of the Debates and Proceedings in the Constitutional Convention of the State of Nevada, . . . July 4, 1864, p. 14.
35 Across the Continent, p. 60.
36 Hubert Howe Bancroft, History of Arizona and New Mexico, 1530–1888, Works, XVII, 720; Bancroft, History of Nevada, Colorado, and Wyoming, 1540–1888, ibid. XXV, 748. Territorial bar associations also petitioned. E.g., Bismarck Tribune, November 11, 1881.
37 William W. Dixon to Maginnis, November [?] 5, 1874, Maginnis Papers. Cf. Decius Wade, "Self-Government in the Territories," International Review, VI (1879), 306.
38 Woolfolk to F. E. Munson, August 3, 1868, Sanders Papers.

purpose of getting rid of his presence." [39] Charles B. Waite of Utah was sent 350 miles from Salt Lake City, with terms so arranged as to require two trips each year.[40] The burdens of extra duties, of course, fell on judges still relatively acceptable. When the Wyoming legislature created a sage-brush district to rid the territory of W. W. Peck, it made a special appropriation to compensate his colleagues for their extra labors and expenses. The territorial delegate and a special agent from the county most concerned successfully defended the redistricting to Congress, while the sheriff kept the courthouse locked.[41] In some cases two out of three judges were in disfavor. The Montana legislature sent Justices Hosmer and Munson to unorganized and uninhabited districts after they refused to recognize the legislative sessions of 1865–66 and 1866–67.[42] A Washington act of 1868 similarly "put pretty much all the Territory into one judicial district with the design to legislate so far as practicable the other judges out of office." [43] Congress took away the legislatures' power to assign judges in Montana, Idaho, and Utah.[44] Elsewhere the old power and the old practices continued, though the Santa Fé *Post* remarked with some chagrin, of the sage-brush districting of Chief Justice Joseph G. Palen, that "the members of . . . the Legislature sent him to the hottest locality over which they had jurisdiction, [and] regret that their jurisdiction is so limited." [45]

Attacks on individual appointees were spectacular and often successful, but they necessarily had limited effect as attacks on territorial justice taken altogether as long as judges and sessions were too few for the traffic. Populations and litigation increased faster than transportation improved, while the number of judges remained unchanged. In 1858 Congress, after suggestion from a New Mexico judge,[46] authorized judges to hold sessions of district court in more than one county in a judicial district, to hear causes where the United States was not a party.[47] Such sessions were established in at

[39] *Rocky Mountain News*, August 31, 1864.

[40] Stephen S. Harding to Seward, February 3, 1863, TP, Utah, II, 567–72.

[41] Governor Hoyt conspired in a scheme by which the territorial bar endorsed Peck for a New Mexico judgeship, but the New Mexico delegate "fumed" until Peck's name was withdrawn. Cheyenne *Daily Sun*, June 14, 1889.

[42] J. H. Hosmer, ed., "Biographical Sketch of Hezekiah L. Hosmer," *Contributions to the Historical Society of Montana*, III (1900), 297–98.

[43] *Cong. Globe* (40 Cong., 2 Sess.), p. 3709; Washington *Statutes* (1 Biennial Sess., 1867–68), pp. 23–25.

[44] Acts of March 2, 1867, *Statutes*, XIV, 426, 427; Act of July 27, 1868, *ibid.*, XV, 242.

[45] January 3, 1872.

[46] Kirby Benedict to Jeremiah S. Black, November 28, 1857, Department of Justice Files, Attorney-General's Papers.

[47] Act of June 14, 1858, *Statutes*, XI, 366.

least six territories.[48] A seventh, Arizona, had county courts of a different sort after 1885: judges chosen by county electors had jurisdiction concurrently with the district judges.[49] Sessions held under the Law of 1858 merely added to the duties of federal judges. To the extent that they were already fully occupied, assigning them to county duty meant increased territorial expenses, and a very limited improvement in justice on the whole. In any case it meant no substantial move toward a territorially controlled judiciary.

Genuine rivalry to the federal system of courts came principally as lower judicial organs under territorial authority gained larger jurisdictions. Justices of the peace, probate judges, and the like were more numerous than presidential appointees, and hence more available; depending on territorial authority for appointment and pay, they were more amenable to territorial influence and demands. The respect they paid to territorial opinion was reciprocated. Judge Richard E. Sloan, whose long service in Arizona began at the end of this period, recalled the difficulty of convictions in United States courts for offenses against the United States. Territorial law seemed more important than federal.[50] Probate judges were naturally of great importance in Utah: the power which disposed of estates might strike at the economic foundations of a polygamous society. In 1852 the legislature provided that they should have "power to exercise original jurisdiction, both civil and criminal, and as well in chancery as at common law," with appellate jurisdiction over lower courts.[51] The result of their wide jurisdiction was that "practically all the legal business, except a few cases in which the United States was a party, was transacted in the probate courts of the Territory." [52] An official Mormon historian freely admits the intent to restrict jurisdiction of federal judges.[53] Chief Justice Schaeffer wrote, "We are largely in the power of the probate judge, who may refuse or neglect to aid in furnishing a list of jurors, and who as a general thing is not friendly to the federal courts." [54] Powers of the legislature to grant a larger

48 Nevada *Laws* (1 Sess., 1861), pp. 289–91; Dakota *General Laws* (1 Sess., 1862), pp. 262–66; Nebraska *Revised Statutes* (1866), pp. 53–55; Wyoming *General Laws* (1 Sess., 1869), p. 390; New Mexico *Compiled Laws* (1884), p. 348.

49 Arizona *Acts, Resolutions and Memorials* (13 Sess., 1885), pp. 95–100, 254–59, 284–89, 305–10. Cf. *Ex parte* Lothrop, 118 *U.S.* 113, upholding the right of the legislature to establish inferior courts.

50 Sloan, *op. cit.*, p. 92.

51 Hubert Howe Bancroft, *History of Utah, 1540–1887, Works*, XXVI, 487.

52 R. N. Baskin, *Reminiscences of Early Utah*, p. 59. Baskin comments on Brigham Young's claim that the Mountain Meadows affair was not investigated because the United States judges were not in the territory. By territorial law, the probate courts had jurisdiction. *Ibid.*, pp. 116, 117–18.

53 Roberts, *op. cit.*, IV, 194.

54 *Annual Report of the Attorney General . . . 1877*, pp. 79–80.

jurisdiction and to assign administrative functions to probate judges were, however, upheld by the law officer of the Department of State [55] and by the Supreme Court, which pointed out in 1872, "The theory upon which the various governments for portions of the territory of the United States have been organized, has ever been that of leaving to the inhabitants all the powers of self-government consistent with the supremacy and supervision of National authority, and with certain fundamental principles established by Congress." [56] Meantime, however, the territorial courts were taking a less friendly view of probate jurisdiction,[57] and the Supreme Court followed suit in 1874.[58] Congress in the same year reined in judicial processes in Utah sharply, restricting lower jurisdictions and taking powers from local officers.[59] In 1882 the United States took charge of probate judges' appointments. Immediately territorial autonomists attempted to restrict instead of expand probate powers.[60] The probate court was a device to be discarded when outworn.

Utah was not the only territory which developed a wider probate jurisdiction. The Nevada constitutional convention of 1859 protested because the Mormons had usurped functions of United States judges: "They have conferred upon Probate Judges the sole right to select juries in civil and criminal cases. . . . They have also given to said judges and justices of the peace absolute jurisdiction in all civil and criminal cases." [61] Yet the Nevada legislature two years later gave probate judges appellate jurisdiction over justices' courts and an original civil jurisdiction which infringed very widely on the district courts.[62] In Washington after 1857 probate judges held monthly "criminal terms"; as in Nevada, they had jurisdiction in civil cases involving amounts up to $500.[63] The legislatures made

[55] Draft letter [E. Peshine Smith] to J. Wilson Shaffer, August 2, 1870, TP, Utah, II, 709–11.

[56] Clinton *et al. v.* Englebrecht, 13 *Wallace* 441. The point of the decision, as of Chief Justice Schaeffer's complaint, was the creation of an administrative body, the county court, of which probate judges were members, to choose jurors for sessions of district courts. Utah *Compiled Laws* (1876), p. 123.

[57] In decisions of 1869, 1870, 1871, and 1873. *Rocky Mountain News,* May 3, 1871; Cast *v.* Cast, 1 *Utah* 112. The earlier attitude had been tolerant. Bancroft, *Utah,* p. 490.

[58] Ferris *v.* Higby, 20 *Wallace* 375.

[59] Act of June 23, 1874, *Statutes,* XVIII, 253–56.

[60] "Report of the Utah Commission," September 24, 1888, *Report of the Secretary of the Interior . . . 1888,* III, 673.

[61] Facsimile of (Genoa, Nevada) *Territorial Enterprise,* July 30, 1859, in Myron Angel, ed., *History of Nevada,* p. 70; cf. *ibid.,* p. 40.

[62] Nevada *Laws* (1 Sess., 1861–62), pp. 177, 418; *ibid.* (2 Sess., 1862–63), pp. 82–83; *ibid.* (3 Sess., 1863–64), p. 41; cf. *ibid.,* pp. 164–66.

[63] Washington *Statutes* (4 Sess., 1857), pp. 13–17; cf. *ibid.* (10 Sess., 1863), p. 200.

similar provisions in Nebraska,[64] Colorado,[65] and Idaho.[66] Congress tolerated probate jurisdiction outside of Utah. An act of 1863 extended the limit for Colorado from $100 to $2,000; [67] an act of 1867 allowed limited civil and criminal jurisdiction to probate courts in Montana.[68]

Justices of the peace also took over some of the work of district judges, chiefly by congressional license. The organic acts denied them jurisdiction over land cases,[69] and over civil cases involving more than $100. Congress raised the $100 limit to $300 for Colorado,[70] Arizona,[71] Washington, Idaho, Montana,[72] and Wyoming.[73] The expanded jurisdiction was necessary because some district courts met only once a year. Such infrequency in meetings amounted "almost to a denial of justice." [74] Like Congress, territorial legislatures favored the justices' courts, although more deviously. In Utah, as elsewhere, justices were forbidden to hear land cases, but they held hearings to determine jurisdiction, which amounted to the same thing.[75] In Washington a plaintiff was not entitled to costs in actions which he initiated in district court in preference to the justice's court.[76] Thus the lower judiciary tended to take up much of the increment in the business of the higher as territories became more thickly settled. The probate judges and the justices of the peace, sometimes with Congress' expressed approval and encouragement, probably took over far more of the district judges' work than the more colorful miners' courts ever did.

The extra-legal popular or miners' courts paralleled the federal system only in emergencies, without advancing formal claim to equivalent jurisdiction. Only a few miners' codes offered substitutes for the general "legal tribunals . . . and fountains of justice which

[64] Ordinary powers and jurisdiction of justices of the peace. Nebraska *Revised Statutes* (1866), p. 534.
[65] Jurisdiction to $2,000. Colorado *Revised Statutes* (1868), pp. 334, 526–27, 530. The original limit was $100. Colorado *Laws* (1 Sess., 1861), p. 382.
[66] Jurisdiction to $800. Idaho *General Laws* (2 Sess., 1864), p. 194. Probate jurisdiction had been introduced by the organic act, which applied the statutes of Washington Territory. T. J. Moore *v.* Henry Koubly, 1 *Idaho* 55.
[67] Act of March 2, 1863, *Statutes,* XII, 700.
[68] Act of March 2, 1867, *ibid.,* XIV, 426.
[69] For Arizona, Act of March 23, 1870, *ibid.,* XVI, 77.
[70] Act of March 2, 1863, *ibid.,* XII, 700.
[71] Act of March 23, 1870, *ibid.,* XVI, 77.
[72] Act of January 19, 1883, *ibid.,* XXII, 407.
[73] Act of January 28, 1885, *ibid.,* XXIII, 287.
[74] *House Reports* (46 Cong., 2 Sess.), No. 472.
[75] People *v.* Hiram House, 4 *Utah* 369.
[76] Washington *Laws* (1870), p. 126. The Supreme Court of Utah denied validity of a Utah law denying costs in district court where the value of property involved was less than $100. Hepworth *et al. v.* Gardner *et al.,* 11 *Pacific Reporter* 566.

every American citizen should enjoy"; [77] most were limited to regulation of mining and closely related subjects.[78] The people of Carson County, refusing to accept the Mormon probate judges, impaneled a jury in the absence of a regular district judge.[79] Montana was organized only nominally under the Idaho and Dakota governments up to the spring of 1864; until establishment of a complete judicial system under the territorial act, there was "the comical solecism of a judicial tribunal authorized by law [the probate and justices' courts] exercising authority over the petty transactions . . . while the larger contentions were determined by an unauthorized and volunteer tribunal." [80] In 1865 there were thirty-five executions by the vigilance committee, none by the civil authorities.[81] As populations and governments became stabilized, the miners' codes were absorbed into territorial and national law; the popular courts of later years were not based on covenant in the absence of territorial justice but on mass indignation at its inadequacy in amount or kind. As late as 1878 Governor Brayman of Idaho advised ignoring the courts of Alturas County, in favor of arbitration or of miners' meetings.[82] Such advice was rare; the basis for it was not.

The judicial system was one of the weakest parts of the territorial institution. Its weakness did not lie in any formal discrimination against the territories. Territorial courts were constitutionally distinct from United States courts, but almost undifferentiated in forms of administrative practice.[83] The important differences (and grievances) were that territorial judges were selected with no more deference to local feeling than territorial governors and secretaries, and that the whole system failed to allow for distances, costs, and other peculiarities of the high plain and mountain wests. Territorial courts did not suit because the territories were of the West. Likewise, being typically western, the territories resisted—and survived—the experience. Rival jurisdictions, rising out of popular dissatisfaction, eased the pressure, though they could not cure basic shortcomings. Nor was there more or less reform in the judiciary than in any other segment of territorial government. It was tolerable and lasted only because it fitted loosely though badly, and because the prospect of early statehood lay always before westerner and easterner alike.

[77] From the Gold Hill code of 1859. Lord, *op. cit.*, p. 42.
[78] Curtis H. Lindley, *A Treatise on the American Law relating to Mines and Mineral Lands*, I, 73–74.
[79] Lord, *op. cit.*, p. 41.
[80] Sanders, "Courts of Montana," pp. 1–9.
[81] E. W. Carpenter, "A Glimpse of Montana," *Overland*, II (1869), p. 382.
[82] *Idaho Tri-Weekly Statesman*, February 21, 1878, cited in Blase, *op. cit.*, p. 49.
[83] While statutory restrictions on leaves applied to judges, for instance, leaves were issued by the attorney-general. Abram Bergen to Boutwell, June 28, 1869, Treasury Judiciary Correspondence.

Chapter VI

APPOINTMENTS: PRACTICES AND POLICIES

THE statistical picture of the federal personnel in the territories offers fair evidence of opportunism on the parts of appointing officers and appointees alike. There was never a territorial service in the sense that imperialist powers developed colonial services. The first suggestions of a trained staff of administrators for American dependencies came after 1898. Professor Bourne, writing in 1899, gave an explanation which reflected the general impression if not the fact: "Our previous annexations of territory, with the possible exception of Alaska, have never involved questions of administration essentially different from those [with] which our public men have been familiar." [1] The typical territorial officer was inexperienced at the outset, and did not retain office long enough to become experienced. Of the 424 governors, secretaries, and judges of the period 1861–90, only thirty-two had served previously in any of the three offices.[2] Of these, some were all but technically reappointed, after intervals such as that of an unfriendly administration; some of these reassignments had much to do with patronage and little to do with the good of the service. Sixty served more than the four years for which they were commissioned, but 288 served for shorter periods.[3] The presidents were not solely responsible for such brevity of tenure: there were at least 110 removals but also no less than 115 resignations in the thirty-year period.[4]

[1] Edward G. Bourne, "A Trained Colonial Civil Service," *North American Review*, CLXIX (1899), 528–29. Cf. Theodore Roosevelt, Jr., *Colonial Policies of the United States*, p. 99, and Earl S. Pomeroy, "The American Colonial Office," *Mississippi Valley Historical Review*, XXIX (1944), 521–32.

[2] *Infra*, Appendix. An amendment offered to the Montana bill would have provided "that any of the officers now appointed . . . for the Territory of Idaho . . . may without any new commission be assigned . . . to the new Territory." *Cong. Globe* (38 Cong., 1 Sess.), p. 1168.

[3] Forty-six served single four-year terms. Elvin L. Valentine states that the average term of governors (1787–1912) was three and a half years, and that only twenty exceeded four years. Valentine, "The American Territorial Governor," pp. 43–44.

[4] Some resignations were requested; some followed on changes of administration. Expired terms were often equivalent to removals. The figures are incomplete and their significance is uncertain because relevant data were not preserved methodically in departmental files and not always stated in nominations.

Presidential policies in appointment varied from an emphasis on pleasing eastern politicians in 1870 to an emphasis on pleasing western politicians in 1890.[5] Candidates' interests varied from those of Secretary William Sanborn, who sought office in Arizona for the sake of his health,[6] to those of Governor James M. Ashley, who said that he went to Montana "for the express purpose of making this strong hold of democracy, Republican." [7] Too often appointments were "of young men or men out of employment, who would not be assigned to like positions in the States . . . or . . . broken-down politicians." [8] Some had bad reputations; few had acquaintance with western problems. The tenor and bulk of charges filed against officers suggest that if the average territorial officer was not a scoundrel in both official and private capacity, he was at least capable of arousing bitter enmity. Yet few charges cannot be discounted on the scores of intraterritorial divisions and of prejudice against appointed, non-resident officers.[9] Those proved dishonest or incompetent probably were outnumbered by those who attained high position and respect in new surroundings.[10] The most basic objection of westerners to territorial appointees was not that they were unfit but that they represented outside authority and an unpopular form of government.

Presidents did not always find it easy to keep their own choices in

[5] In the following rough analysis of types of recommendations filed anterior to nominations of governors and secretaries, each unit represents a type of recommendation (represented singly or plurally) for a nominee. "Territorial bodies" refers to legislatures, political conventions, bar associations, and other groups.

RECOMMENDATIONS

Presidency	State & national politicians	Territorial officers	Territorial bodies	Delegates
Lincoln	23	8	8	6
Johnson	10	10	7	5
Grant, 1869–73	25	4	2	4
Grant, 1873–77	6	2	2	2
Hayes	7	4	3	1
Arthur	10	5	2	2
Cleveland, 1885–89	10	9	12	4
Harrison, 1889-90	7	2	15	9

[6] W. Hartsuff to Chandler, November 3, 1865, State Appointments Files.
[7] Ashley to Fish, January 23, 1870, Fish Papers. He was accused of seeking a senatorship. Cong. Globe (40 Cong., 3 Sess.), Appendix, p. 218.
[8] William M. Stewart in Cong. Rec. (50 Cong., 1 Sess.), p. 6459.
[9] Wade, op. cit., p. 306.
[10] Men such as L. B. Prince (New Mexico), Elisha P. Ferry, Roger S. Greene (Washington), William P. Kellogg (Nebraska), John L. Routt (Colorado), and Decius S. Wade (Montana), all appointed as non-residents.

territorial offices. Low salaries, frontier discomforts, and endless ad ministrative difficulties discouraged most newcomers. According to former delegate Charles D. Poston, Arizona had been "a tarrying post for every political tramp for many years." All the governors had left the territory, but théy were "not much to blame," for Arizona had "been a poor goose to pluck." [11] None was more enthusiastic about the mountain country than William Gilpin, author of *The Mission of the North American People,* but as governor of Colorado he complained of having "the *legislature,* the *Indians,* the *military,* the *courts,* and this *wonderful population*—30,000 (all *Males*)—to manage, without a single skilled assistant." [12] Not a few regarded territorial service as exile, a political and physical Siberia. Some refused to serve even after the Senate had confirmed their nominations; many more resigned after brief periods in office.

Lincoln had an unusual opportunity in the territorial patronage. In 1861 he removed fifteen Democrats from territorial offices and accepted resignations from three more, retaining only four. Between 1861 and 1864 he was able to fill thirty offices in six new territories. Still "the pressure for place" at times overcame his own inclinations,[13] which were never implacably opposed to the use of patronage for party or politician.[14] Others were ready to promise territorial patronage for him. While Chairman James M. Ashley of the House Committee on Territories prepared bills to organize Idaho and Arizona, he promised an appointment in return for support for his own reëlection in 1862.[15] The several new territories of Lincoln's presidency were none too many for the demands of Congress. The bill organizing Arizona according to one story owed its passage to a judicious distribution of offices among lame ducks. C. D. Poston, who represented Arizona interests, implies that Ashley and Benjamin F. Wade advised this strategy:

He [Ashley?] said there were a number of members of the expiring Congress, who had been defeated in their own districts for the next term, who wanted to go West and offer their political services to the "galoots," and if they could

11 *History of Arizona Territory,* p. 210.

12 *Rocky Mountain News,* December 21, 1861.

13 John Conness to Johnson, May 31, 1865, State Appointments Files (under W. H. Wallace). Lincoln endorsed a recommendation from Hannibal Hamlin for Henry P. Torsey as secretary of Montana: "The Vice President says I promised to make the appointment, & I suppose I must make it." Hamlin to Lincoln, March 1, 1864, State Appointment Files.

14 Few instances suggest the restraint and purity of purpose attributed to him by Charles Anderson Dana in *Recollections of the Civil War,* pp. 74–75. For criticism of Dana's reliability, see Earl S. Pomeroy, "Lincoln, the Thirteenth Amendment, and the Admission of Nevada," *Pacific Historical Review,* XII (1943), pp. 362–68.

15 John Dixon to B. F. Wade, February 24, 1863, Wade Papers.

be grouped, and a satisfactory slate made, they would have influence enough to carry the bill through Congress. Consequently an "oyster supper" was organized to which the "lame ducks" were invited, and then and there the slate was made and the Territory was virtually organized.[16]

Certainly lame ducks flocked to Arizona and other territories. On the other hand, one of the most important holdovers from Buchanan's administration was Chief Justice Benedict of New Mexico, attacked as a Douglas Democrat but retained and reappointed as one of the President's old friends from Illinois.[17]

Johnson's territorial nominees were victims of the Tenure of Office Act. It is not true, however, that "no appointments . . . were confirmed . . . except the nominees were first recommended or indorsed by the Radical Members of Congress." [18] He was able to name a few Democrats [19] and even to pay an occasional political debt. Green Clay Smith of Kentucky, a rival for the vice-presidential nomination in 1864 who coöperated with the administration after the election, received the governorship of Montana.[20] Loyal officers pledged their support to the president and received his.[21]

Wyoming and Idaho were the greatest sufferers from radical opposition. J. M. Ashley had attacked the bill to organize Wyoming as a scheme for officeholders,[22] and although the radicals did not defeat it, they kept the offices vacant. Ten months passed before officers reached and organized the territory.[23] Republicans of Cheyenne offered to bear the expense if Johnson would send officers without waiting for confirmation: "The judges of Dacotah refused to hold court here and we are worse off than if we were not organized." [24] Secretary of the Interior James Harlan urged that the situation afforded "sufficient reason for an executive construction of all merely

16 *History of Arizona Territory*, p. 209.

17 Ralph Emerson Twitchell, "Kirby Benedict," *Old Santa Fe*, I (1913), 51, 83.

18 *Diary of Gideon Welles*, II, 126 note.

19 Men such as Justice Perry E. Brocchus and Chief Justice John S. Watts of New Mexico and Secretary Thomas F. Meagher of Montana, who described himself as a "Jacksonian Democrat." Meagher to Johnson, January 20, 1866, Johnson Papers.

20 Green Clay Goodloe, "Governor Green Clay Smith," *Contributions to the Montana Historical Society*, VII (1910), 217–18.

21 Opposite the signatures in such a message from New Mexican officials are Johnson's endorsements, "confirmed" and "not confirmed." R. B. Mitchell *et al.* to Johnson, September 27, 1866, Johnson, "Papers." Protestations of loyalty were less anxious than those under Grant, but give the impression of at least equal sincerity.

22 *Cong. Globe* (40 Cong., 2 Sess.), pp. 4344–45.

23 Governor Campbell's proclamation districting the territory was dated May 19, 1869. "Message of Governor Campbell . . . October 12, 1869," p. 3, TP, Wyoming, p. 23.

24 E. P. Snow to Seward, August 8, 1868, *ibid.*, pp. 7–9.

doubtful legal questions in favor of immediate organization." [25] Idaho faced not delay in organization but prolonged subjection to discredited officeholders. Governor David W. Ballard, removed early in January, 1867,[26] and, to resolve doubts voiced by cautious departmental lawyers,[27] suspended in August,[28] continued in office while the Senate refused to accept three different nominees to succeed him. A new governor did not appear and remain at his duties until nearly five years after Ballard's removal.[29] Evidence of his incompetence and dishonesty was such that the Indian office refused to act through him and Secretary McCulloch urged the use of military force to remove him,[30] but Johnson was powerless or chose to be cautious. The territorial secretary had a reputation for peculation and misconduct such as would ordinarily have justified prompt removal; protected by departmental construction of the Tenure of Office Act,[31] he continued in office until removed in 1868, only to be restored by Grant. The Senate refused to confirm nominations of successors to Governor William Pickering of Washington, who was accused of incompetency as well as of radicalism,[32] and to Secretary Frank Hall of Colorado.[33]

Fortunately for Johnson and for the territories, not all vacancies occurred at the height of radical strength, or attracted concerted radical opposition. Being politically isolated, however, the President generally lacked reliable information on which to base his selections. He often turned to Senator James W. Nesmith,[34] whose recommendation in turn was probably responsible for the influence of Delegate Edward D. Holbrook of Idaho.[35] Dependence on territorial advice

[25] Harlan to Seward, September 25, 1868, *ibid.*, pp. 19–20.

[26] *Senate Executive Journal*, XV, 76.

[27] Memorandum, E. P. Smith, May 1, 1867, TP, Idaho, I, 341–47; J. M. Binckley to Seward, July 30, 1867, *ibid.*, II, 105–6.

[28] Seward to Ballard, August 28, 1867, "Domestic Letters," LXXVII, 37. See William Turrentine Jackson, "Indian Affairs and Politics in Idaho Territory, 1863–1870," *Pacific Historical Review*, XIV (1945), 311–25.

[29] Hailey, *op. cit.*, pp. 164–65.

[30] *Diary of Gideon Welles*, III, 186; *supra*, p. 17.

[31] Memorandum, Charges against S. R. Howlett . . . , E. P. Smith, June 11, 1867, TP, Idaho, I, 365–68.

[32] Memorandum, Governor of Washington Territory, n.d., State Appointments File.

[33] Alexander Cummings to Seward, September 8, 1866, State Appointments File; Hall to Fish, October 2, 1871, TP, Colorado, I, 353.

[34] E.g., Johnson endorsed charges against Pickering (apparently in favor of G. E. Cole), "If Senator Nesmith desires this appointment now, let it be made." State Appointment Files.

[35] *Infra,* p. 84.

involved Johnson in intraterritorial rivalries and sometimes brought forward men of questionable fitness, not easily displaced.[36] The revival of conventional political influences in 1869 did not erase all difficulties in territorial appointments. Grant made 137 appointments to 45 offices: 25 did not take office. He did not find a governor of Idaho until December 1871, nearly five years after Johnson had tried to remove Governor Ballard. But Grant was the worst enemy of the service. More than Johnson, he watched for signs of personal loyalty and disloyalty. In consequence the territorial correspondence was choked with anxious protestations of political faith and violent charges of political betrayal. Removals on such grounds were many and sudden. James M. Ashley, former Radical chairman of the House Committee on Territories, appointed governor of Montana, complained that he "had but just unpacked my furniture when" removed [37]—perhaps because he had been accused of criticizing Grant's appointments, or of being a friend of Charles Sumner.[38] Governor Emery of Utah brought about the removal of Secretary Black, a political rival, on charges of denouncing Grant.[39]

For advice Grant often turned, as Johnson had done, to an Oregon senator, in this case John H. Mitchell. Mitchell endorsed candidates on a baldly political basis,[40] intervened in departmental channels,[41] and, together with certain colleagues from the Pacific Coast, exercised a sort of guardianship over the northwestern territories. Idaho, Governor Brayman said later, was "a political dependency of Oregon. Senator (Atty. Genl) Williams and others of his class controlled appointments here. In rewarding political and personal services, men unfit and unacceptable in Oregon, were billeted upon Idaho." [42] Members of Congress tended to expect to influence patronage in territories adjoining their home states: the East, politically speaking, included Kansas, Oregon, and California as well as New York and Pennsylvania. Mitchell's greatest influence was in Washington, Idaho, and Utah. California-Nevada control was most effective in

---

[36] *Infra*, p. 74.
[37] Ashley to Seward, December 20, 1869, TP, Montana, I, 186–87.
[38] Helena *Weekly Herald*, clipping, n.d., enclosed in H. E. Fisk to Grant, March 29, 1870, State Appointments File; D. Wilson to Fish, January 13, 1870, State Department Miscellaneous Letters; Charles S. Ashley, "Governor Ashley's Biography and Messages," *Contributions to the Historical Society of Montana*, VI (1907), 194.
[39] G. A. Black to Schurz, April 9, 1877, Interior Appointment File 141.
[40] E.g., "His [D. P. Thompson's] appointment [as governor of Idaho] would be *invaluable* to the *Republican party* in Oregon in our next campaign." Mitchell to Grant, November 24, 1875, Interior Appointment File 134.
[41] E.g., receiving the resignation of Governor Woods of Utah. Woods to Grant, November 8, 1873, *ibid.* 138.
[42] Brayman to J. F. Christiancy, March 27, 1877, *ibid.* 140 (under Curtis).

Arizona and New Mexico, while Dakota depended on Minnesota.
Territorial parties acknowledged the situation by addressing an appeal, for instance, to "U.S. Senators from the Pacific Coast States." [43]
Politicians generally, whether from East or West, claimed and received shares of territorial appointments for their states. Delivering
a governorship was both proof of personal political power [44] and
means of maintaining the party's hold on a state. The older states
conceded no priority in influence to the states along the territorial
frontier. Zachariah Chandler argued on behalf of his candidate for
the governorship of New Mexico,

> Michigan is almost without representation in Territorial appointments
> while Kansas is *well taken care of.* . . . [If] the appointment lies between
> Michigan and Kansas, . . . it ought not to lie there long. Michigan never
> wavers *any where.* She is found at the ballot box, at conventions in the
> Senate, House of Representatives *everywhere* & 1,250,000 such people are
> not excelled even by Kansas.[45]

Notions of specific quotas of territorial appointments for the states
were fairly prevalent. When Congress considered partitioning Dakota in 1874, there were " 'states' already made up, by the Politicians
for the officers—Gov, Sec, Judges, etc." [46] Thus pressed, Grant extended favors freely—and withdrew them almost as fast as he gave
them out.[47] The very number of Grant's appointments illustrates this
trait: there was little certainty of tenure in the face of constantly
contending influences.

Favors were purely personal as well as political. John Rawlins'
friendship gave the secretaryship of Dakota to T. M. Wilkins, and
until Rawlins' death kept it for him despite private and official
misconduct.[48] When Secretary Edwin S. McCook of Dakota was

[43] L. F. Carter and G. Goodrich (chairman of the Idaho Republican and Democratic committees) to Mitchell *et al.,* December 26, 1878, enclosed in Mitchell *et al.*
to President, January 20, 1879, *ibid.* 166.

[44] Senator J. M. Thayer was told that procuring the governorship of Utah for
Silas A. Strickland would be "as strong an argument as can be given the Ligislature
[*sic*] in favor of your re-election." J. E. Lancaster to Thayer, November 7, 1870,
State Appointments File.

[45] Chandler to Fish, July 16, 1871, *ibid.*

[46] W. K. Rogers to Hayes, October 13, 1874, Hayes Papers. Cf. R. C. Schenck to
Fish, December 9, 1870, Fish Papers.

[47] When Stephen B. Elkins had a friend appointed as secretary of New Mexico,
the incumbent's congressional sponsors protested that "his removal . . . would
impress the people of Wisconsin very unfavorably—and we therefore earnestly
ask that he may be restored." Grant ordered reappointment "to correct an injustice
that has unintentionally been done." T. O. Howe *et al.* to Grant, May 29, 1876,
Interior Appointment File 140.

[48] Affidavit, G. W. Kingsbury, March 24, 1870; J. B. S. Todd to Grant, May 15,
1870, State Appointments File. Wilkins to Grant, March 20, 1872, TP, Dakota, I,
287–88.

murdered, his father-in-law, Oscar A. Whitney, succeeded as a matter of "justice to the memory of the late Secretary—justice also to his bereaved family." [49] Both Wilkins and Whitney, however, found themselves out of office as soon as Grant's sentimentality had spent itself. The surest and safest appeal lay in a record of service in the Union Army and of personal loyalty to Grant (rather than loyalty to the party). Grant occasionally was willing to overlook party irregularity in firm administration supporters. [50]

During the Hayes administration political influences were less turbulent and competitive, though not unimportant in the placement process. Hayes made relatively few territorial appointments. When he decided on replacements, after due deliberation, he tended to allow incumbents to finish their terms before substituting his own men. [51]

While congressmen under Hayes had not the ready access to territorial patronage that they had had in the Grant period, states received their quotas of appointments and political creditors their dividends. Governor R. J. Oglesby apparently administered the "share of Territorial appointments" pertaining to the state of Illinois. [52] The governorship of Dakota went to an applicant who asked if "New Hampshire, from whose citizens no Territorial Governor has ever been appointed, [is not] worthy of recognition at this time?" [53] To John C. Frémont went the governorship of Arizona for claims dating from the election of 1864. [54] At least two men who had helped Hayes in 1876–1877 received governorships: Lew Wallace, who had witnessed returning board counts in Louisiana and Florida, went to New Mexico, [55] while Willian A. Howard, credited with turning Michigan's vote to Hayes at the Cincinnati convention, went to Dakota. [56] Reformers in and outside the administration gave no thought to extending civil service reform or its spirit to the territories.

[49] W. P. Dewey to Delano, September 12, 1873, Interior Appointment File 139.

[50] E.g., J. B. Brown, secretary of Wyoming, 1873–75, a Democrat until 1872, but recommended as a victim of Democratic persecution for his active support of Grant. O. P. Morton to Grant, February 5, 1873, ibid. 142.

[51] Thus A. Worth Spates was promised the secretaryship of Wyoming at least three months, and recommended for it eleven months, before Secretary French's term expired. Spates to Hayes, December 18, 1878, and passim, ibid. 142.

[52] R. J. Oglesby to Frank H. Hurlbut, April 3, 1877; C. L. Fort to Hurlbut, March 12, 1877, ibid. 139.

[53] N. G. Ordway to Hayes, January 1, 1879, ibid. 167.

[54] Frémont to Chandler, May 23, 1878; Jessie B. Frémont to Hayes, July 7, 18[81?], Hayes Papers.

[55] Wallace to Chandler, February 7, 1877, Chandler Papers.

[56] A. H. Morrison to Hayes, December 31, 1877, Hayes Papers; Bismarck Tribune, April 16, 1880; Harriette May Dilla, The Politics of Michigan, 1865–1878, pp. 190–91.

Politicians continued to influence appointments in all administrations: there was no other way to relieve their pressure or to fill the offices they coveted. As large scale mining, railroad, and stock-raising organizations increased their control of western economies, however, the corporation executive vied for influence with the politician. The first considerable evidence of open pressure from eastern businessmen as such appeared under Arthur. A Pennsylvania railroad president wrote frankly,

> Having probably the largest interests in the territory of Idaho, we naturally feel an interest in its Government. . . . Inasmuch, as a few Philadelphians included in our Corporation, have invested several Millions of Dollars in the Territory we feel that Philadelphia has very strong claims.[57]

"Neither I nor my associates," said C. P. Huntington, urging retention of Chief Justice S. B. Axtell of New Mexico, "have any case likely to come before him, although we are interested as large property holders in the maintenance of good government in the Territory."[58] A resident of Arizona complained that "California & Nevada are claiming the privilege of naming a governor & secretary for the Territory on account of their great interest there."[59] Yet it is difficult to say whether "business" was much more influential than in earlier years when it was more customary to sign letters of recommendation as alderman or veteran than as stockholder or banker. Since businessmen, unlike congressmen, came from territories as well as from states, they might speak even for local public opinion instead of for their economic interests.

Cleveland's policy in territorial appointments was a gratifying surprise to Republican incumbents and a source of anguish to starved Democratic office-seekers. "I presume it will take Mr. Cleveland about thirty days to reach my case after the fourth of March, when I expect to be displaced," wrote Secretary Nicholas H. Owings of Washington Territory.[60] Owings remained long enough to be displaced by a nominee of Harrison. Some others were almost as fortunate. In his first year Cleveland removed only seven territorial officials, generally waiting for vacancies to occur naturally.

Expediency rather than idealism may have restrained the President. It was a very real condition which confronted him when one of Arthur's appointees had new Democratic affiliations, or when an emergency demanded that a strong governor continue. Secretary

[57] P. A. B. Widener to Arthur, December 29, 1883, Interior Appointment File 166. The candidate, W. M. Bunn, also had important political support.
[58] Huntington to Arthur, June 24, 1884, Justice Appointment Papers, New Mexico.
[59] Reuben Wood to Arthur, January 17, 1882, Interior Appointment File 163.
[60] Owings to Hayes, March 1, 1885, Hayes Papers.

Owings' brother was publisher of the Brooklyn *Union-Argus,* a Republican newspaper which supported Cleveland.[61] Supporters of Governor Watson C. Squire of Washington argued that his removal "would be construed as disapproval of Squires Course in upholding Law & suppressing Violence against [the] Chinese," [62] and the danger of riots was not over. Similarly, Mark Hanna and James W. Savage, as government directors of the Union Pacific, urged that, while Governor Francis E. Warren of Wyoming *"should be removed,* his dismissal would be a triumph for those who sympathized with the Rock Spring rioters." [63] Secretary Thomas of Utah found protection in his usefulness to the Utah Commission.[64] Cleveland was awake to the need for experience and continuity in major offices as well as minor; tolerating Republicans in individual cases amounted almost to a general rule of no removals except for unfitness.

The Republicans who continued in office outraged Democratic spoilsmen who had difficulty in accommodating themselves even to the administration's very limited program of civil service reform. A flood of protests and charges poured into the departments, appealing to partisanship that could not be forgotten overnight. The annoyance of political agitation balanced the efficiency of experience. Governor Gilbert A. Pierce of Dakota resigned with a tribute to Cleveland's "spirit of tolerance":

Offices of this character were made an exception to the rules governing removal from office laid down by you at the opening of your administartion [*sic*], but you have . . . never by act or word indicated that my continuance in the office was not entirely acceptable.

I tender my resignation now because the pressure for the place subjects you to constant annoyance, and because I feel my own usefulness is impaired by the constant agitation of the question of change.[65]

Democrats had accumulated a great appetite for office during twenty-four years of exile. They were, moreover, more concerned with extending party influence in territories of Republican tendency than Republicans would have been. Statehood was near at hand for several territories which might be Democratic states if a Democratic president gave proper encouragement to the territorial wings of the party. A supporter of Edmund G. Ross for governor of New Mexico

[61] H. C. King to D. S. Lamont, March 10, 1885; A. McLean to Lamont, April 4, 1885; A. M. Bliss to Lamont, April 16, 1885, Interior Appointment File 242.
[62] W. H. White *et al.* to Cleveland, February 23 [1886], *ibid.* 238. *Infra,* p. 86.
[63] Hanna and Savage to Cleveland, October 14, 1885, *ibid.* 239. Pyle says that Hill advised Cleveland on Northwest and Dakota appointments. Joseph Gilpin Pyle, *The Life of James J. Hill,* I, 426–27.
[64] Pettigrew to A. H. Garland, April 30, 1885, Interior Appointment File 242.
[65] Pierce to Cleveland, November 15, 1886, *ibid.* 164.

wrote, "I do not know him personally but I find he is strongly endorsed by the leading citizens, men . . . whose influence will be felt to hold New Mexico as a Democratic ally when she assumes the dignity of a State which she will soon do. . . ." [66] While Governor Pierce and his Republican colleagues remained in office, Republicans remained in possession of the minor patronage which federal officers controlled under territorial law.[67] It was so in Washington, where Democrats called for removal of Governor Squire: "The appointment should be made . . . soon as the governor has considerable patronage and will have Something to do with the next general election." [68] The administration's good intentions were weakened by such attrition within the party. Cleveland's removals were more numerous and more political after 1886.

The Republican sweep of territorial offices in 1889 was immediate and uncompromising. The Omnibus Bill had passed; it was important to keep the advantage from the Democrats. Boss Quay endorsed a statement of "the political necessity which exists for the . . . appointment of Republicans . . . in order that the election Machinery may be in friendly hands pending the formation of the state [of Idaho]. . . . It will . . . insure the admission of another Republican State into the Union." [69]

Harrison disposed of most of the Democratic governors and secretaries within his second week in office. Justices, perhaps because less important politically in the admission process, lingered until fall or beyond under stays of political execution. Some officers received brusque telegraphed requests for their resignations; [70] one new appointee arrived before his predecessor had notice of his removal.[71] Secretary Michael L. McCormack of Dakota was refused two additional weeks in office to make out his reports.[72]

Harrison's partisanship was strict but not unfamiliar. It was new only in degree and speed of application. It surprised no one because Harrison pretended only to traditionalism, and because Cleveland had not been able to establish a tradition of non-partisanship, in

[66] L. R. Bacon to Cleveland, May 9, 1885, *ibid.* 237.

[67] W. B. McConnell to Cleveland, October 21, 1886, *ibid.* 235. In Wyoming there was the additional danger that the Republican court would prevent removal of Republican appointees. J. C. Friend *et al.* to W. D. Hill, January 23, 1886, *ibid.* 239 (under Warren).

[68] T. H. Cann to W. R. Morrison, September 4, 1885, *ibid.* 238 (under Semple).

[69] S. L. Wright to W. L. Elkins and Widener, March 19, 1889, enclosed in Elkins & Widener to Quay, March 20, 1889, *ibid.* 430.

[70] E.g., W. C. Hall to Noble, May 4, 1889; Hall to Noble, May 5, 1889, *ibid.*, 241.

[71] G. W. Lane to Noble, June 3, 1889, *ibid.*

[72] M. L. McCormack to Noble, March 8, 1889, *ibid.* 240; Noble to McCormack, March 11, 1889, March 12, 1889, Interior, Appointment Letters, IX, 440 1/2, 440.

territorial or in national opinion. The excitement of the admission process answered or overshadowed any criticism, and there were few critics. Territorial opinion tended rather to praise Harrison for a really new departure: he was the first president to appoint territorial residents generally and successfully.

Non-resident appointments had been subjects of frequent argument and occasional experiment long before 1889. They were never obligatory, and Congress did not apply even the freehold qualification of the Ordinance of 1787 to the trans-Mississippi west and Florida.

The number of nominees claiming territorial residence had fluctuated without rising much above one-third of the total in any administration before 1889.[73] The number of actual and accepted residents probably was much smaller. The facts of residence as stated in nominations and commissions were often merely what the men concerned wanted them to be. It was possible to establish legal territorial residence before acquiring a territorial point of view. Lewis Wolfley is known as the first resident governor of Arizona (1889–90),[74] though Richard C. McCormick (1866–69) and C. M. Zulick (1885–89) had claimed Arizona residence. McCormick had been territorial secretary, appointed from New York in 1863; Zulick was surrogate in New Jersey six months before his commission.[75] Yet Governor Elisha P. Ferry of Washington (1872–80) was considered

[73] The following table represents numbers of residents and non-residents nominated to be governor, secretary, or judge (including nominations rejected and reappointments of nominees of predecessors).

| President | Residents | | | | Non-residents | | | |
	G	S	J	Total	G	S	J	Total
Lincoln	6	5	10	21	13	13	43	69
Johnson	6	8	8	22	11	11	17	39
Grant	6	10	21	37	28	24	40	92
Hayes	1	2	8	11	10	6	26	42
Garfield	.? 0	0	0	0	1	0	2	3
Arthur	2	4	6	12	10	3	21	34
Cleveland	9	2	12	23	3	2	20	34
Harrison, 1889–90	10	5	14	29	0	0	5	5

[74] Effie R. Keen, "Arizona's Governors," *Arizona Historical Review*, III (1930), No. 13, p. 11.
[75] Zulick to J. R. McPherson, June 8, 1885, Interior Appointment File 234. R. E. Sloan considered himself the "first bona fide resident" judge of Arizona (*op. cit.*, p. 79), despite claims of Justices J. De Forrest Porter and Joseph H. Kibbey. Kibbey's two-year residence (Keen, "Arizona's Governors," p. 16) may have been overlooked because of his unpopularity and political appointment. Sloan, *op. cit.*, pp. 76–77; *St. Louis Republic*, April 27, 1892; Abram Humphries, "Removal of Territorial Judges," *American Law Review*, XXVI (1892), 471.

a resident, though twice commissioned as from Illinois.[76] Territorial citizens reserved the informal designation of "bona fide resident" for men whom they accepted, regardless of legal qualifications or of eastern political connections.

Aside from considerations of patronage, there were always persuasive arguments for limiting offices to Easterners. During the Civil War, the danger of general disloyalty and the "Pacific Republic" project increased the "importance of having *good reliable Republicans*" in office, in the words of Secretary Arny of New Mexico, who advised Seward "to ignore all applications from persons in New Mexico, and *appoint well known and reliable Republicans* who have never been here." [77] "There are candidates here," wrote Chief Justice Hall of Colorado, "but it will be unsafe . . . to appoint them." [78]

Appointment of residents was often more of a concession to popular demands than a fulfillment of administrative needs. A former delegate from Dakota said in 1866 that "outside the officials, there is not a man . . . that has the legal knowledge or qualification" for a judgeship.[79] Some residents when appointed proved to be dishonest: these included two of the greediest embezzlers of government funds.[80] Residents were not easily chosen, for candidates and their backers were often unknown and might obtain endorsements by fraud or even by threat. In Arizona in 1885 petitions circulated freely "for Federal appointments, at from fifty cents to one dollar for each subscriber." [81] Governor John W. Hoyt of Wyoming reportedly obtained a legislative memorial for his reappointment "by an intimation that certain Territorial appointments would not be made." [82] The best of testimonials were no guarantee of satisfaction in the face of intraterritorial rivalries, as bitter as any in the states. Attacks against residents might be as savage as against non-residents: to appoint a member of any faction was to embarrass the party as a whole. Two leading Idaho Republicans argued that "the appointment of . . . any man from the Territory at present as Governor will only keep up a factional fight in the Republican party Better appoint a

[76] Francis Tarbell to Brents, December 12, 1879; P. P. Canoll to Brents, January 3, 1880, Interior Appointments File 168.

[77] Arny to Seward, January 6, 1865, TP, New Mexico, III, 1–5.

[78] Benjamin F. Hall to Seward, October 30, 1861, TP, Colorado, I, 32.

[79] J. B. S. Todd to Harlan, June 20, 1866, Johnson Papers. Todd's statement must be considered in light of his rivalry with Delegate W. A. Burleigh, who controlled Dakota appointments under Johnson.

[80] Webb of Montana (*supra*, p. 34) and Gilson of Idaho (*supra*, p. 30).

[81] Poston to Cleveland, April 4, 1885, Interior Appointment File 234.

[82] F. J. Stanton to J. A. Logan, April 3, 1882, *ibid.* 169.

new man for the sake of peace." [83] Generally the executive impulse to
appoint from the territories was sporadic and needed no better
answer.

Some of Lincoln's few appointments of residents suggest a simple
strategy to hold the territories to the Union and to the party. New
Mexico in particular smoldered with secessionism; Utah, astride the
central route to the West Coast, was to be suspect for many years
after the war of 1857. Appointment of a man like Delegate Miguel
A. Otero as secretary of New Mexico may well have been designed to
"strengthen the attachment of the people to the union, and to pre-
serve the Territory from internal discontent and protect it from the
anticipated invasion from without." [84] Both he and Henry Connelly,
nominated as governor, were residents, recommended by the territorial delegate, but the Senate rejected Otero's nomination, and the
territory went temporarily to the Confederacy, which met a grievance
of long standing by organizing the territory of Arizona.[85] Lincoln appointed only two residents in Utah, but he asked the territorial delegate for suggestions, and a church historian says that his course
was "uniformly considerate" and "designed . . . to conciliate ex-
Governor Young and the Mormons." [86] He apparently gave attention
to an appeal from Nebraska not to send Easterners: "We have beaten
the democracy with all their patronage by telling the people that the
republican party would give the offices to actual residents. We shall
have no party left in the territory if this promise is not in part at least
performed." [87] Appeals from the East ordinarily were urgent enough,
however, to keep the territorial patronage in its accustomed channels.
Perhaps because the rapidity of the admission process gave him little
opportunity, Lincoln did not even make special concessions to residents of prospective new states.

[83] D. Bacon and R. A. Sidebotham to H. H. Bingham, January 25, 1884, ibid.
166. Cf. (relative to Arizona) L. T. Eggers to Noble, September 8, 1890, ibid. 348
(under Murphy).

[84] John S. Watts to Seward, March 13, 1861, State Appointments File. Rejection
of Otero's nomination in favor of that of a man like Holmes, informer as well as
defaulter (Santa Fé Gazette, October 4, 1862, October 18, 1862), suggests how little
Congress appreciated the strategy of warding off Confederate appeals to dissatisfaction.

[85] See Loomis M. Ganaway, "New Mexico and the Sectional Controversy, 1846–
1861," New Mexico Historical Review, XVIII (1943), 342–43.

[86] Edward W. Tullidge, The History of Salt Lake City and Its Founders, pp. 249,
325. It was said that in 1865 half or two-thirds of federal officials in Utah were
polygamists. Bowles, op. cit., 109. In Utah appointment of anyone tolerant of
Mormonism was the practical equivalent of a resident appointment.

[87] A. S. Paddock to Seward, March 27, 1861, State Appointments File. Cf. S. G.
Daily to Lincoln, April 4, 1861, ibid.

The political emergency of the Civil War did not permit a policy of resident appointments; neither reform nor practical politics during the next twenty years demanded it. Johnson nominated a good number of territorial residents, perhaps because of his isolation from the ordinary Congressional advisers. For convenience and for the sake of peace in the executive offices, governors had some influence then and thereafter in the nomination of secretaries; available candidates were likely to be residents.[88] Grant seemed friendly to a joint territorial request for "home rule" in 1872,[89] but the following year said that men from the states were necessary to hold together the territorial wings of the party.[90] Shortly before, the surveyor-general of Dakota had written that "it is better . . . to take new men for appointees, those entirely outside of the territory and who are in no way embarrassed with former complications." [91] Still residence was often a recommendation, if seldom a qualification. In 1876, according to the New York *Sun*, Republicans planned to pass a territorial "home rule" bill in the event of Democratic victory, to limit patronage.[92]

Before the election of 1884, the Democratic House passed a bill requiring residence for governors,[93] while the Republican Senate defended traditional practices:

In many instances, owing to party complications and unhealthy alliances . . . , it was almost impossible to select impartial and unprejudiced persons . . . from residents. . . . It often happens that schemes exist in the Territories, or a certain policy prevails that Congress is anxious to suppress . . . , with which every resident otherwise fit to be governor is not only identified, but is exerting himself to maintain . . . , and to limit the selection to residents . . . would in such cases amount to encouraging strife and discord. . . .

The Territories being the common property of the United States . . . , the committee can see no good reason why these Territorial officers may not be selected from the States having an interest in these Territories.[94]

A month later, however, the Republican convention at Chicago adopted a position essentially similar to that of the House, though without restricting it to governors or recommending a statutory re-

[88] Brayman to Christiancy, March 27, 1877, Interior Appointment File 140 (under Curtis); William M. Bunn to Teller, October 18, 1884, *Annual Report of the Secretary of the Interior . . . 1884*, II, 552; *supra*, pp. 66–67, 84–85.
[89] Armstrong, *Early Empire Builders*, 220.
[90] *Ibid*. 270. He referred in particular to Dakota.
[91] W. P. Dewey to Delano, November 25, 1873, Interior Appointment File 139.
[92] Quoted in Cheyenne *Wyoming Weekly Herald*, May 6, 1876; cf. H. R. 179 and H. R. 2792, *House Journal* (44 Cong., 1 Sess.), pp. 51, 621.
[93] H. R. 4713. *House Reports* (48 Cong., 1 Sess.), No. 477, p. 1.
[94] *Senate Reports* (48 Cong., 1 Sess.), No. 496, pp. 1–2.

quirement.[95] The Democrats followed suit in July.[96] Thus both parties grew generous as the territories matured and as the contest of 1884 approached. After the Democratic victory in the fall the Republican delegate from Wyoming warned that generosity was still good politics: the people

do not want a sick man or a politician sent from elsewhere. The prominent republicans say very freely that they had rather have a decent resident democrat fill the place than the best non-resident republican. . . . . . You know, that if the republican party would again come into power . . . that it must be done through the progressive western States and Territories.[97]

Francis E. Warren, the prominent Wyoming rancher whom Arthur named as governor during his last month in office, remained as governor until November of 1886, aided by the Union Pacific[98] and by a split among Wyoming Democrats.[99] Then he was suspended after charges of enclosing government land and of collusion in a territorial "salary grab."[100] His successor, another resident, was asked to resign after a month in office when it appeared that he, too, was implicated in illegal enclosures.[101]

By 1886–87 Cleveland was besieged by eastern spoilsmen on the one side and by Land Office Commissioner Sparks on the other. Reform in the territories meant conservation, not home rule or even civil service reform, and leading territorial politicians were likely to be leading landowners as well. Governor Samuel T. Hauser of Montana, like Warren, disagreed with the policies of Commissioner Sparks and resigned, for that reason or because of the pressure of private affairs.[102] He was succeeded by a former governor of Ken-

[95] *Official Proceedings of the Republican National Convention . . . 1884*, p. 93. The resolution as offered by A. H. Stebbins of Arizona read, "from the bona fide residents of the Territory, and in accordance with the wishes of the people thereof." *Ibid.*, p. 44.
[96] Referring to "Federal officers for the Territories" rather than merely to governors. *Official Proceedings of the National Democratic Convention . . . 1884*, pp. 199, 203.
[97] Joseph M. Carey to Teller, January 26, 1885, Interior Appointment File 239.
[98] *Supra*, p. 71.
[99] Rawlins *Journal*, February 28, 1885; Laramie *Boomerang*, February 20, 1885.
[100] Warren later stated, while under attack for "jumping cornerstones," that he had been removed "for criticizing Commissioner Sparks in my annual report in 1886." New York *World*, June 27, 1889. Charges filed in 1885–86, however, related mainly to finances; land fencing was mentioned in 1885 (not in 1886) without emphasis. Interior Appointment File 340, *passim*.
[101] George W. Baxter to H. E. Johnson, June 2, 1888, *ibid.* 239.
[102] Hauser's resignation refers briefly to private demands. Hauser to Cleveland, December 13, 1886, *ibid*, 236. Warren later said that Sparks demanded removal of himself and Hauser for comments made in their annual reports, but that Hauser, being a Democrat, was allowed to resign. Francis Emroy Warren, Dictation, pp.

tucky; [103] the new governor of Wyoming had run for the governorship in Kansas.[104] After 1886, Cleveland nominated fewer residents. The House Committee on Territories receded from the stand it had taken against eastern appointments under a Republican president in 1884, reporting that "while . . . whenever practicable the Territorial offices should be filled by appointment of . . . qualified electors . . . it would be unwise to require by statute that this should be done in all cases." [105] The author of this report himself was appointed as chief justice of Washington in 1888.[106]

The Democratic platform of 1888 attacked the Republicans for stopping admission bills but omitted all mention of appointments.[107] The Republicans, whose turn it was to be emphatic, resolved that "pending the preparation for statehood all officers thereof should be selected from the bona fide residents and citizens of the Territories wherein they are to serve." [108]

It was easy for Republicans to renounce territorial patronage in 1889: the reward of a few months of virtuous abstinence was to be a sizeable block of Republican votes in Congress. In some quarters resident appointments were regarded as provisional grants of self-government pending formal congressional action in the form of admission. A banner in the streets of Cheyenne read "Hurrah for Home Rule and Statehood; Vox Populi, Vox Dei; Warren." [109] Cleveland's intentions may have been relatively disinterested, but they met with unpropitious circumstances. Harrison from the first made strictly partisan appointments, from among partisans within the territories. Far limiting his resident appointments to territories facing immediate statehood, however, he extended them also to Utah, New Mexico, and Arizona.

Republicans in the territories received the party's promise in good faith, and prepared to accept nominations amicably, regardless of factions. In some cases they made concerted suggestions. The Rock Springs *Independent*, reminding Wyoming Republicans that discord among Democrats had led to the removal of Governor Baxter (1885–86) and "the infliction of Moonlight," urged a prearranged dis-

33–34. Warren's criticisms were far more extensive; Stevenson of Idaho also criticized the land laws but continued in office. *Report of the Secretary of the Interior for 1886*, II, 834, 1006–16, 849–51.

[103] John W. Wade, "Hon. Preston Hopkins Leslie; a Short Sketch of his Life," *Contributions of the Historical Society of Montana*, VII (1910), 203–14.

[104] T. P. Fenlon to Cleveland, November 10, 1886, Interior Appointment File 239.

[105] *House Reports*, (49 Cong., I Sess.), No. 2581.

[106] Cf. *Cong. Rec.* (50 Cong., 2 Sess.), No. 822.

[107] *American Annual Cyclopedia . . . 1888*, p. 774.

[108] *Official Proceedings of the Republican National Convention . . . 1888*, p. 110.

[109] Cheyenne *Daily Sun*, April 10, 1889.

tribution of offices among factions and sections.[110] The Wyoming Territorial Republican Committee conducted a preference poll of its members, and found all replying in favor of former Governor Warren.[111] North Dakota Republicans in Washington convened to nominate Luther B. Richardson as secretary.[112] The Montana delegate consulted territorial political leaders by telegraph and agreed with them on B. F. White for the governorship.[113] Harrison's attention to such suggestions, and the territorial parties' acquiescence in appointments made, doubtless helped to make his policy more successful than Cleveland's had been.

The practice of appointing residents, perhaps because further admissions were always imminent, continued until the admission of the forty-eighth state in 1912.[114] Appointments after 1889 were not the constant grievance they had been in the territories; they largely ceased to be political spoils in the states. But any prospects for a territorial service of trained, experienced administrators fell away with the cry of "carpetbagger." There is no clear reason that this, the actual course of events, was not the better course from the point of view of free western political development, whatever it was from the point of view of administrative efficiency. By 1912, when Alaska achieved full territorial status, or even by 1861, territorial government was far more organic, satisfactorily organic, far less systematic, than the organic acts themselves indicate. Practices and policies in appointment, both before and after 1889, were significantly incompatible with the growth of a territorial system.

[110] January 24, 1889.
[111] A. D. Kelley to Carey, March 10, 1889, Interior Appointment File 431.
[112] Copy of proceedings, March 6, 1889, enclosed in Harrison Allen to Noble, March 8, 1889, ibid. 430.
[113] Thomas H. Carter to Noble, March 23, 1889, ibid.
[114] Note also the practice generally obtaining in Hawaii under the acts of April 4, 1900 (Statutes, XXXI, 153) and July 9, 1921 (ibid., XLII, 116). When President Roosevelt asked permission to appoint a non-resident, the minority of the House Committee on Territories and Insular Possessions reported that "Appointment of any person governor other than a resident would place this Territory in the status of a colonial possession to be ruled arbitrarily. . . . The right of any part of the United States to representative government has always been recognized for Hawaii as well as for the rest of the United States." House Reports (73 Cong., 1 Sess.), No. 168, p. 3; see also Earl S. Pomeroy, "Election of the Governor of Puerto Rico," Southwestern Social Science Quarterly, XXIII (1943), 357.

Chapter VII

THE DELEGATE IN TERRITORIAL RELATIONS

THE territorial delegate increased in stature appreciably between 1861 and 1890. Without the formal powers of a congressman, he acquired more of a congressman's influence and general functions. He was disseminator of information, lobbyist, agent of territorial officers, of the territorial legislature, and of his constituency, self-constituted dispenser of patronage. He interceded at times in almost every process of control over the territories, and generally no one challenged his right to intercede.

The statutory powers of the delegate did not change appreciably after the Ordinance of 1787, giving him "a seat in Congress, with a right of debating, but not of voting," [1] and the Act of 1817, which belatedly assigned him to the House of Representatives,[2] over twenty-two years after the seating of a delegate from the Territory South of the River Ohio.[3]

Delegates were members of occasional select committees in early years, and also of the Committee of the Whole.[4] The first regular assignment of a delegate to committee duty was under a rule of 1871 providing "from among the Delegates from the Territories an additional member of the Committee on the Territories." In committee, as on the floor of the House, he had no vote. According to Representative Randall of the Committee on Rules, the object of the assignment was "simply to facilitate legislation, and to make that legislation intelligent and wise." [5] The *Rocky Mountain News* saw

---

[1] Confirmed in the Act of August 7, 1789, *Statutes*, I, 50–53. *Journals of the Continental Congress*, XXXII, 339. In 1880 Downey of Wyoming introduced an amendment to give each territory one member in the House. *Cong. Rec.* (46 Cong., 2 Sess.), p. 1941.

[2] Act of March 3, 1817, *Statutes*, III, 363.

[3] *Annals of Congress* (3 Cong.), IV, 884–88, 888–90, 891.

[4] *Cong. Globe* (42 Cong., 2 Sess.), p. 118; cf. *House Reports* (27 Cong., 1 Sess.), No. 10, p. 5, and ·*House Journal* (12 Cong., I Sess.), pp. 84, 247, cited in Asher Crosby Hinds, *Hinds' Precedents of the House of Representatives*, II, Secs., 1299, 1301, p. 865.

[5] The rule also placed the District of Columbia's delegate on the District committee. *Cong. Globe* (42 Cong., 2 Sess.), pp. 117–18.

an important increase in influence, "a recognition of territorial rights as unexpected as it is gratifying."[6] Further committee appointments followed in 1876, 1880, and 1887,[7] bringing the total to nine. The rule of 1871 presupposed that the single delegate on the Committee on the Territories would be "the representative of the opinions of . . . the nine representatives of the Territories." Representative Randall explained that "the Delegates have formed among themselves as it were a *quasi* committee, that they meet together both socially and in a legislative sense."[8]

Concerted action of delegates for particular purposes was not new. They had memorialized the Senate in 1843 and 1844 for appointment of a standing Committee on the Territories.[9] During the early sixties, however, sectional jealousy made close relations difficult. The New Mexico-Colorado boundary question arose repeatedly,[10] and Coloradans had hot words for their neighbors.[11] Delegates denounced Utah and Mormonism freely then and in later years,[12] perhaps in the belief that Utah's reputation stood in the way of the other territories. Delegates William H. Clagett and Martin Maginnis of Montana were particularly emphatic in advocating strict regulation,[13] while the Mormon population in southern Idaho made the "Mormon issue" there appealing to both parties.[14] In 1865 and thereafter, delegates passed over some of their differences to the extent of signing petitions jointly, sometimes in collaboration with western senators and representatives, urging legislation or appointments.[15] By 1867 they asked a room "for the common use of the Delegates from the Territories, which they can use for meetings for consultation."[16]

Organization of delegates into a committee seems to have taken place late in 1871. Their intention, according to the *Rocky Moun-*

6 December 20, 1871.

7 Indian Affairs, Mines and Mining, Public Lands (1876); Coinage, Weights and Measures, Agriculture, Military Affairs, Post Office and Post-Roads (1880); Private Land Claims (1887). *Hinds' Precedents*, II, Sec. 1297, p. 864.

8 *Cong. Globe* (42 Cong., 2 Sess.), p. 118.

9 *Senate Journal* (27 Cong., 3 Sess.), p. 113; *ibid.* (28 Cong., 1 Sess.), p. 166.

10 *Cong. Globe* (37 Cong., 2 Sess.), p. 2025; Santa Fé *Gazette*, February 20, 1864; Santa Fé *Weekly Gazette*, February 18, 1865.

11 E.g., *Rocky Mountain News*, March 19, 1863.

12 E.g., *ibid.*, April 16, 1863.

13 B. F. Hall to Maginnis, January 14, 1882, Maginnis Papers; W. W. Dixon, "Sketch of the Life and Character of William H. Clagett," *Contributions to the Historical Society of Montana*, IV (1903), 251.

14 Fred T. Dubois to Arthur, April 14, 1884, Interior Appointment File 240 (under Curtis).

15 E.g., Holbrook *et al.* to Johnson, n.d., State Appointments File (under Murphy, nominated 1867); Conness *et al.* to Johnson, February 13, 1866, Johnson Papers.

16 *Cong. Globe* (40 Cong., 1 Sess.), p. 8.

tain News, was to act "so far as practicable, in connection with the standing committee on territories. . . . They will also consult with and aid each other in the preparation and passage of measures through both houses. They style themselves the 'territorial syndicate.' " [17] The "syndicate" requested Grant to appoint only residents to territorial offices, and received a favorable reply.[18] It invited the President, Vice-President, Speaker of the House, and members of the committees on the territories to a dinner where there was discussion of greater representation for the territories. The *Denver News* saw pleasing prospects:

> Never have the delegates of the territories been more united than now to promote their respective interests. They have a territorial organization of their own and hold frequent consultations. They represent individually both political parties, but are a unit concerning the affairs of the territories.[19]

The territorial syndicate did unite delegates on bills of general interest as never before. It appointed a member, Maginnis of Montana, to take charge of a "general [railroad subsidy] bill on which the delegates have after much wrangling agreed to unite in case *they fail to get their special bills* through." [20] After Grant the committee slipped from sight, if it still existed, but concerted action continued. The delegates' approval of a bill was a point in its favor; [21] occasionally they recommended appointments jointly.[22] In 1884 they authorized two representatives to the Democratic national convention.[23] Such coöperation probably did much to advance the prestige of the office of delegate and the influence of individuals as well as of the group.

The rôle of the delegate has been much minimized. "Playing congressman without a vote or a place on any committee . . . ," said ex-Governor Evans of Colorado in 1870, "a Territorial delegate . . . , so far as his official position is concerned, is by no means so

[17] December 27, 1871.

[18] Armstrong, *Early Empire Builders*, p. 220; *supra*, p. 76.

[19] Quoted in *Daily New Mexican*, March 22, 1872. Official recognition came in 1874 with allotment of stationery and a clerk to "the territorial Delegates, as a committee." *House Journal* (43 Cong., 1 Sess.), p. 819. Cf. New York *Herald*, March 11, 1872.

[20] Maginnis to Sanders, February 14 [1876?], Sanders Papers; Virginia City *Montanian*, October 14, 1875.

[21] *Cong. Rec.* (46 Cong., 3 Sess.), p. 287; *ibid.* (47 Cong., 1 Sess.), p. 6819.

[22] Copy, Marcus A. Smith *et al.* to Harrison, March 5, 1889, Interior Appointment File 429 (under Poston); C. S. Voorhees to Lamar, May 21, 1885, *ibid.* 236 (under Stevenson).

[23] S. T. Hauser, governor of Montana, 1885–86, and Samuel Word, attorney for the Utah and Northern Railway. Word to Daniel Manning, April 8, 1885, *ibid.* (under Hauser).

influential as a private citizen of a stete [sic] in the lobby." [24] Arguments for statehood frequently included similar deprecations: "As a Territory, Colorado has a Delegate in Congress; an agent without a vote, and without even a voice except by courtesy and at rare intervals. . . . He has no vote—nothing to sell, and in consequence can buy nothing. All he gets is by favor." [25] Yet congressmen sought out the delegates before advancing bills affecting the territories; delegates canvassed committees and individual Congressmen, and in turn were called upon to give information,[26] or to attend committee meetings.[27] As a delegate from Washington Territory later recalled, "Delegates . . . were regarded as quite an influential body of men, and were usually able, by scattering through the House, by use of personal persuasion, by attendance before committees and receiving favorable reports, to get a part, at least, of what they desired for their Territories." [28]

On the floor of the House delegates could speak and did speak on all types of business. There are few evidences that their arguments on large questions of policy were of much weight against a prevailing indifference in congressional opinion. They were concerned more successfully with matters of detail, administrative rather than legislative. Thus territorial legislatures and officers found it convenient to request minor special appropriations through their delegates. Secretary of the Interior John W. Noble, when asked to help in securing funds for the Idaho Insane Asylum, referred the case to the delegate with the comment "that an appropriation . . . should be made . . . ; but according to the practice of this Department the presentation and advocacy of this measure falls rather upon you as a delegate than upon me as Secretary." [29] Occasional appropriations won by delegates were for prizes as rich as the Denver Mint, for which, according to Speaker Colfax, Delegate Bennet of Colorado was "certainly entitled to the largest share of credit. . . . The Committee on Ways and Means . . . found that nearly all the members of the House had had it explained to them in advance by your Delegate, and it passed therefore, with scarcely an opposition or debate." [30]

In the matter of appointments delegates played a considerable part, of much significance in the general operation of territorial control.

[24] *Rocky Mountain News,* August 31, 1870.
[25] *Ibid.,* May 4, 1864.
[26] E.g., *Senate Reports* (48 Cong., 1 Sess.), No. 462, p. 1.
[27] E.g., Seattle *Weekly Post-Intelligencer,* January 20, 1882.
[28] *Memoirs of Orange Jacobs,* p. 111.
[29] Noble to Dubois, December 18, 1889, Interior Miscellaneous Letter Book, XXX, 477–78.
[30] *Rocky Mountain News,* August 7, 1862.

From the first they claimed some right to give advice. "I, as the Delegate ought to know better who deserve appointments in the Territory than any non-resident even though he be Senator of the U.S.," wrote Daily of Nebraska to the President in 1861.[31] Lincoln did hearken to suggestions of the territorial delegates of New Mexico and Utah, where it was his policy to conciliate local opinion.[32] But the territorial patronage was to be largely eastern for many years to come. Under Lincoln there was readier response to delegates' requests for removals than to their nominations. Even a Democrat, George E. Cole of Washington, was elected delegate (1863–65) on a pledge to remove all office holders.[33]

Johnson gave to certain delegates an unusual amount of confidence and an unusual amount of patronage in their territories, though there is no certainty that he favored them as delegates rather than as friends of the administration. Senator James W. Nesmith of Oregon recommended Delegate Edward D. Holbrook of Idaho, *"The only man left in Congress, from our Coast who is your friend as mine.* Whatever representations he makes to you in regard to Federal appointments you can rely upon as correct." [34] Johnson did rely on Holbrook (though the radicals blocked some of the more important appointments) and for apparently similar reasons on Dr. Walter A. Burleigh of Dakota, who insisted on "the right of our Citizens to be heard in the selection of the Federal Officers." [35] The administration conceded enough influence to J. Francisco Chaves of New Mexico so that a Pennsylvania congressman invoked his favor in asking for a judgeship: "I have no doubt that it would afford Col Chavis . . . to see me gratified in this or any other appointment in his territory." [36] Eloquent testimonial to the influence of some delegates is the censure and ridicule others met when their influence fell below the accustomed level. "Clever has introduced another bill into Congress!" taunted the *New Mexican,* a partisan of Chaves. "How about appointments for friends? He hasn't been able yet to

[31] Daily to Lincoln, April 4, 1861, State Appointments File.

[32] The outgoing delegate of Utah referred to an interview he had with the President that day, wherein Lincoln had suggested that the delegates furnish (for the President's consideration) a list of names for the various offices of Utah territory. Among those mentioned was J. F. Kinney, appointed chief justice. W. H. Hooper to Lincoln, March 22, 1861, State Appointments File; *supra,* p. 75.

[33] J. G. Sparks to Wallace, December 16, 1863, Wallace Papers.

[34] J. W. Nesmith to Johnson, April 29, 1867, State Appointments File.

[35] Burleigh to Johnson, August 9, 1865, Johnson Papers; Kingsbury, *op. cit.,* I, 435.

[36] S. M. Pettis to Grant, August 24, 1869, State Appointments File (under Wetter).

introduce any of the latter to office. What a representation!" [37] The
unhappy Clever had complained privately to Johnson that "sending
strangers from other States . . . weakens the influence in the Territory of any Delegate." [38] The Yankton *Dakotian* dwelt on Delegate
J. B. S. Todd's inability to "gain an audience even in the lobby
rooms of the . . . Senate, and much less secure the *confirmation* of
the much sought and signed for Brigadiership [for which Todd was
a candidate], or any other small Dakota appointment." [39] The measure of a delegate at election time was not simply his policies but
the amount of his patronage. Holbrook found that to receive patronage in the White House was to lose it in the Senate; a constituent
warned him, "It is expected that you will secure the appointment of
some efficient man. . . . Are you aware that the people will hold
you accountable for any dereliction in this matter?" [40] The successful candidate in the Colorado election of 1866 ran on a pledge to
remove the governor. "Voters of Colorado," warned the *Rocky
Mountain News*, "if you do not want this piece of double concen-
trated scum of a triple extract of meanness, craft and hypicrisy [*sic*]
continued in power over you, vote for Geo M. Chilcott." [41]

Johnson could offer nominations but not confirmations; as Grant
renewed executive relationships with Congress in 1869, the influence
of delegates in the White House declined for a time. Solomon L.
Spink of Dakota found his patronage sharply limited; the voters
were accustomed to more favors and elected a Democrat to succeed
him.[42] At least two delegates, however, had a modicum of influence.
Stephen B. Elkins foreshadowed his later career by dextrous manipu-
lations of appointments for New Mexico. Elkins claimed,

President Grant had appointed a friend of mine Secretary [John Pratt] and
relieved Ritch. This friend . . . was afterward appointed to a foreign con-
sulship. . . . Ritch then came on to Washington and importuned me to
allow him to be reappointed. . . . Grant would not do it unless by my
consent and I consented. . . . This was all done however to make way for

[37] Quoted in Santa Fé *Weekly Gazette*, April 4, 1868. Yet he apparently had
Secretary Heath removed. Memorandum, E. P. S[mith], n.d. (stamped January 9,
1868), TP, New Mexico, III, 127.
[38] C. P. Clever to Johnson, January 27, 1868, Justice Appointment Papers, New
Mexico.
[39] August 5, 1862.
[40] C. F. Parnell to Holbrook, July 8, 1867, enclosed in Holbrook to Johnson,
July 22, 1867, TP, Idaho, II, 97–98.
[41] August 1, 1866. Governor Cummings resigned after representations from the
outgoing delegate. Allen A. Bradford to Johnson, February 7, 1867, TP, Colorado,
I, 284–85.
[42] Kingsbury, *op. cit.*, I, 548–49.

the nephew of Senator Sherman who is (now to be made) U.S. Marshal in New Mexico.[43]

In Colorado, Chaffee was credited with much power until he fell out with the President, by tradition, over a poker game.[44] These were exceptional instances; the emergence of a committee of delegates probably illustrates the need to combine small influences rather than the joining of influences already considerable in their individual rights.

The influence of delegates on appointments did revive and continue during the years after Grant, whether from policy or from accident. Expressions such as "I insist upon the appointment" [45] suggest an established right to be heard. A Democratic president was wise to listen even to a Republican delegate, for Republican votes might defeat his territorial nominations in the Senate.[46] The Republican Governor Benjamin F. Potts of Montana asked Democratic Delegate Maginnis to urge Republican President Hayes to reappoint him.[47] A delegate's opposition was a matter of serious concern to a candidate: Delegate Voorhees of Washington successfully opposed the candidacy of Eugene Semple for the governorship over a two-year period.[48]

Delegates also concerned themselves with a variety of lesser matters. "The business of the territories is done through the departments," said Judge Granville G. Bennett of Dakota, arguing that a delegate need not be of the party in power in Congress.[49] A Montana journalist said that the duties of delegate were "to toil and moil over Indian reservations and post offices in the East for us." [50]

Some of this business was of a decidedly routine order—a request for a governor's leave of absence,[51] selection of books for the territorial library,[52] consultation on Indian affairs.[53] There was also a

43 Words in parentheses are crossed out. Elkins to John P. Jones, October 27, 1881, Interior Appointment File 171. *Supra.* p. 68, note 47.

44 Charles S. Thomas, "The Pioneer Bar of Colorado," *Colorado Magazine,* I (1924), 201; Ellis, *op. cit.,* p. 89.

45 John Hailey to Lamar, June 10, 1886, Interior Appointment File 236.

46 E. W. Miller to Cleveland, November 15, 1886, *ibid.* 235.

47 Hauser to Maginnis, April 26, 1877, Maginnis Papers.

48 D. W. Voorhees to H. C. Semple, May 20, 1885; J. F. King to Cleveland, March 21, 1887, Interior Appointment File 238, and *passim.*

49 Bismarck *Tribune,* October 30, 1878.

50 G. M. Baker to Maginnis, n.d. [November, 1882?], Maginnis Papers.

51 William T. Jones to Fish, May 23, 1872, TP, Wyoming, 39. A leave might be suspended on a delegate's representations as well. Fish to Wetter, December 2, 1870, Domestic Letters, LXXXVII, 168.

52 Bennet to John P. Usher, March 24, 1863, Interior Miscellaneous File 197; Usher to Bennet, March 31, 1863, Interior Miscellaneous Sent, press copies (Department of the Interior), IV, 182.

53 Schurz to Maginnis, January 22, 1879, Maginnis Papers.

substantial amount of minor patronage not connected with the territorial system but recognized as partly within the delegate's influence. R. F. Pettigrew as delegate from Dakota contested the governor's control over certain post offices, and was sustained by Senator O. H. Platt.[54] A delegate expected to control the public printing,[55] military appointments for the territory,[56] and even a few minor appointments in Washington.[57]

Once their influence was on the way to becoming extensive, delegates could add to it by making judicious concessions to politicians of higher rank.[58] They could not trade in votes, for they had none of their own, and none to promise while statehood was only a possibility, but they could allot their crumbs of patronage. When there was slight chance of having a first choice appointed, it might be politic to support, perhaps, a brother of the Secretary of the Interior.[59] Easterners might have use for a delegate's influence in intraterritorial politics. Jay Gould asked the Democratic delegate from Montana to support a railroad tax exemption and subsidy bill.[60] Territorial votes at national nominating conventions occasionally were important,[61] and may have been worth concessions to territorial opinion as represented through the delegate.

Simple, informal personal persuasion may have been as helpful to delegates as concrete bargains. "There is a sort of generous feeling existing between many members of the National House who have served many years together," wrote a Congressman, "and . . . there is a disposition to aid and assist one another." [62] Delegates often had influence independent of their territorial constituencies. Many had come west originally bearing federal commissions; officers commonly aspired to be returned to Congress even when they had reasonably secure tenure as governor, secretary, or judge. The difference in income and the opportunity to return to the East probably are sufficient explanations of this tendency. C. D. Poston tells of how the federal officers starting out to organize Arizona "quarreled all the way across the plains about who should be the first dele-

---

[54] Richard Franklin Pettigrew, *Imperial Washington*, pp. 153–54, 156.

[55] Schurz to Jefferson P. Kidder, January 28, 1879, Interior Miscellaneous Letter Book, XIII, 168.

[56] Nelson A. Miles to Maginnis, November 8, 1878, Maginnis Papers.

[57] Copy, Philetus Sawyer to Windom, May 11, 1889, enclosed in John G. Carlisle to Vilas, April 3, 1894, Vilas Papers.

[58] Kingsbury, *op. cit.*, I, 673.

[59] Recommending James H. Teller as secretary of Dakota suggests an effort to please. Pettigrew to H. M. Teller, October 16, 1886, Interior Appointment File 170.

[60] Gould to Maginnis, September 7, 1878, Maginnis Papers.

[61] Sloan, *op. cit.*, 204–9; Santa Fé *Weekly Gazette*, February 18, 1865.

[62] Leopold Morse to Cleveland, March 28, 1885, Interior Appointment File 236 (under Maginnis).

gate to Congress from a Territory they had never seen." As delegate
Poston drew $7200 in mileage; even paying $15 a gallon for whiskey
probably left him a comfortable residue.[63] The Dalles (Oregon)
Mountaineer took a sour view in asserting that governors were
"usually obscure strikers, who do the dirty work of parties, and
being sent out as governors, assume proconsular powers, and en-
deavor to 'mold public sentiment' into sending them to Congress." [64]
Rivalries among federal officers for nominations were at the basis
of a large part of charges brought against them. It is not improbable
that men with contacts strong enough to send them out to the territories in the first place renewed these contacts to help them in lesser
matters when they returned to sit in Congress.

General interest in elections for delegate probably attests to the
influence and importance of the post as well as to the pleasures of
life in Washington. Party battles were as fierce as in the elections for
senator and representative; party issues were drawn as broadly as
in the states. In later years there might be the impression that the
territory had voted in a presidential election; [65] the terms "delegate"
and "representative" were sometimes used interchangeably.[66] No
territorial population, except possibly that of New Mexico, was old
enough to be much isolated from political currents and practices in
the states. Delegates brought home knowledge of national political
methods and controversies; [67] the election of delegates helped to sustain interest in national affairs. An old settler of Dakota who had
voted in the East for Lincoln in 1860 might or might not vote for
Harrison in 1892, but at least he was no more likely to vote against
Harrison or to stay away from the polls than was a neighbor who had
moved only as far west as Minnesota.

Perhaps the delegate was important to his constituency because
they did not know how unimportant he was. Certainly he had no
powers and few privileges by statute; if there was proof that he had
influence in a particular case, it was likely to be the influence of the
lobbyist or former congressman, the influence of Holbrook, the President's supporter, the influence of Elkins, the speculator. Whatever
the reason, his interventions served to protect territorial interests
from defects in the system of territorial control where there was not

[63] Charles D. Poston, "Building a State in Apache Land," *Overland Monthly*,
Ser. 2, XXIV (1894), 407–8.
[64] *Rocky Mountain News*, December 11, 1862.
[65] [W.P.A., Washington (State),] *Told by the Pioneers*, II, 15.
[66] *Rocky Mountain News*, December 14, 1861; Keen, *op. cit.*, p. 8.
[67] One writer suggests that J. F. Chaves, as presiding officer of the legislative
council of New Mexico, owed his parliamentary skill to having observed Colfax
in the House. Frank W. Clancy in Paul A. F. Walter, Frank W. Clancy, and
M. A. Otero, *Colonel José Francisco Chaves, 1833–1924*, p. 5.

sufficient protection in still other defects. Appointed officers, often negligent or neglected as links in the federal connection, were supplanted in some degree by this voteless agent.[68]

[68] According to Snow, "The appointed Governors and Secretaries have regarded themselves as responsible entirely to the people and the elected Senate and House of Representatives of the respective Territories, and the delegate . . . has been recognized as the link between each Territory and the Union." Alpheus H. Snow, *The Administration of Dependencies*, p. 576.

Chapter VIII

THE COMMITTEES ON TERRITORIES

THE congressional committees on territories were usually on the periphery of supervisory operations. They had much to do with legislation for the territories, which tended to grow more administrative toward the end of the territorial period. The Senate committee held a check on appointments. With the day-to-day practical details both had little contact and little concern.

Under the Articles, a select committee drew up instructions to the governor of the Northwest Territory.[1] It was similar in membership to other committees concerned with western matters.[2] Under the Constitution, when Congress delegated the exercise of much of its authority over the territories to the president,[3] there was at first no standing committee on the territories. In the House, territorial business drifted into short-lived select committees and into four different standing committees before the founding of the Committee on the Territories, December 13, 1825.[4] Thus decentralization became established in the absence of any group regularly constituted to revive and apply to territorial business "the modes of procedure adopted by the late Congress, who were both a Legislative and Executive body." [5]

As set down in 1825, the duties of the House Committee with respect to the territories were "to examine into their legislative, civil, and criminal proceedings, and to devise and report to the House such means, as, in their opinion, may be necessary to secure the rights and privileges of residents and nonresidents." [6] A revision of 1880 described the jurisdiction as over subjects relating "to Territorial legislation, the revision thereof, and affecting Territories or the admission of States." [7]

The Senate committee was eighteen years later in establishment,

---

[1] *Journals of the Continental Congress,* XXXIV, 473–74.

[2] *Ibid.,* 297, 298, 320, 405, 423, *passim.*

[3] Act of August 7, 1789, *Statutes,* I, 52–53.

[4] Ways and Means (1795), Public Lands (1805), Judiciary (1813), and Indian Affairs (1821). Lauros G. McConachie, *Congressional Committees,* pp. 359–61.

[5] Gerry in *Annals,* II, 1464, cited in McConachie, *op. cit.,* 89.

[6] *House Journal* (19 Cong., 1 Sess.), p. 46.

[7] *Cong. Rec.* (46 Cong., 2 Sess.), p. 205.

though the Senate was at least as much concerned with territorial affairs as the House was. In 1843 three delegates urged appointment of a committee on territories: [8] the Senate adopted the resolution to create the committee, to "take charge of all territorial business," on March 25, 1844.[9] The practical jurisdictions of both committees were much narrower than is suggested by their titles or by the rules governing them. In the House territorial appropriations pertained to the Committee on Ways and Means (until 1865) and the Committee on Appropriations,[10] and judicial matters to the Committee on the Judiciary. On the other hand, the House Committee on the Territories acted at times on bills relating to territorial judicial affairs,[11] land grants in a state and two territories,[12] a United States penitentiary in Dakota,[13] and Indian removal.[14] Of especial interest is the reference of a reconstruction bill in 1862.[15]

Similar conditions prevailed in the Senate. Senator Evans had opposed founding the Senate Committee because "still bills of the Territories, having reference to appropriations, and the disposition of lands, &c., would have to be referred to the committees appropriately having charge of these subjects." [16] This proved to be true. Yet the Committee did consider bills on matters as various as judicial organization,[17] the administration of Yellowstone Park,[18] the California-Nevada boundary,[19] and southern reconstruction.[20]

The Senate committee was by far the more active of the two in extra-legislative matters, perhaps because of its function in confirming appointments. While considering executive nominations, it sometimes inquired into charges and recommendations.[21] There are

---

8 *Senate Journal* (27 Cong., 3 Sess.), p. 113.

9 *Ibid.* (28 Cong., 1 Sess.), p. 189; *Cong. Globe* (28 Cong., 1 Sess.), p. 428.

10 The practice of distributing appropriation bills among other committees during the years 1879–85 (McConachie, *op. cit.*, 374–75) did not apply to territorial bills.

11 *House Reports* (46 Cong., 2 Sess.), No. 470; *ibid.* (48 Cong., 1 Sess.), No. 254; etc.

12 *Ibid.* (50 Cong., 1 Sess.), No. 71.

13 *Ibid.* (46 Cong., 2 Sess.), No. 138.

14 *Ibid.*, No. 474.

15 *House Journal* (37 Cong., 2 Sess.), pp. 115, 155, 208, 437–39.

16 *Cong. Globe* (28 Cong., 1 Sess.), p. 395.

17 *Senate Reports* (46 Cong., 2 Sess.), No. 455.

18 *Ibid.* (47 Cong., 2 Sess.), No. 911.

19 *Ibid.* (48 Cong., 2 Sess.), No. 1009.

20 A bill (S. 201) for cotton cultivation in South Carolina islands and other lands. *Cong. Globe* (37 Cong., 2 Sess.), pp. 940–41. A bill (S. 45) "to set apart a portion of the State of Texas for the use of persons of African descent." *Senate Reports* (38 Cong., 1 Sess.), No. 8.

21 E.g., Samuel Butler to Schurz, December 19, 1880, Interior Appointment File 166.

occasional recommendations by committee members themselves,[22] though not enough to suggest that they had extraordinary concern or influence on account of their membership. The committee apparently made no visits to the territories as happened later in the Beveridge investigation of Arizona; [23] it might, however, call in territorial officials on rare occasions.[24]

The House committee received an especially large number of resolutions introduced by delegates, in addition to memorials from territorial legislatures and communications from the departments. The House had no formal functions relative to appointments, although an influential committee member might claim a right to be heard in the department concerned. When James M. Ashley was in Denver in 1865, Governor Alexander Cummings consulted him on matters such as the removal of executive officers.[25]

Legislation on the government of the territories was more frequent and more detailed in the period 1861–90 than before, but many of the bills should be considered together, as directed toward single purposes. For the most part these purposes, such as suppression of polygamy in Utah and restriction of costs of legislative sessions, pertained to only a small part of the territorial system. In general, by indifference or by intent, Congress left internal affairs to the decision of the local legislatures. As the House Committee on Territories commented in 1884:

If . . . injustice is done . . . , the local legislature would be much more familiar with all the facts than Congress could possibly be, and its facilities for examining fully into the whole matter . . . are much better than those of Congress. To legislate upon such matters was the object of the creation of the . . . Territorial legislature, and Congress ought not to interpose in subjects of local legislation unless it is manifest there has been an abuse of power by the Territorial legislature. The legislature of Idaho having been in

---

[22] Cullom procured appointment of C. S. Zane, his law partner, as justice of Utah. Shelby M. Cullom, *Fifty Years of Public Service*, pp. 205, 206. Committee members indicated to Johnson that I. L. Gibbs would be confirmed as governor of Idaho. D. W. Bliss to Johnson, August 14, 1867, State Appointments File; W. W. Parker to Johnson, August 15, 1867, TP Idaho, II, 123.

[23] Cf. a suggestion to visit a proposed territory of Oklahoma. *Senate Reports* (43 Cong., 1 Sess.), No. 465.

[24] Leave from the departmental superior was necessary. J. Burrows to Kirkwood, December 24, 1881, Interior Appointment File 167 (under Murray).

[25] Cummings to Seward, January 9, 1866, TP Colorado, I, 148. Ashley wrote in 1865 that recommendations for appointments from Governor Evans of Colorado were to be recognized "when endorsed by the Chairman of the Committee on Territories," and that some had been so made. Ashley to Seward, May 22, 1865, State Appointments File. During his visit to Utah in 1865, petitions were addressed to Schuyler Colfax for the appointment of O. H. Irish as governor. Roberts, *op. cit.*, V, 179–80.

session . . . and failed . . . to make any reapportionment, it is reasonable to suppose there existed something . . . to justify the failure. . . .[26]

Exclusively committee administration of the territories would have been difficult, though not impossible, even had Congress wished to retain the exercise of immediate control. As an example of what could be done, the Senate Committee inquired into the refusal of the Utah legislature to print a message of Governor Harding, and, in pursuance of a Senate resolution, rebuked the legislature by affirming the propriety of the message and having a thousand printed copies sent to the Governor.[27] Yet when the two committees were first appointed, territorial affairs had been managed through other agencies for from thirty-six to fifty-four years. The committees were not constituted for administrative action. Ultimately delegates were represented on the House Committee, but appointments, one of their major concerns, were reserved to the Senate. Both bodies were, like other committees, of mixed party membership, and rivalries were stirred by few questions as much as by the admission of new states. Few members had prior or subsequent part in territorial affairs. Most were from the East; in each session on the average more than three-fourths of the members of the House committee were new, more than half of the members of the Senate committee.[28] James M. Ashley and Benjamin F. Wade, chairmen of the Civil War period, were chiefly concerned with political considerations in state-making. O. H. Platt, Senate chairman during the 1880's, may have applied some of his experience to the very different problem of insular dependencies.[29] In the intervening period such questions as polygamy occupied an unduly large part of the committees' time. When interest in control was at best halting in the departments, it is not to be expected that Congress would overcome such obstacles to administer territorial affairs regularly through the committee system.

[26] *House Reports* (48 Cong., 1 Sess.), No. 440, p. 1. The Senate Committee endorsed a similar policy. *Senate Reports* (49 Cong., 1 Sess.), No. 1249, p. 1.

[27] *Ibid.* (37 Cong., 3 Sess.), No. 87; *Senate Journal* (37 Cong., 3 Sess.), p. 249.

[28] Computation made from committee rolls of the thirty-seventh to fifty-first Congresses.

[29] Louis A. Coolidge, *An Old-Fashioned Senator: Orville H. Platt, of Connecticut*, p. 146.

Chapter IX

THE SYSTEM AND THE PEOPLE

THE historian of frontier politics necessarily has a peripheral function in frontier historiography, peripheral even though the frontier was always politically minded. The natural environment was more proximate than the institutional. The territorial system constituted only a few phases of formal government where formal government was not all of what little government there was. It may be that its chief significance is negative: being weak, it allowed a freer play of other influence, personal, economic, physiographical, spiritual.

The territory had no immutable function. It was always a frontier unit in a very loose sense in that its boundaries overlapped a frontier of fur traders or miners or farmers. Sometimes it was a unit staked out by the general government to advance or to mold western settlement. Whether following or preceding first settlement, it tended increasingly to be a frontier unit in that it was dominated and molded by the frontier and by frontiersmen.

The Ordinance of 1787 was for a frontier to come rather than for a frontier in being. The dying Congress of the Confederation, preoccupied by the financial strictures of a young country and badgered by land speculators, described a political framework to attract land settlers. It was the peculiarly good fortune of the United States and of the settlers along the Ohio that the Ordinance came when it did. The Cincinnati's demands in 1783 had looked to a semi-independent soldiers' state; Jefferson's Ordinance of 1784 sketched out states but no preliminary stages of dependency. After July 1787, while grievances accumulated, the United States seemed to lose capacity for legislation over a two-year period, and it shortly developed sectional and partisan jealousies which might have prejudiced development of a liberal and far-sighted plan for control of dependent territories. By 1803 the Federalists were sure that they had not contemplated free and unlimited admission of states at Philadelphia in September of 1787,[1] whatever the Congress had done when it passed the Ordinance at New York in July.

---

[1] Morris wrote to Henry W. Livingston (December 4, 1803), "I always thought that, when we should acquire Canada and Louisiana, it would be proper to govern them as provinces, and allow them no voice in our councils. In wording the third

In the early national period the individual land purchasers who benefited by the great Ordinance generally followed along after the first territorial officers. Not until 1800 did the line of settlement reach beyond the line of the states. Then it enclosed a narrow strip of settlement along the Ohio as far as the Muskingum in Northwest Territory. In no case, except Florida, did the conventional census reporter's line of six inhabitants to the square mile appear in a territory for more than one census year: statehood followed fairly promptly on settlement. In no case, until the admission of Nevada in 1864, did the line of the states reach beyond the line of settlement: settlement preceded statehood. Land could not be occupied legally before the surveyor-general of the territory had staked it out; it could not be occupied safely before governor, secretary, and judges had arrived and instituted regular government.

The American pioneer, however, characteristically did not always wait for what was legal and safe. Within the territories pioneers pushed out of the settled regions, demanding new surveys and new county organizations, roads and military protection. Beyond the existing territories they still pushed out, eventually demanding, because it became customary to have it, new territorial organization. Initial settlement preceded government in Orleans, Louisiana, Oregon, New Mexico, and Utah territories. In Orleans and in Utah the new regime was not welcome, but in general by 1836 territorial government had become traditional enough and popular enough in form to be included among normal frontier demands.

Simply as a unit of land sale, the territory never fully justified itself. It was not enough to bring the land office to the settler in 1800. In each territorial act Congress provided for a territorial surveyor-general, whose bailiwick coincided with the new political unit while as independent of it as the systems of post offices and post roads. But within the territory the surveyor seldom kept up with the advance guard of the frontier of settlement. He lagged behind even during the relatively steady and orderly advance into the Old Northwest, held back by lack of funds as well as by the process of quitting Indian titles. With the advance into the high plains, where the government quarter-section gave way to railroad land grants, to cattle ranges and mineral claims, the formal land office claim lost still more of its former significance. The old line of six to the square mile likewise had little meaning in stock and mining country: even a half century after Turner noted the passing of the frontier, the Rocky Mountain and Great Basin areas were merely dotted with islands of settlement. The old frontier line remained apparently fixed at the

section of the fourth article, I went as far as circumstances would permit to establish the exclusion." Jared Sparks, *Life of Gouverneur Morris*, III, 192.

hundred and third meridian, beyond which a frontier has passed, but a frontier different from that of the fertile, well-watered Ohio Valley farm.

Closely related to the territory of land sales was the territory of Indian control. Protection against the aborigines was, indeed, often of greater concern to the settler than the formal bounding of the land he farmed. The Ohio Associates could have sold few farms in districts where previous settlers had gained possession by purchase but lost it by the tomahawk. The United States itself had responsibility for the safety of settlers and for the peaceable disposition of Indian relations. Soon after passing the Ordinance of 1787, Congress united the functions of territorial governor and superintendent of Indian affairs.

Combining the governorship and the Indian administration was clearly a measure of economy. It had a certain logic as long as Indian relations were on a diplomatic basis and as long as territorial affairs were administered in the Department of State. It had some rough convenience, if not logic, in representing in one officer the contrary interests of the civil administration under the Department of State and of the Indian administration under the Office of Indian Affairs and the Department of the Interior. James M. Ashley told the House, "You cannot more cheaply and more economically govern these Indians than by having your Territories cut up, and your Governors appointed to superintend and take charge of those Indians." [2]

That there was no necessary economy in such an arrangement was apparent as soon as Governor St. Clair retreated before Little Turtle in 1791, but it was not until 1870 that the combination of responsibilities was discontinued. By this time territorial organization had extended beyond the ninety-fifth meridian, into districts where the civil governorship alone was no part-time assignment. In any region there was a natural incompatibility between the duties of a political officer, dependent for political favor on a constituency of settlers, and the duties of an administrator charged with the protection of aborigines who were the enemies of those same settlers.

Indian administration, strictly speaking, had never been a part of the territorial system. Congress merely borrowed the territory as a geographical unit and the governor as an individual to make a paper disposition of the Indian problem. Essentially and constitutionally the territory was a unit of the national domain over which the Congress had municipal authority, a unit with only such privileges of self-government as Congress chose to grant. Especially in the early period, roughly to 1816, national authority was paramount both in law and in practice: the territory was a unit for the transmission of

[2] *Cong. Globe* (38 Cong., 1 Sess.), p. 1169; *ibid.* (40 Cong., 2 Sess.), pp. 2800–1.

authority, for political control. After 1816 national authority continued unimpaired, but the privileges of self-government gained dominance in the operations of territorial machinery.

As a unit of political control, the early territory followed as much on Congress' familiarity with the eighteenth-century British crown colony as on any sentiment for free republican institutions. A popularly elected legislature probably would have contributed more expense than wisdom to the workings of government in a sparsely populated wilderness; [3] this is suggested in the experiences of the later territories, which had full-fledged legislatures from the start. The military rule in Louisiana (1803-4) reflected to a considerable extent the national bewilderment at the problem of governing a huge, newly acquired region with a population unaccustomed to representative government. During those early years Congress tended to turn over the knotty problems of frontier government to its own agencies instead of to the agents of the frontier constituencies.

The territory with appointed legislative council, as sketched out in the Ordinance of 1787, eventually gave way to the territory with completely elective legislature. The newer form was less a unit of control than a framework for self-government. When the people chose both branches of the legislature, the general structure of government differed from the ordinary structure of state government only in the appointment of governor, secretary, and judges at Washington. Missouri reached this stage in 1816, followed by Arkansas (1820), Florida (1826), and Michigan (1827); after 1827 Congress established no more continental territories with legislatures appointed in whole or in part. The older form might have been more efficient, from the Congressional point of view, but the newer seemed less autocratic to the settlers and to a more democratically inclined Congress. [4]

As the territory came under popular control, it came more nearly to satisfy popular demands. By 1858 the citizens of the old Minnesota Territory west of the new state boundary had organized their own territory. The citizens of the Pike's Peak region of Kansas Territory followed with the Territory of Jefferson in 1859. These territory-makers were no less spirited than the state-makers of the early national period, no less devoted to republican principles or jealous of outside interference. Their attempts show a curious misunderstanding of constitutional law. They also mark the great changes that had

[3] See Trimble, *op. cit.*, p. 246, where he points out the greater efficiency of the Canadian political unit.

[4] Turner points out that even the origins of the territorial system of 1787 must be traced to the Ohio Valley itself (which demanded something like it) as well as to the Ordinance of 1787 and New England. Frederick J. Turner, *The Frontier in American History*, pp. 168–69.

occurred, since the time of the state of Franklin (1784–88), in the territorial institution and its reputation. Incidentally, the grievance of the territory-maker gives point to what can be inferred from the map: that large territories such as Indiana of 1800 or Kansas of 1854 were too large to be effective frontier units of administration or of self-government. But the people of Illinois had wanted separate territorial organization because of the burden of going to the capital of Indiana at Vincennes, while the Pike's Peak miners wanted it because of the advantage of going to their own capital.

Self-government developed both within and without the territorial system proper. In the first months of territorial existence, even after 1827, there could be no self-government within the system, for the system itself was incomplete. The governor necessarily exercised autocratic powers in establishing the capital, calling elections, defining judicial districts. Even beyond the period of organization, there was often a period of political pump-priming in which the legislature met but found little wealth to tax, in which the small national subsidy covered all or most of the expenses of territorial government.

With the legislature once established, however, there soon appeared counties and municipalities, probate judges and justices of the peace, constituting a fabric of local government little different from local government in the states. On the territorial scale, the people elected a legislature which created departments and offices, laid and collected taxes, erected buildings, raised a militia; the people elected a delegate who was in many respects the equivalent of a congressman. When statehood came, the transition was slight, for the new state's constitutional convention found the system established by national law and territorial law under the organic act not very different from the systems of the older states whose constitutions were the convention's models.

As a framework for self-government, the territory also permitted types of political self-expression decidedly not implied in the organic act. The appointed governor, secretary, or judge had, in practice, local as well as national responsibilities. In election years he aspired to return to Washington as territorial delegate. Between elections he had to court territorial favor for mere continuance in office, if not for reappointment. Always there was prospect of office under statehood, especially of a senatorship.

The officer who did not go to Congress faced a considerable dependence on the legislature. Congress had been wise to deny it the best weapon of the colonial assembly, complete control over the governor's salary. But legislatures learned to vote "increased compensation," ostensibly because salaries were insufficient to maintain competent officers; the effect was that officers had to demonstrate their competency by acting in agreement with the legislative will. Judges could be controlled in this way or through the legislature's power to define judicial districts and to establish lower courts. A stubborn judge was likely to find himself holding court in a desert, while the cases he might have heard went to his colleagues or to probate judges and justices of the peace. In the background were the miners' courts and vigilante courts, most active in emergencies.

The territory of self-government thus looked to statehood. By the time statehood approached, national financial aid normally had become relatively insignificant. Appointed officers had divided loyalties. The bulk of governmental operations proceeded in little wise differently from operations after admission. The leavening of new political reforms did not wait for Congress to pass an admission act. The dispute over the recall of judges in Arizona, and its outcome, were fitting display of the political development of the last of the continental territories, at the closing of the political frontier.

The West is both independent and dependent in spirit. The physiographical environment demands expenditures and inter-regional coördination beyond the competence of single state organizations. Still the explanation of western dependence lies partly in the territorial experience. The normal national subsidy to territorial government, however small, was a natural vehicle for additional subsidies during the territorial period, and a precedent for requests for subsidies after admission. From requests for larger contingent and legislative accounts, there were natural steps to the diversion of such funds to other uses; [5] from requests for books or surveying instruments,[6] to memorials for poor and agricultural relief.[7] The United States built a few buildings for territorial purposes, and territorial authorities came to regard such favors as a natural right. One of the strongest arguments against statehood was the loss of the congressional appropriation. Though territorial taxes covered all but perhaps a tenth of territorial and local government expenses, that tenth included expenses most often in controversy and hence best known.

[5] E.g., a New Mexico act of January 3, 1859, authorizing compensation for law code commissioners (properly paid by territorial funds) out of the legislative fund, "and not otherwise." Copy, Arny to R. Solfer, November 21, 1863, enclosed in copy, S. E. Chittenden to Chase, December 26, 1863, Treasury A.B., LXXXII, 203–6.

[6] Frémont to Schurz, March 2, 1880, Interior Miscellaneous File 252; Schurz to Frémont, March 16, 1880, Interior Miscellaneous Letter Book, XIV, 369.

[7] John L. Pennington to Delano, September 9, 1874, Interior Miscellaneous File 200; Lewis Wolfley to Noble, May 8, 1889, ibid. 253.

Through these financial ties, through the plain fact of temporary political dependency, the "denizen of the territory involuntarily becomes a nationalist." [8]
Independence of national authority, on the other hand, was a tendency even in financial matters. While always eager to take larger sums from the national Treasury, legislatures at times appropriated generously to increase salaries, in order to control federal officers or to insure their honesty and efficiency. They memorialized for increased judicial service, but financed locally-controlled courts intended to take cases from the supreme and district courts. In some degree most territorial populations shared the sentiments of Confederate sympathizers in Arizona who "wanted Federal money, but . . . did not want Federal Government." [9]
Direct resistance to congressional legislation was infrequent, but little more infrequent than legislation of regulatory or restrictive character. Some of this was passed at the suggestion of delegates, and therefore not likely to provoke opposition. Certain prohibitions might be evaded over long periods: the machinery for disallowance worked slowly and uncertainly.[10] Positive intervention in cases where it was not easy to ignore or defeat it was resented actively. Delegates had sharp words for "experimental legislation" and for "tinkering" where residents knew their own needs. Delegate George M. Chilcott of Colorado hoped that "the members [of Congress] . . . will at least allow the Delegates . . . the privilege of making application on behalf of their people whenever the latter desire changes in the laws." [11]
Resistance to outside authority was practical, not doctrinal. There were few arguments on a constitutional basis for general territorial autonomy after 1861.[12] One of the earliest fatalities in the Civil War was the doctrine of territorial sovereignty. But having no doctrinal

8 Kingsbury, op. cit., II, 1596.
9 History of Arizona, 210.
10 The Senate Committee on Territories urged a bill to prohibit special legislation: "It is true that all Territorial legislation is now subject to be annulled or modified by act of Congress. But experience has shown that it is very difficult to exercise this power wisely." Senate Reports (49 Cong., 1 Sess.), No. 1327, p. 2.
11 Cong. Globe (40 Cong., 3 Sess.), pp. 457–58.
12 Arguments in the Douglas tradition had advanced to the point that "the people sua sponte, and not from any extrinsic grant of power, may form a government for the inchoate State, or Territory. . . . But neither admission nor rejection can give Federal power any greater control over the non-Federal—the mere State concerns and laws of the people. . . . If the right to organize a territorial government . . . is a power incident to the admission of new States, still it would give no municipal power over the territory so organized." Durbin Ward, On the Government of the Territories, pp. 18, 10.

defense, territorial autonomists likewise found no doctrinal limitations to their wants and grievances. Occasionally they would have controlled even activities of the United States government which lay outside the territorial system. "We ought too to have the privelidge [*sic*], yes—the right to elect our Territorial officials," wrote a Montana patriot apropos of the Indian administration.[13]

General unrest under territorial government was closely identified with resistance to appointed officers. The legal limits on their numbers apparently enabled legislators to work together more harmoniously to override the governor's vetoes. "The members of both houses seem to have combined against the executive," complained the Bismarck *Tribune*, "but when Dakota becomes a state and the membership of the legislature is enlarged vetoes will begin to be considered as they deserve." [14] They could restrict the governor's power of appointment by withholding confirmation or by passing territorial tenure of office acts on the national model.[15] Governor Ordway of Dakota reported "a systematic effort for several years past to thwart U.S. officials in the discharge of their duties." [16]

Certain legislative tactics had decidedly personal implications. Judges were "sage-brush" districted; allowances of officers were raised, lowered, withheld for offense or for simple unpopularity. Insults were both violent and systematic. The New Mexico legislature printed a governor's message with a preamble referring to the "false, erroneous absurd and ill-sounding ideas therein contained." [17] Newspapers took up the part of the legislators, exhausting the vials of frontier invective on officers who were unfortunate enough to be Republicans when they should have been Democrats, Stalwarts where they should have been Halfbreeds—or simply appointed Easterners instead of elected Westerners.

Non-residence was a stigma for any officer; he was suspect from the beginning. It was clear that men from the states, without supplementary incomes, were at least under great disadvantages in living on consistently low federal salaries. If they starved, they showed that they were driven west by their incompetence; if they prospered, they showed that they were dishonest. When officers tried to maintain old business connections, their absences might be real grievances.[18]

Distrust of officers without independent incomes was hardly less

[13] I. H. D. Street to Maginnis, February 5, 1865, Maginnis Papers.
[14] February 25, 1881.
[15] *Cong. Globe* (41 Cong., 3 Sess.), pp. 970–71.
[16] Ordway to Hayes, January 13, 1880, Hayes Papers.
[17] Santa Fé *Gazette*, December 20, 1862.
[18] As during the Dakota Indian wars of 1862. Armstrong, *op. cit.*, pp. 81–82.

than distrust of officers whose incomes came from outside the territories. Men who tried to live on their salaries were potentially corrupt, but they might be corrupted in the territorial interest, even by the legislature itself. Men with material interests in the states might be even less likely to share the territorial point of view. A Dakota journalist complained in 1862 that "not a government official has built a house, fenced a lot, or expended $200 in the territory since its organization." [19] Governor A. P. K. Safford, arriving in Arizona in 1869, found territorial affairs in confusion because of the acting governor's residing in Mexico: "The former officers . . . had either resigned or been removed and had nearly all left the Territory. The Executive Office was closed; and the few books and papers to be found were covered with dust and looked as if they had not been disturbed for many months." [20] A petition for removal of a governor of Wyoming averred that "he does not mingle with our people, and get acquainted with our wants and our interests, or identify himself in any way with our citizens." [21] The Santa Fé Weekly Gazette favored appointment of residents because they would spend their salaries in New Mexico "instead of sending them to the States and adding them to the wealth of communities of which we know nothing." [22]

Even apart from questions of income and property, and of devotion to official duties, territorial wants and interests were held to be unique and quite impenetrable to eastern understanding. According to Tullidge's Quarterly Magazine,

> The situation here is different to that of any State or Territory in the Union, and as a natural consequence, a resident of any other section knows little of the real necessities of Utah.
> No matter how well fitted a man might be for the executive department of his own State, that does not by any means fit him to fill the position of Governor of Utah.[23]

Governors from the states were no doubt satisfactory in other territories, but "not so . . . with respect for New Mexico," complained a resident. "Nearly a whole term is here required to fit an intelligent

[19] Armstrong, op. cit., p. 79. On November 2, 1862, he reported that the governor had entered with his family for the first time (p. 84), and on February 10, 1863, that with one exception all officers had been living in Sioux City, Iowa, during the past year. Ibid., p. 101.

[20] "Narrative of A.P.K. Safford, Ex-Govr. of Arizona . . ." (unpublished dictation), pp. 40–41.

[21] H. J. Gurney et al. to Grant, n.d. [1874?], Interior Appointment File 138 (under Campbell).

[22] October 21, 1868.

[23] "The Governorship of Utah," II (1883), 18, 19.

appointee for Governor from the East for his duties." [24] The fundamental irreconcilability of eastern officers and western constituencies
is well described by the Bismarck *Tribune,* which sympathized with
a New England governor in his difficulties with the legislature:

The members [of the Dakota legislature] are nearly all Americans, of
vigorous age and habits, capable of thinking and acting for themselves.
Their controversy with the governor was the result of their independence,
and knowledge of the wants of their constituents. They had been with the
people and learned of them, while he was fresh from New England where
business runs in the same old ruts year after year, and where the vigorous
manhood, to be found in the west, is rarely developed. There a town meeting
would be held to determine whether to replace the county school yard out-
house, while here public buildings are erected in anticipation of business
certain to come long before the bonds given in payment fall due. The people
of Dakota, too, feel that they are abundantly able to govern themselves and
no matter how good and pure the man who is sent from the outside to govern
them, a natural opposition to him springs up at once. This was true of the
late Governor Howard, one of the purest and best of men . . . , but he came
merely to govern, the people thought, and was looked upon very much as
the governors sent from England were regarded by our forefathers. True,
the United States pays the expenses of the territory . . . , but we do not ask
them to foot the bills. . . . The people of the territory are willing and
anxious to pay their own expenses in return for the right to name their
governor and other officers.
Governor Ordway was right in almost every instance where there was a
difference between him and the legislature, looking at matters from a New
England viewpoint, . . . but [his] . . . way of doing things does not meet
with the approval of our people who open new countries and build in a
single season. [25]

While most territorial citizens protested against individual officeholders and individual laws as they appeared, there was a considerable and growing body of opinion critical of the territorial status
itself. From comparing an unpopular governor with an agent of
George III, it was natural to go on to describe the territories as
"mere colonies, occupying much the same relation to the General
Government as the colonies did to the British government prior to

[24] S. W. Bonner to Kirkwood, March 8, 1881, Interior Appointment File 167.
The Colorado legislature asked for a resident chief justice because of the "novel
and peculiar" problems in western mining law. Henry Dudley Teeter, "Hon. Moses
Hallett," *Magazine of Western History,* IX (1889), 613–14.
[25] March 18, 1881. The *Tribune* had predicted that Ordway's "fidelity to the
people will be appreciated when his carpet bag garb is worn out and the people
become willing to recognize him as a citizen of Dakota. Governor Ordway came
to Dakota to remain and though he labored under the disadvantage of bringing
a federal commission with him, he will survive the wrath of the politicians."
February 25, 1881.

the Revolution." [26] Delegate Maginnis of Montana told the House
in 1884 that

the present Territorial system . . . is the most infamous system of colonial
government that was ever seen on the face of the globe. . . . [The territories]
are the colonies of your Republic, situated three thousand miles away from
Washington by land, as the thirteen colonies were situated three thousand
miles away from London by water. And it is a strange thing that the fathers
of our Republic . . . established a colonial government as much worse
than that which they revolted against as one form of such government can
be worse than another.[27]

Stressing colonial aspects was so customary that the *Rocky Mountain
News* could greet news of admission legislation with the comment,
"The Colorado bill has passed both branches of Congress, and Colorado is now in America." [28] According to the Vermillion *Republican,* Dakotans were

not even wards of the government, but a party subject to the whims of
political leaders, the intrigues of schemers and the mining of party rats. . . .
When shall we slough off this chrysalis or bondage and be free, independent
and self governing? When some political party shall think it for their
benefit to allow us the common rights and privileges of American citizens,
and not till then.[29]

By the time of the Omnibus Bill, the defects of territorial administration in general and of non-resident appointments in particular
were freely aired in both territories and states. The Minneapolis
Tribune commented, "The admission of four new States will give the
Northwest the greatest boom it has had for many years. Carpet-bag
rule is not promotive of vigorous development." [30] Under Arthur
Democrats orated in Congress against "carpet-bag officials who have
been intriguing, blundering, and domineering in the Territories as
they used to do in the South." [31] After 1885 minority Republicans
saw the error of Democratic non-residence: not all carpet-baggers
were Northerners. Senator Stewart of Nevada said that territories
"are treated as alien lands; as a sort of Botany Bay for the rest of
the United States to which to banish broken-down politicians and
needy individuals." [32] In a few cases it is possible that the real concern of territorial citizens with the problem of non-residence was

[26] *Cong. Globe* (38 Cong., 1 Sess.), p. 1171.
[27] *Cong. Rec.* (48 Cong., 1 Sess.), p. 2780.
[28] May 9, 1866.
[29] Quoted in Bismarck *Weekly Tribune,* June 28, 1878.
[30] Quoted in *Public Opinion,* VI (1889), 459.
[31] Ben Tillman in *Cong. Rec.* (48 Cong., 1 Sess.), p. 2783.
[32] *Ibid.* (50 Cong., 1 Sess.), p. 6459.

less than the concern of eastern politicians who framed party declarations with an eye to future western electoral votes. Montana Democrats were secretly content to have a Republican governor because "it will keep the [Republican] party divided and we stand a much better show to defeat them in the elections."³³ Later the Helena editor, Alexander M. Woolfolk, remarked "It would be a master stroke of policy for the democrats to keep him [Governor Potts] in office, as a stalwart governor would be a constant 'thorn in the flesh.'"³⁴ Democrats in Dakota may have wished Governor Ordway to remain in office because his opposition to statehood would turn the territory to them;³⁵ many Republicans already had gone over to the Democrats because of Hayes's non-resident appointments.³⁶ No president could satisfy territorial opinion by his appointments. The territorial system cannot be credited with the responsibility for western political insurgency, but undoubtedly presidential appointments among residents or nonresidents kept factional divisions fresh in the territorial wing of the president's party.

The mere existence of major party organizations in the territories, however broken into factions, may be a better key to the nature of the territorial system than the hotly worded perorations of party leaders. The tone of contemporary protests in itself warns against taking them at face value. While there might be no great difference between the territory and the British colony from the point of view of sovereignty,³⁷ the spirit and the operation of territorial control were unique. Monroe in 1786 pointed out the chief novelty intended: "It is in effect to be a Colonial Gov^t similar to that w^h prevail'd in these States previous to the revolution, with this remarkable & important difference that when such district shall contain the number of the least numerous of the '13. original States for the time being' they shall be admitted into the confederacy."³⁸ The difference was greater than could be foreseen in the eighteenth century. However unpopular appointed non-resident officers might be, they could not be very foreign to men who had preceded them from the states by only a few years. A considerable number became acknowledged leaders, remaining after their terms had expired, filling local offices, writing justifications of territorial causes and advertise-

³³ P. W. McAdoo to Maginnis, March 14, 1877, Maginnis Papers.
³⁴ Woolfolk to Maginnis, March 26, 1882, ibid.
³⁵ Bismarck Tribune, March 26, 1881.
³⁶ Bismarck Tri-Weekly Tribune, April 6, 1878.
³⁷ Alexander Johnston in John J. Lalor, ed., Cyclopedia of Political Science, III, 914.
³⁸ Monroe to Jefferson, May 11, 1786, Monroe, Writings, I, 127.

ments for territorial resources.[39] Citizens resented the territorial status not only because they were Westerners, but also because recently they had been Easterners. A group of attorneys of eastern Montana complained to Congress, "The inhabitants of this part of the Territory being very largely of a class accustomed to the due and orderly administration of justice in the older States, cannot but feel that the present judicial arrangements . . . are wholly inadequate." [40] The Washington legislature asked Congress "to establish an act authorizing American citizens . . . to choose their own Governors and Judges." [41] There was not time for the shifting populations of territories to achieve a colonial point of view, as there was not time for those left in the states to work out the attitudes of imperialism.

Control was ineffective rather than either tyrannical or generously moderate. Even the anti-polygamy program, which was markedly exceptional to the ordinary course of territorial administration,[42] showed only what might be attempted. Polygamy persisted during over thirty years of territorial government in Utah. Normally control over the territories was designed to operate over only a fraction of governmental activities, and normally it fell far short of its purpose. Congress delegated supervision to the president and to three departments, but no department consolidated its functions. Correspondence was never canalized through a single office, as later became necessary in the administration of the overseas dependencies.[43]

Poor government in the territories is seldom traceable only to lack of self-government, unless it be that in the long run it was a

[39] An extended list of such writings of officers might be made, including William Frederick Milton Arny, *Interesting Items Regarding New Mexico;* John N. Irwin, "Claims to Statehood: Arizona," *North American Review,* CLVI (1893), 354–59; L. Bradford Prince, *New Mexico. It is Entitled to Statehood;* William Gillet Ritch, *Illustrated New Mexico.*

[40] *House Reports* (46 Cong., 2 Sess.), No. 470, p. 3.

[41] Washington *Laws* (6 Sess., 1859), p. 90.

[42] Senator Edmunds, defending woman suffrage in Washington, although the Edmunds Bill forbade it in Utah, said, "There can be no parallel or coincidence in the situation of affairs in Utah and in any other Territory. . . . The case of Utah is unique; it is separate; it can have no parallel or relation to any other question. . . ." *Cong. Rec.* (49 Cong., 1 Sess.), p. 3262.

[43] An executive order of May 11, 1907 required "all official communications or reports from and to executive officers of the territories and territorial possessions" or United States officers stationed in the territories to be transmitted through the Department of the Interior. Copy in Register of Appointments (Department of the Interior). Later estimates of appropriations were submitted to the Department (Act of July 16, 1914, *Statutes,* XXXVIII, 479), and accounts and vouchers were examined by the Secretary and settled by the Auditor for the Department (Act of March 4, 1915, *Statutes,* XXXVIII, 1021). Of greater significance was the establishment of the Division of Territories and Island Possessions on May 20, 1934. Pomeroy, "The American Colonial Office," *Mississippi Valley Historical Review,* XXX, 529.

consequence of divided responsibilities. Often government might have been improved by more active direction from Washington. W. J. Trimble concluded that the great defect of the territorial system in the mountain West was "the slowness of administration in comparison to the sudden needs of mining camps." In this respect territorial and county action was no better than congressional action. "The fundamental trouble was that a system of government which had been evolved for the needs of an agricultural population, in regions generally not rugged, failed to meet the demands of communities of miners in mountainous regions." [44] Yet a system which kept its agents uninstructed, without funds or responsibility for funds, without protection from political interference, should not be described inferentially as adequate for any part of the country, Old Northwest or Far West.

The system was bad, but probably it was not much worse than the systems of state government which were the only practicable alternative. If it was worse, it may have been so partly because of the popular impression that it was hopeless and without honor. "A State signifies law and order," pronounced the Colorado Springs *Gazette*, "a Territory violence and disorder." [45] The territorial form did not guarantee against anarchy, nor did it necessarily cause it. American mining camp procedure in the territories, which may have followed on the "looseness and ineffectiveness of the American territorial machinery," [46] was not dissimilar to mining camp procedure in the states. An alternative of arbitrary, centralized control may have been physically possible after the extension of rapid communication to the Pacific in 1861 and 1869. "When . . . our communication across the continent is complete," said Senator James A. McDougall in 1862, discussing the suppression of polygamy in Utah, "then we can take jurisdiction where we have power, and can employ power for the purpose of correcting these abuses." [47] As a matter of practical politics centralization could not have been conceived in the East or tolerated in the West.

To find and define the effects of the territorial system in American politics is a task far greater than to define the system itself. While there was more a lack of governance than actual misgovernment in the growing years of the mountain West, national control could represent quite positively oppression and assistance, foreign inter-

44 Trimble, *op. cit.*, p. 227.
45 June 10, 1876.
46 Trimble, *op. cit.*, p. 227. Trimble contrasts the British and American systems as concentration under an efficient executive against "representative government, under hampering conditions, working tardily and faithfully towards order, and meeting local or occasional reinforcement." *Ibid.*, p. 246.
47 *Cong. Globe* (37 Cong., 2 Sess.), p. 2507.

vention and patriotic attachment. The territorial West was at least neither wholeheartedly individualistic and independent nor predominantly dependent and colonial under the system. Its political complexions came to be unpredictable, insurgent; yet they were not Tory-Governor and Whig-Assembly, but Democratic and Republican. There was to be insurgency, but California had insurgency, the mining camp, federal grants-in-aid without passing through the territorial stage. The constitution makers of 1889 checked the powers of the new state legislatures as if territorial legislatures had never defied carpet-bag governors. "The West is a rich museum of political forms and experimentation that will reward study." [48] Ordinances and laws and appointments alone are not the exhibits or the key.

[48] Frederick J. Turner, "The West as a Field for Historical Study," *Annual Report of the American Historical Assn. . . . 1896,* I (1897), 285.

Appendix I

LIST OF TERRITORIAL OFFICERS
1861 to 1890

THIS list of governors, secretaries, and judges is designed primarily to illustrate practices and problems in administration. For that reason names of nominees not commissioned are included (names of all those who did not serve being starred), and, for those commissioned, brief indications of how tenure was terminated. In these respects, as well as in extending beyond 1873, this list differs from the "List of Territorial Officials, 1789–1872" included in Carter, *Territorial Papers*, I (Preliminary Printing), 3–33.

As far as possible information is official; thus residence is designated as in nominations and commissions, though actual residence may be known unofficially to be different; and the official distinction between removals and resignations by departmental request is respected. Renominations are omitted, but all commissions, including temporary or recess commissions, are listed. Dates of actual service in the territories are too uncertain for general tabulation. Where possible there is indication, by reference to names of successors, of the continuity in particular judgeships.

Sources include the *Journal of the Executive Proceedings of the Senate;* MS volumes entitled "Consular and Miscellaneous Officers, 1789–1868," "Miscellaneous Officers, 1807–1876," "Commissions of Judges," II and III (State Department Archives, The National Archives); Appointment Letters, memoranda in Appointment Files, a MS volume entitled "Bureau Officers, Territorial and Miscellaneous, 1879–1908" (Department of the Interior, National Archives); the *Dictionary of American Biography*, local historical series, newspapers.

Nominee	Residence	Date of Nomination	Date of Commission	How succeeded
		NEW MEXICO: GOVERNORS		
Abraham Rencher	N.C.	12/19/57	8/17/57	Removed
			1/18/58	
Henry Connelly	N.M.	7/8/61	5/24/61	Deceased
		12/23/61	7/16/62	
Robert Byington Mitchell	Kas.	12/20/65	1/15/66	Removed, suspended, resigned
Charles Campbell Crow * [1]	Ala.	4/3/69	4/17/69	Did not take oath
William Anderson Pile	Mo.	12/6/69	5/28/69	
			12/21/69	
Willard Warner *	Ala.		5/19/71	Declined
Marsh Giddings [2]	Mich.	12/6/71	7/27/71	Deceased
			12/19/71	
Samuel Beach Axtell [3]	Calif.	12/9/75	7/1/75	Suspended
			12/16/75	
Lewis Wallace	Ind.	12/4/78	9/3/78	Resigned
			12/16/78	
Lionel Allen Sheldon	Ohio	3/23/81	5/5/81	Expired
Edmund Gibson Ross	N.M.	12/10/85	5/27/85	Removed
			4/20/86	
LeBaron Bradford Prince [4]	N.M.	4/1/89	4/2/89	Expired

* Did not serve.
[1] Secretary Utah, 1870.
[2] Consul-general Calcutta, 1870.
[3] Chief justice N.M., 1882–85; governor Utah, 1874–75.
[4] Chief justice N.M., 1878–82.

NEW MEXICO: SECRETARIES

Nominee	Residence	Date of Nomination	Date of Commission	How succeeded
Alexander M. Jackson	Miss.	6/3?/58	9/16/57, 6/3/58	Resigned
Miguel Antonio Otero [5]	N.M.	7/8–9?/61	5/24/61	Rejected
James H. Holmes	N.M.	7/22/61	7/26/61	Removed
Alonzo S. Upham*	N.Y.	4/2?/62		Tabled 7/12/62
William Frederick Milton Arny [6]	Kas.	1/7/63	7/31/62, 2/18/63	Removed
George P. Este *	Ohio	12/30/65	1/15/66	Unaccepted
Herman H. Heath	Neb.	1/7/67	2/1/67	Removed
Edward L. Perkins	Pa.	4/3/69	4/9/69	Resigned by request
Henry Wetter	N.M.	1/10/70	2/14/70	Resigned
William Frederick Milton Arny [7]	N.M.		6/30/72	Removed
William G. Ritch [8]	Wis.	3/17/73	3/18/73	Removed
John Pratt *		5/18/76	5/22/76	Removed
William G. Ritch [9]	Wis.	6/2/76	6/28/76, 6/28/80	Expired
Samuel A. Losch	Pa.	6/26/84	7/2/84	Suspended
George W. Lane	N.Y.	12/14/85	8/7/85, 5/5/86	Removed
Benjamin M. Thomas	N.M.	12/5/89	5/27/89, 12/30/89	Deceased

[5] Delegate N.M., 1856–61.
[6] Secretary N.M., 1872–73.
[7] Secretary N.M., 1862–65.
[8] Secretary N.M., 1876–84.
[9] Secretary N.M., 1873–76.

NEW MEXICO: JUDGES

Nominee	Residence	Date of Nomination	Date of Commission	How succeeded
Kirby Benedict	Ill.	4/2/53	4/5/53	
#			4/18/57	
			5/15/58	
			#6/14/58	
			#6/6/62	
William C. Blackwood	Mo.	2/11/59	2/16/59	Removed (Knapp)
Perry E. Brocchus [10]	Md.	1/14/61	1/24/61	Removed (Hubbell)
Sidney A. Hubbell [11]	N.M.	7/9/61	4/30/61	Resigned (Brocchus)
			7/22/61	
Joseph Gillett Knapp	Wis.	8/5/61	8/5/61	Removed (Hubbell)
Perry E. Brocchus [12]	Md.	1/5/64	7/18/63	Superseded (Hubbell)
Nathaniel Usher [13]	Ind.		8/10/64	(Gooding)
David S. Gooding *	Ind.		8/10/64	Declined (Vinton)
Sidney A. Hubbell [14]	N.M.	1/17/65	8/10/64	Resigned (Brocchus)
David P. Vinton	Ind.	2/21/65	2/23/65	
Henry Sherman *	Ind.		5/10/65	Declined
Joab Houghton	N.M.	12/20/65	6/15/65	Removed (Bergen, Johnson)
			3/21/66	
John P. Slough #	D.C.		1/26/66	Deceased

Chief justice.
[10] Justice N.M., 1854–58, 1863–64, 1867–69; justice Utah, 1850–54.
[11] Justice N.M., 1864–67.
[12] Justice N.M., 1854–58, 1861, 1867–69; justice Utah, 1850–54.
[13] Nominated U.S. district attorney Indiana, 12/20/65.
[14] Justice N.M., 1861–63.

Nominee	Residence	Date of Nomination	Date of Commission	How succeeded
Perry E. Brocchus [15]	Md.	7/20/67	7/20/67	Removed (Johnson, Bergen)
John Sebrie Watts # [16]	N.M.	3/19/68	7/11/68	Removed
Hezekiah S. Johnson	Pa.	4/13/69	4/15/69 3/20/73	Deceased 1876 (Redick)
Joseph G. Palen #	N.Y.	4/13/69	4/15/69 3/20/73	Deceased
Abram Bergen		4/13/69	4/15/69	Resigned (Tweed, Waters)
Charles A. Tweed * [17]	Mo.	12/13/69		
Benjamin F. Waters [18]		4/22/70	4/29/70	Resigned (Lewis)
Joseph R. Lewis * [19]		5/10/71	5/15/71	Declined
Daniel B. Johnson, Jr.		12/6/71	7/18/71 12/11/71	Resigned (Bristol)
Warren Bristol [20]	Minn.	4/15/72	4/24/72 3/9/76	Expired (Peck)
Henry L. Waldo #	N.M.	1/6/76	1/10/76	Resigned
John J. Redick		5/16/76	5/22/76	Resigned (McLin)
Samuel B. McLin *	N.M.	10/17/77		Rejected
Samuel Chipman Parks [21]	Ill.	1/14/78	1/22/78	Transferred (Bell)
Charles McCandless #	Pa.	2/14/78	3/18/78	Resigned (Prince)
LeBaron Bradford Prince # [22]	N.Y.	12/18/78	1/14/79	Resigned

[15] Justice N.M., 1854–58, 1861, 1863–64; justice Utah, 1850–54.
[16] Justice N.M., 1851–54; delegate N.M., 1861–63.
[17] Justice Ariz., 1870–78.
[18] Chief justice Idaho, 1870.
[19] Justice Idaho, 1869–71?; justice Wash., 1871–75, chief justice, 1875–79.
[20] Justice N.M., 1880–84.
[21] Justice Idaho, 1863–65?; justice Wy., 1882–86.
[22] Governor N.M., 1889–93.

Nominee	Residence	Date of Nomination	Date of Commission	How succeeded
William Ware Peck * 23	Wy.	3/9/80		Unconfirmed (Pettis)
Solomon Newton Pettis * 24	Pa.	3/24/80		Rejected (Pelham)
Charles Pelham *	Ala.	6/14/80		Rejected
Warren Bristol 25	Minn.	12/7/80	12/14/80	Resigned (Wilson)
Joseph Bell	N.Y.	1/6/82	1/11/82	Resigned (Brinker)
Samuel Beach Axtell # 26	Ohio	6/14/82	7/13/82	Resigned
Stephen F. Wilson	Pa.	12/4/84	10/16/84	Suspended (Fleming)
			2/20/85	
William H. Brinker	Mo.	12/14/85	4/17/85	Resigned by request
			2/2/86	
William A. Vincent #			5/11/85	Suspended
William B. Fleming				Resigned (Henderson)
William F. Henderson	Ark.	12/14/85	10/8/85	Resigned (McFie)
			7/27/86	
Elisha Van Long #	Ind.	12/14/85	6/23/86	Resigned
Reuben A. Reeves	Tex.	2/28/87	3/3/87	Resigned (Whiteman)
John R. McFie	N.M.	3/19/89	3/23/89	Expired
William H. Whiteman	N.M.	12/5/89	4/16/89	Resigned (Seeds)
William D. Lee	N.M.	12/5/89	4/16/89	
			3/4/90	
James O'Brien	Minn.	2/10/90	2/25/90	
Edward P. Seeds	Iowa	7/17/90	7/24/90	
Alfred A. Freeman	Tenn.	9/29/90	10/1/90	Expired

23 Justice Wy., 1877–81.
24 Justice Colo., 1861–62; justice Wy., 1880.
25 Justice N.M., 1872–80.
26 Governor N.M., 1875–78; governor Utah, 1874–75.

UTAH: GOVERNORS

Nominee	Residence	Date of Nomination	Date of Commission	How succeeded
Alfred Cumming	Mo.	12/19/57	7/11/57 1/18/58	Removed
John W. Dawson	Ind.	12/23/61	10/3/61	Rejected
Stephen S. Harding [27]	Ind.	3/24/62	3/31/62	Resigned
James Duane Doty [28]	Utah	1/6/64	6/2/63 2/2/64	Deceased 6/13/65
Charles Durkee	Wis.	12/19/65	7/17/65 12/21/65	To expire
J. Wilson Shaffer	Ill.	12/16/69	1/17/70	Deceased 10/31/70
Vernon H. Vaughan [29]	Ala.		11/1/70	
Silas A. Strickland *	Neb.	1/12/71		Nomination withdrawn
George L. Woods [30]	Ore.	1/23/71	2/2/71	Expired
Samuel Beach Axtell [31]		12/15/74	2/2/75	Resigned
George W. Emery	Tenn.	12/9/75	7/1/75 12/13/75	Expired
Eli H. Murray	Ky.	1/15/80	1/27/80	Resigned by request
Caleb Walton West [32]	Ky.	4/5/86	1/28/84 4/21/86	Resigned by request

27 Chief justice Colo., 1863–66.
28 Justice Mich., 1823–32; governor Wis., 1841–44; delegate Wis., 1839–41; superintendent Indian affairs Utah, 1861–63.
29 Secretary Utah, 1870.
30 Justice Idaho, 1866.
31 Governor N.M., 1875–78; chief justice N.M., 1882–85.
32 Governor Utah, 1893–96.

Nominee	Residence	Date of Nomination	Date of Commission	How succeeded
Arthur Lloyd Thomas [33]	Utah	12/5/89	5/6/89	Removed
Caleb Walton West [34]	Utah	4/7/93	12/30/89	Admission
			4/14/93	

UTAH: SECRETARIES

Nominee	Residence	Date of Nomination	Date of Commission	How succeeded
Francis H. Wootton	Md.	4/9/60	4/19/60	Resigned
Frank Fuller	N.H.	7/9/61	7/15/61	Removed
Amos Reed [35]	Utah	1/6/64	9/4/63	Resigned
			2/2/64	
Edwin Higgins	Mich.	12/17/67	12/20/67	Removed
S. A. Mann	Nev.	4/3/69	4/7/69	
Charles Campbell Crowe * [36]	Ala.	5/24/70		Deceased
Vernon H. Vaughan [37]	Ala.	7/11/70	7/13/70	
George A. Black	Utah	1/16/71	2/2/71	Removed
			2/2/75	
Moses M. Blane	Ill.	5/18/76	6/8/76	Resigned
Levi P. Luckey	Ill.	1/8/77	2/13/77	Resigned
Arthur Lloyd Thomas [38]	Pa.	4/7/79	5/1/79	Resigned
			5/1/83	

33 Secretary Utah, 1879–87.
34 Governor Utah, 1886–89.
35 Indian agent.
36 Governor New Mexico, 1869.
37 Governor Utah, 1870–71.
38 Governor Utah, 1889–93.

Nominee	Residence	Date of Nomination	Date of Commission	How succeeded
William C. Hall	Utah	1/4/88	3/26/87 1/16/88	Resigned by request
Elijah Sells	Utah	12/5/89	5/6/89	Removed
Charles C. Richards	Utah		12/30/89 5/6/93 9/2/93	Admission

UTAH: JUDGES

Nominee	Residence	Date of Nomination	Date of Commission	How succeeded
Robert P. Flenniken	Pa.	4/9/60	5/11/60	Removed (Waite)
John Fitch Kinney # 39	Neb.	6/26/60	6/27/60	Removed
Henry R. Crosbie	Ore.	1/30/61	8/1/60 2/21/61	Removed (Drake)
Thomas J. Drake	Mich.	1/27/62	2/3/62 2/16/66	Resigned (Strickland)
Charles Burlingame Waite	Ill.	1/27/62	2/3/62	Resigned (McCurdy)
John Titus # 40	Pa.	1/5/64	5/6/63	Expired
Solomon P. McCurdy * #	Mo.	4/13/64 #1/23/68	1/20/64 4/21/64	Chief justice (Hoge)
Edwin O. Perrin *	N.Y.	6/23/68		Rejected
Charles C. Wilson #	Ill.	7/25/68	7/25/68	Rejected
Enos D. Hoge		1/23/68		Unconfirmed, removed (Hawley)
Obed F. Strickland	Mich.	4/1/69	4/5/69	Resigned (Emerson)

39 Chief justice Utah, 1854–57; delegate Utah, 1863–65.
40 Justice Ariz., 1869–70; chief justice Ariz., 1870–74.

Nominee	Residence	Date of Nomination	Date of Commission	How succeeded
Cyrus M. Hawley	Ill.	4/15/69	4/19/69	Expired (Boreman)
James Bedell McKean #	N.Y.	5/24/70	6/17/70	
			6/2/74	
Philip H. Emerson [40a]	Mich.	3/7/73	3/10/73	Resigned (Powers)
Jacob S. Boreman [41]	Mo.	3/13/73	3/20/73	Resigned (Twiss)
			4/11/77	
			10/30/77	
Isaac C. Parker * #	Mo.	3/16/75		Nomination withdrawn
David P. Lowe #	Kas.	3/18/75	3/19/75	
Alexander White #	Iowa		9/11/75	
John M. Coghlan #	Calif.	3/29/76	3/28/76	Resigned
Michael Schaeffer #	Ill.	4/19/76	4/20/76	Removed
David T. Corbin * #	S.C.	4/2/79		Rejected
John A. Hunter #	Mo.	7/1/79	7/1/79	Expired
Stephen P. Twiss	Mo.	12/7/80	12/3/80	Expired (Boreman)
			12/14/80	
Philip H. Emerson	Utah		5/16/81	Resigned
Charles Shuster Zane # [42]	Ill.	7/2/84	7/5/84	Expired
Jacob S. Boreman [43]	Utah	12/20/84	1/7/85	Expired (Anderson)
			4/20/85	
Orlando Woodworth Powers	Mich.	1/5/86		Nomination withdrawn (Henderson)
Henry P. Henderson	Mich.	7/20/86	8/2/86	To expire (Miner)
John W. Judd	Tenn.	7/9/88	7/19/88	Resigned (Blackburn)

[40a] Justice Utah, 1881–85.
[41] Justice Utah, 1885–89.
[42] Chief justice Utah, 1889–94.
[43] Justice Utah, 1873–80.

Nominee	Residence	Date of Nomination	Date of Commission	How succeeded
Elliott Sandford #	N.Y.	7/9/88	7/20/88	Removed
Thomas J. Anderson	Iowa	1/14/89	2/11/89	Resigned (Bartch)
John W. Blackburn	Utah	12/16/89	10/11/89 2/27/90	Removed (Smith)
Charles Shuster Zane # [44]	Utah	12/5/89	1/7/90	Expired
James A. Miner	Mich.	6/20/90	8/2/90	Expired (King)
George W. Bartch	Utah	1/4/93	1/13/93	Statehood
Harvey W. Smith	Utah	8/16/93	5/8/93 8/29/93	Deceased (Rolapp)
Samuel A. Merrit #	Utah	1/8/94	1/17/94	Statehood
William H. King	Utah	7/6/94	8/2/94	Statehood
Henry H. Rolapp	Utah	12/4/95	11/30/95	Statehood
WASHINGTON: GOVERNORS				
Richard Dickerson Gholson	Ky.	3/4/59	3/5/59	Resigned
William Henson Wallace [45]	Wash.	7/8-9?/61	4/9/61 7/16/61 8/7/61	Resigned
William Pickering	Ill.	12/5/61	12/19/61 1/9/66	Removed
George Edward Cole [46]	Wash.	12/12/66	11/21/66	Rejected
Charles E. DeLong *	Nev.	4/15/67		Rejected
Marshall F. Moore [47]	Ohio	4/19/67	4/20/67	Removed

44 Chief justice Utah, 1884–88.
45 Delegate Wash., 1861–63; governor Idaho, 1863–64; delegate Idaho, 1864–65.
46 Delegate Wash., 1863–65.
47 Secretary Colo., 1867.

Nominee	Residence	Date of Nomination	Date of Commission	How succeeded
Alvin Flanders [48]	Wash.	4/3/69	4/5/69	Removed
Edward Selig Salomon	Ill.	1/10/70	3/14/70	Resigned by request
James F. Legate *	Kas.		1/26/72	
Elisha P. Ferry [49]	Ill.	4/24/72	4/26/72	Expired
			4/26/76	
William A. Newell [50]	N.J.	4/7/80	4/26/80	Expired
Watson Carvasso Squire	Wash.	7/1/84	7/2/84	Removed
Eugene Semple	Wash.	1/4/88	4/9/87	Removed
			1/16/88	
Miles C. Moore	Wash.	3/21/89	3/23/89	Statehood

WASHINGTON: SECRETARIES

Nominee	Residence	Date of Nomination	Date of Commission	How succeeded
Henry M. McGill	Ohio	12/19/59	9/30/59	Removed
			1/16/60	
Leander J. S. Turney	Ill.	7/8-9/61	4/9/61	Removed
			7/16/61	
			8/7/61	
Elwood Evans [51]	Wash.	1/7/63	10/18/62	Renomination rejected
			2/18/63	
Ezra L. Smith	Wash.	4/15/67	4/16/67	Removed
James Scott	Ohio	4/3/69	4/7/69	
Joseph C. Clements	Ohio	12/21/70	1/27/71	Resigned

[48] Delegate Wash., 1867–69.
[49] Surveyor-general Wash., 1869.
[50] Indian inspector, 1884–85.
[51] Justice Wash., 1869.

Nominee	Residence	Date of Nomination	Date of Commission	How succeeded
Henry G. Struve	Wash.	12/3/72	10/17/72	Expired
			12/12/72	Expired
Nicholas H. Owings	Colo.	2/2/77	2/5/77	
			2/5/81	
			2/5/85	
Oliver C. White	Wash.	3/21/89	3/23/89	Statehood

WASHINGTON: JUDGES

Nominee	Residence	Date of Nomination	Date of Commission	How succeeded
Obadiah Benton McFadden #	Pa.	2/1/54	2/2/54	Chief justice (Strong)
William Strong	Wash.	5/27/58	6/4/58	Removed
Edward C. Fitzhugh	Wash.	5/27/58	6/4/58	Removed (Wyche)
Christopher C. Hewitt #	Wash.	6/2/58	6/4/58	Removed (Oliphant)
	Wash.	7/9/61	4/9/61	Removed
			7/26/61	
			3/21/65	
			1/22/66	
James E. Wyche	Mich.	7/9/61	4/9/61	Removed (Evans)
	Miss.		7/22/61	
			3/21/65	
			1/22/66	
Ethelbert Patterson Oliphant	Pa.	7/9/61	4/15/61	Resigned (Darwin)
			7/22/61	
			3/21/65	
Charles Ben Darwin	Ohio	1/5/66	2/25/66	Removed (Dennison)
B. F. Dennison #		6/12/68	7/9/68	Chief justice (Jacobs)
		4/15/69	4/8/69	

Nominee	Residence	Date of Nomination	Date of Commission	How succeeded
Elwood Evans * 52	Wash.	4/5/69	4/14/69	Chief justice (Lewis)
Orange Jacobs 53	Ore.	4/12/69	4/14/69	
#		1/17/70	3/17/70	
			4/7/74	
James K. Kennedy	Wash.	4/12/69	4/14/69	Resigned (Lewis)
Roger Sherman Greene 54	Wis.	6/18/70	7/9/70	Chief justice (Hoyt)
	Wash.		6/19/74	
	D.C.		5/23/78	
Joseph R. Lewis 55	Idaho	3/14/71	3/21/71	Chief justice (Wingard)
#	Wash.	1/16/75	1/26/75	Expired
Samuel C. Wingard 56	Wash.	1/16/75	1/26/75	Suspended (Langford)
			12/20/78	
			2/27/83	
Roger Sherman Greene # 57	Wash.	12/20/78	1/16/79	Expired
			1/29/83	
John Philo Hoyt 58	Mich.	12/20/78	1/16/79	Expired (Allyn)
			1/29/83	
George Turner	Ala.	7/4/84	7/5/84	Resigned (Nash)
William G. Langford	Wash.	12/4/85	1/29/87	Statehood
Frank Allyn	Iowa	2/4/87	2/22/87	Statehood

52 Secretary Wash., 1862–67.
53 Delegate Wash., 1875–79.
54 Chief justice Wash., 1879–87.
55 Justice Idaho, 1869–71; justice N.M., 1871.
56 U.S. attorney.
57 Justice Wash., 1870–79.
58 Secretary Ariz., 1876–77; governor Ariz., 1877–78; governor Idaho, 1878.

Nominee	Residence	Date of Nomination	Date of Commission	How succeeded
Richard A. Jones #	Ore.	2/4/87	2/22/87	Deceased
Lucius B. Nash	Wash.	2/27/88	3/14/88	Statehood
Charles E. Boyle # 59	Pa.	9/4/88	9/ /88	Deceased
Thomas Burke #	Wash.	12/19/88	12/ /88	Resigned
Cornelius Holgate Hanford #	Wash.	3/12/89	3/ /88	Statehood

NEBRASKA: GOVERNORS

Nominee	Residence	Date of Nomination	Date of Commission	How succeeded
Samuel W. Black	Neb.	2/3/59	2/8/59	Removed
Alvin Saunders	Iowa	3/26/61	3/27/61	Statehood
			4/13/65	
			1/9/66	

NEBRASKA: SECRETARIES

Nominee	Residence	Date of Nomination	Date of Commission	How succeeded
Julius Sterling Morton	Neb.	4/15/58	6/14/58	Removed
Algernon Sidney Paddock 60	Neb.	7/8-9?/61	4/27/61	Statehood
			7/16/61	
			8/4/66	

NEBRASKA: JUDGES

Nominee	Residence	Date of Nomination	Date of Commission	How succeeded
Eleazer Wakely	Wis.	1/21/57	1/22/57	Removed (Lockwood)
			1/24/61	
Augustus Hall #	Iowa	12/22/57	12/3/57	Deceased 2/1/61
Joseph Miller	Ohio	3/4/59	3/5/59	Removed (Milligan)

59 House Committee on Territories, 1886.
60 Governor Wy., 1868; Utah Commission, 1882–86.

Nominee	Residence	Date of Nomination	Date of Commission	How succeeded
William Pitt Kellogg # [61]	Ill.	3/25/61	3/27/61 4/17/65 1/15/66	Statehood
Sam Milligan *	Tenn.	3/25/61	3/27/61	Failed to assume duties (Streeter)
William F. Lockwood	Neb.	7/9/61	4/27/61 7/23/61 7/23/65 2/15/66	Statehood
Joseph E. Streeter	Ill.	12/9/61	10/15/61 1/22/62	Deceased (Ketchum)
Winthrop Welles Ketchum	Pa.	3/10/63	3/11/63	Resigned (Dundy)
Elmer S. Dundy	Neb.	1/5/64	6/2/63	Statehood

COLORADO: GOVERNORS

Nominee	Residence	Date of Nomination	Date of Commission	How succeeded
William Gilpin	Colo.	3/21/61	3/25/61	Removed
John Evans	Ill.	3/18/62	3/26/62	Resigned by request
Alexander Cummings	Pa.	12/19/65	8/8/65 1/26/66	Resigned
A. Cameron Hunt [62]	Colo.	7/19/67	5/10/67 11/29/67	Removed
Edward Moody McCook [63]	Colo.	4/15/69	4/17/69	To expire; declined reappointment

[61] Senate Committee on Territories, 1877–81; House Committee, 1881–83.
[62] U.S. marshal.
[63] Governor Colo., 1874–75.

Nominee	Residence	Date of Nomination	Date of Commission	How succeeded
Samuel Hitt Elbert [64]	Colo.	3/19/73	4/17/73	Removed
Edward Moody McCook [65]	Colo.	1/27/74	6/19/74	Resigned
John Long Routt	Ill.	2/8/75	2/8/75	Statehood
COLORADO: SECRETARIES				
Lewis Ledyard Weld	Colo.	3/21/61	3/25/61	Resigned
Samuel Hitt Elbert [66]	Neb.	4/9?/62	4/14/62	Resigned 1/1/66
Frank Hall [67]	Colo.	2/13/66	4/10/66	Nomination not submitted
James R. Hood *			9/25/66	
Hiram Pitt Bennet [68]	Colo.	3/21/67		Rejected
Henry M. Slade * [69]	Ohio	4/4/67		Rejected
Marshall F. Moore * [70]	Ohio	4/13/67		Rejected
Frank Hall [71]	Colo.	4/3/69	4/7/69	Removed
			4/7/73	
John W. Jenkins	Va.	1/27/74	2/12/74	Suspended
John Taffe	Neb.	12/9/75	7/2/75	Statehood
			12/9/75	

[64] Secretary Colo., 1862–66.
[65] Governor Colo., 1869–73.
[66] Governor Colo., 1873–74.
[67] Secretary Colo., 1869–74.
[68] Delegate Colo., 1861–65.
[69] Secretary Wy., 1869.
[70] Governor Wash., 1867–69.
[71] Secretary Colo., 1866.

COLORADO: JUDGES

Nominee	Residence	Date of Nomination	Date of Commission	How succeeded
Benjamin Franklin Hall #	N.Y.	3/21/61	3/25/61	Resigned
Solomon Newton Pettis [72]	Pa.	3/21/61	3/25/61	Resigned (Bradford)
Charles Lee Armour	Md.	3/21/61	3/28/61	
Allen Alexander Bradford [73]	Colo.	6/2/62	6/6/62	
Stephen S. Harding # [74]	Ind.	1/5/64	7/18/63	Resigned
			4/7/64	
William H. Gale	N.Y.	12/20/65	6/10/65	
			1/15/66	
Charles F. Holly	Colo.	12/20/65	6/10/65	Removed (Gorsline)
			1/22/66	
Moses Hallett #	Colo.	3/20/66	4/10/66	Statehood
			4/6/70	
			4/7/74	
William R. Gorsline	N.Y.	5/28/66	6/18/66	Expired (Belford)
Christian Eyster	Pa.	12/ /66	8/11/66	
			3/2/67	(Wells)
James B. Belford	Ind.	6/7/70	6/17/70	
			5/27/74	(Stone)
Ebenezer T. Wells	Colo.	2/3/71	2/8/71	Expired (Brazee)
Andrew W. Brazee	N.Y.	2/5/75	2/24/75	Statehood
Amherst W. Stone	Colo.	2/5/75	2/24/75	Statehood

[72] Justice N.M., 1880; justice Wy., 1880.
[73] Delegate Colo., 1865–67, 1869–71.
[74] Governor Utah, 1862–63.

Nominee	Residence	Date of Nomination	Date of Commission	How succeeded
		NEVADA: GOVERNOR		
James Warren Nye	N.Y.	3/20/61	3/22/61	Statehood
		NEVADA: SECRETARY		
Orion M. Clemens	Mo.	3/23/61	3/27/61	Statehood
		NEVADA: JUDGES		
Horatio M. Jones	Mo.	3/25/61	3/27/61	Resigned (Locke)
Gordon Newell Mott 75	Calif.	3/25/61	3/27/61	Resigned (North)
George Turner #	Ohio	3/25/61	3/27/61	Resigned
John W. North	Nev.	1/5/64	8/20/63 1/20/64	Resigned
Powhatan B. Locke	Mo.	1/5/64	8/31/63 1/20/64	Resigned
		DAKOTA: GOVERNORS		
William Jayne 76	Ill.	3/23/61	3/27/61	Resigned
John Fox Potter *	Wis.	3/4/63	3/9/63	Declined
Newton Edmunds	Dak.	1/6/64	10/6/63 2/2/64	Removed
Andrew Jackson Faulk	Pa.	12/12/66	8/4/66 3/2/67	Removed

75 Delegate Nev., 1863–64.
76 Delegate Dak., 1863–64.

Nominee	Residence	Date of Nomination	Date of Commission	How succeeded
John A. Burbank	Ind.	4/3/69	4/5/69	Resigned by request
			4/5/73	
John L. Pennington [77]	Ala.	12/11/73	1/1/74	Expired
William A. Howard	Mich.	2/15/78	3/12/78	Deceased 4/10/80
Nehemiah G. Ordway	N.H.	5/14/80	5/22/80	Expired
Gilbert Ashville Pierce	Ill.	6/27/84	7/2/84	Resigned
Louis K. Church [78]	Dak.	12/13/86	2/3/87	Resigned
Arthur Calvin Mellette	Dak.	3/12/89	3/13/89	Statehood

DAKOTA: SECRETARIES

Nominee	Residence	Date of Nomination	Date of Commission	How succeeded
John Hutchinson	Kas.	3/23/61	3/27/61	Resigned
Solomon Lewis Spink [79]	Ill.	12/19/65	3/21/65	
			1/10/66	
Turney M. Wilkins	Iowa	4/3/69	4/9/69	Removed
George H. Hand * [80]	Dak	2/21/70		Confirmation reconsidered
George Alexander Batchelder	Mass.	5/10/70	5/20/70	Resigned (removed?)
Edwin Stanton McCook	Ill.?	2/6/72	2/13/72	Deceased 9/11/73
Oscar A. Whitney	Dak.	12/15/73	9/22/73	Resigned
			12/18/73	
George H. Hand [81]	Dak.	12/9/74	10/29/74	Expired
			12/17/74	
			1/16/79	

[77] Internal revenue collector, 1878.
[78] Justice Dak., 1885–87.
[79] Delegate Dak., 1869–71.
[80] Secretary Dak., 1874–83; U.S. district attorney.
[81] Secretary Dak., 1870.

Nominee	Residence	Date of Nomination	Date of Commission	How succeeded
James Harvey Teller	Ohio	2/12/83	2/21/83	Suspended
Michael L. McCormack	Dak.	12/14/85	11/24/85	Removed
			4/6/86	
Luther B. Richardson	Dak.	3/12/89	3/13/89	Statehood

DAKOTA: JUDGES

Nominee	Residence	Date of Nomination	Date of Commission	How succeeded
Philemon Bliss #	Ohio	3/23/61	3/27/61	Superseded
Lorenzo P. Williston 81a	Pa.	3/23/61	3/27/61	Transferred (Bartlett)
Allan A. Burton*	Ky.	3/23/61	3/28/61	Declined (Williams)
Joseph Lanier Williams	Tenn.	7/9/61	6/18/61	Superseded (Gleason)
			7/22/61	
Asa Bartlett	Ill.	6/20/64	6/22/64	Chief justice (Kidder)
#	Dak.	2/16/65	2/23/65	Expired
William E. Gleason	Md.	2/16/65	2/23/65	
Jefferson Parish Kidder 82	Minn.	2/16/65	2/23/65	Resigned (Bennett)
			4/6/69	
			3/18/73	
John W. Boyle	Dak.	12/ /66	8/3/66	Removed (Brookings)
	Dak.		1/26/67	
George W. French # 83	Dak.	4/3/69	4/6/69	Renomination withdrawn; expired
Wilmot W. Brookings	Dak.	4/15/69	4/16/69	Expired (French)

81a Justice Mont., 1864-68.
82 Justice Dak., 1879-84; delegate Dak., 1875-79.
83 Justice Dak., 1873; secretary Wy., 1875-79.

Nominee	Residence	Date of Nomination	Date of Commission	How succeeded
Peter C. Shannon #	Pa.	3/15/73	3/21/73 4/11/77 11/12/77	Resigned
George W. French * [84]	Dak.?	3/15/73	3/24/73	Withdrawn (Barnes)
Alanson H. Barnes	Wis.	3/24/73	3/15/77	Expired (Hudson)
Granville Gaylord Bennett [85]	Dak.	2/5/75	2/24/75	Resigned (Moody)
Gideon Curtis Moody [86]	Dak.	12/5/78	9/20/78 12/12/78	Expired (W. E. Church)
Jefferson Parish Kidder [87]	Dak.	3/24/79	4/2/79 4/27/83	Deceased (Palmer)
Sanford A. Hudson	Wis.	3/10/81	5/4/81	Expired (McConnell)
Alonzo J. Edgerton #	Minn.	12/21/81	12/21/81	Resigned
William E. Church	N.J.	2/27/83	2/28/83	Resigned (Thomas)
Cornelius S. Palmer	Vt.	2/19/84	2/28/84	Expired (Garland)
Frank Sperry *	N.Y.	7/4/84	7/5/84	Withdrawn (Francis)
Seward Smith	Iowa	7/4/84	7/5/84	Suspended (L. K. Church)
William H. Francis [88]	N.J.	7/5/84		Expired (Rose)
William B. McConnell	Dak.	12/14/85	5/8/85 1/20/86	Statehood
Bartlett Tripp	Dak.	12/14/85	11/24/85 1/20/86	Statehood

[84] Chief justice Dak., 1869–73; secretary Wy., 1875–79.
[85] Delegate Dak., 1879–81.
[86] Register in bankruptcy, Yankton.
[87] Justice Dak., 1865–75; delegate Dak., 1875–79.
[88] Receiver of public moneys, Bismarck.

Nominee	Residence	Date of Nomination	Date of Commission	How succeeded
Louis K. Church [89]	N.Y.	12/21/85	5/28/86	Governor (Spencer)
Charles M. Thomas	Ky.	7/26/86	8/2/86	Statehood
James Spencer	N.Y.	1/4/87	1/29/87	Statehood
John E. Carland	Dak.	2/27/88	3/7/88	Resigned (Aikens)
Roderick Rose	Dak.	7/9/88	7/19/88	Statehood
Charles F. Templeton	Dak.	8/22/88	10/ /88	Statehood
Louis W. Crofoot	Dak.	9/13/88	10/ /88	Statehood
Frank R. Aikens	Dak.	3/19/89	3/ /89	Statehood

ARIZONA: GOVERNORS

Nominee	Residence	Date of Nomination	Date of Commission	How succeeded
John Addison Gurley	Ohio	3/7/63	3/19/63	Deceased 8/19/63
John Noble Goodwin [90]	Me.	1/6/64	8/21/63 2/2/64	Resigned
Richard Cunningham McCormick [91]	Ariz.	3/14/66	4/10/66	
Anson Peacely-Killen Safford [92]	Nev.	4/3/69	4/7/69 4/11/73	Expired
John Philo Hoyt [93]	Mich.	10/15/77	4/5/77 10/29/77	Transferred
John Charles Frémont	N.Y.	6/8/78	6/12/78	Resigned
Frederick A. Tritle	Nev.	1/26/82	2/6/82	Resigned
Conrad Meyer Zulick	Ariz.	12/10/85	10/14/85 5/5/86	Removed

89 Governor Dak., 1886–89.
90 Chief justice Ariz., 1863; delegate Ariz., 1865–67.
91 Secretary Ariz., 1863–66; delegate Ariz., 1869–75.
92 Surveyor-general Nev.
93 Secretary Ariz., 1876–77; governor Idaho, 1878; justice Wash., 1879–87.

Nominee	Residence	Date of Nomination	Date of Commission	How succeeded
Lewis Wolfley	Ariz.	3/14/89	3/28/89	Resigned
John Nichol Irwin [94]	Iowa	9/29/90	10/4/90	Resigned 4/18/92
ARIZONA: SECRETARIES				
Richard Cunningham McCormick [95]	N.Y.	3/7/63	3/19/63	Governor
James P. T. Carter	Tenn.	3/ /66	4/10/66	Removed
Coles Bashford [96]	Ariz.	4/3/69	4/8/69	Resigned
			4/11/73	
William Sanborn *	Mich.	12/9/75	2/1/76	Declined
John Philo Hoyt [97]	Mich.	5/22/76	5/24/76	Governor
John J. Gosper	Neb.	10/17/77	4/12/77	Expired
			10/29/77	
Hiram M. Van Arman	Calif.	2/14/82	3/17/82	Resigned
James Asheton Bayard	Md.	12/14/85	11/6/85	Resigned by request
			2/10/86	
Nathan Oakes Murphy [98]	Ariz.	3/18/89	3/21/89	Resigned; governor
ARIZONA: JUDGES				
John Noble Goodwin # [99]	Me.	3/6/63	3/10/63	Resigned; governor
William T. Howell	Mich.	3/6/63	3/10/63	New appointment (Backus)
Joseph P. Allyn	Conn.	3/6/63	3/11/63	Expired (Cartter)

[94] Governor Idaho, 1883–84.
[95] Governor Ariz., 1866–69; delegate Ariz., 1869–75.
[96] Delegate Ariz., 1867–69.
[97] Governor Ariz., 1877–78; governor Idaho, 1878; justice Wash., 1879–87.
[98] Governor Ariz., 1892–94, 1898–1902.
[99] Governor Ariz., 1863–65; delegate Ariz., 1865–67.

Nominee	Residence	Date of Nomination	Date of Commission	How succeeded
William F. Turner #	Iowa	1/5/64	8/22/63 1/20/64 2/5/68	Removed
Henry T. Backus	Mich.	3/10/65	3/11/65	Removed (Reavis)
Harley H. Cartter	Idaho	3/16/67	3/20/67	Chief justice (Tweed)
John Titus 100 #	Pa.	3/15/69	3/19/69 4/18/70	Expired
Isham Reavis	Neb.	4/16/69	4/20/69	Expired (Silent)
Charles A. Tweed	Calif.	4/14/70	4/18/70 3/5/74	Expired (Silent)
J. De Forrest Porter	Neb. Ariz.	2/20/72	2/23/72 2/28/76 2/2/80	Resigned (Pinney)
Edward F. Dunne #	Nev.	3/6/74	3/20/74	Expired
Charles G. W. French #	Calif.	12/13/75	12/16/75 1/13/80	Expired
Charles Silent	Calif.	2/11/78	2/20/78	Resigned (Stillwell)
William Henry Stillwell	N.Y.	12/7/80	12/3/80 1/5/81	To be removed (Hoover)
David H. Pinney	Ill.	6/14/82	6/19/82	Suspended (W. W. Porter)
Wilson W. Hoover	Calif.	7/19/82	8/7/82	Suspended (Sheldon)
A. W. Sheldon	Md.	12/18/83	1/4/84	Deceased (Fitzgerald)
W. F. Fitzgerald	Miss.	3/3/84	3/11/84	Suspended (Barnes)
Sumner Howard #		3/18/84	3/26/84	Suspended, resigned
William H. Barnes	Ill.	12/14/85	10/ /85 5/28/86	Removed (Sloan)

100 Chief justice Utah, 1863–68.

Nominee	Residence	Date of Nomination	Date of Commission	How succeeded
William W. Porter	Calif.	12/21/85	7/26/86	Removed (Kibbey)
John C. Shields #	Mich.	12/14/85	10/ /85	Rejected
James H. Wright #	Mo.	2/4/87	2/22/87	To be removed
Joseph Henry Kibbey	Ariz.	12/16/89	8/5/89	Removed
			2/25/90	
Richard Elihu Sloan 101	Ariz.	12/16/89	10/17/89	Expired
			2/19/90	
Henry C. Gooding #	Ind.	3/13/90	4/26/90	Resigned
Edmund William Wells	Ariz.	2/16/91	2/ /91	Resigned
IDAHO: GOVERNORS				
William Henson Wallace 102	Wash.	3/ /63	3/10/63	Delegate
Caleb Lyon	N.Y.	2/2/64	2/26/64	Removed
David W. Ballard	Ore.	3/14/66	4/10/66	Removed, suspended, expired
John M. Murphy *	Idaho	1/14/67		Rejected
George C. Bates *	Ill.	3/6/67		Unconfirmed
Isaac L. Gibbs *	Idaho	7/19/67		Unconfirmed
Samuel Bard *	Ga.	2/4/70	3/30/70	Resigned
Gilman Marston *	N.Y.	5/24/70	6/7/70	Declined
Alexander H. Connor *	Ind.	12/16/70	1/12/71	
Ebenezer Dumont *	Ind.	3/15/71		Deceased
Thomas Meade Bowen	Ark.	4/17/71	4/19/71	Resigned 9/5/71
Thomas Warren Bennett 103	Ind.	12/6/71	12/14/71	Renomination declined

101 Justice Ariz., 1897–1909; governor Ariz., 1909–12.
102 Governor Wash., 1861; delegate Wash., 1861–63; delegate Idaho, 1864–65.
103 Governor Idaho, 1876; delegate Idaho, 1875–76.

Nominee	Residence	Date of Nomination	Date of Commission	How succeeded
David P. Thompson	Ore.	7/12/76	12/16/75	Resigned
Thomas Warren Bennett * [104]	Idaho	7/18/76	7/24/76	Suspended, reinstated; expired
Mason Brayman	Wis.	6/8/78	8/7/78	Declined
John Philo Hoyt * [105]	Utah	12/6/80	7/12/80	Declined
John B. Neil [106]			12/14/80	Removed
John Nichol Irwin [107]	Iowa	3/1/83	3/2/83	Resigned
William M. Bunn	Pa.	3/3/84	3/26/84	Resigned
Edward A. Stevenson	Idaho	12/10/85	9/29/85	Removed
			2/8/86	
George Laird Shoup [108]	Idaho	3/ /89	4/1/89	Statehood

IDAHO: SECRETARIES

Nominee	Residence	Date of Nomination	Date of Commission	How succeeded
William B. Daniels	Ore.	3/ /63	3/10/63	Resigned
C. DeWitt Smith	D.C.	7/1/64	7/4/64	Deceased 8/19/65
Horace C. Gilson	Idaho	12/19/65	9/4/65	Removed
			1/26/66	
S. R. Howlett	Idaho	7/14/66	7/26/66	Suspended
William H. Parker *		6/5/68		Unconfirmed
William F. Pidgeon * [109]	Ind.	6/21/68		Unconfirmed

[104] Governor Idaho, 1871–75; delegate Idaho, 1875–76.
[105] Secretary Ariz., 1876–77; governor Ariz., 1877–78; governor Wash., 1879–87.
[106] Receiver land office, Salt Lake City.
[107] Governor Ariz., 1890–92.
[108] Senate Committee on Territories, 1891.
[109] Justice Wy., 1868.

Nominee	Residence	Date of Nomination	Date of Commission	How succeeded
Edward Jay Curtis [110]	Idaho	12/6/69	5/4/69 1/24/70 2/5/74	Expired
Robert A. Sidebotham	Idaho	4/1/78	4/29/78	Removed
Theodore Frelinghuysen Singiser [111]	Pa.	12/16/80	12/22/80	Resigned
Edward Leverett Curtis [112]	Idaho	3/3/83	3/3/83	New appointment
David P. B. Pride [113]	Idaho	7/1/84	7/2/84	Resigned
Edward Jay Curtis [114]	Idaho	2/9/85	2/12/85 2/12/89	Statehood

IDAHO: JUDGES

Nominee	Residence	Date of Nomination	Date of Commission	How succeeded
Sidney Edgerton # [115]	Ohio	3/6/63	3/10/63	
Samuel Chipman Parks [116]	Ill.	3/6/63	3/10/63	
Alleck C. Smith	Idaho	3/6/63	3/10/63	
Silas Woodson #	Mo.	6/20/64	7/28/64	
John Rogers McBride #	Ore.	1/28/65	2/14/65	Resigned (Kelley)
Milton Kelley	Idaho	12/20/65	4/17/65 1/15/66 1/24/70	Removed (Woods) Resigned Removed (Whitson)

110 Secretary Idaho, 1885–90.
111 Receiver public moneys, Oxford, Idaho; delegate Idaho, 1883–85.
112 Register land office, Boise, 1884.
113 Register land office, Boise.
114 Secretary Idaho, 1869–78.
115 Governor Montana, 1864–66.
116 Justice N.M., 1878–82; justice Wy., 1882–86.

Nominee	Residence	Date of Nomination	Date of Commission	How succeeded
George L. Woods * 117	Ore.	1/20/66		Withdrawn (Cummins)
John Cummins	Idaho	5/18/66	5/29/66	Removed (Baker)
John H. Baker *		2/21/67		Unconfirmed
Richard B. Carpenter *		3/15/67		Unconfirmed
George A. Hawley *		7/20/67		Unconfirmed
Richard T. Miller		3/26/68	7/1/68	Removed (Lewis)
Thomas J. Bowers #		7/15/68	7/18/68	Removed
David Noggle #	Wis.	4/7/69	4/9/69	Removed; resigned
			3/18/73	
Joseph R. Lewis 118	Mo.	4/13/69	4/15/69	Resigned
Benjamin J. Waters * # 119	Ore.	3/9/70		Withdrawn
William C. Whitson	Idaho	7/13/70	7/13/70	Deceased (Prickett)
			6/19/74	
Madison E. Hollister #	Ill.	3/16/71	3/20/71	Chief justice (Clark)
John Clark	Idaho	12/22/74	1/14/75	Resigned
Henry E. Prickett	Idaho	12/22/74	1/14/75	Expired (Buck)
	Idaho	1/13/76	1/19/76	Expired (Broderick)
			1/21/80	
William G. Thompson #	Iowa	1/20/79	1/23/79	Resigned
John T. Morgan #	Ill.	5/19/79	6/10/79	Suspended
			7/5/84	
Norman Buck	Idaho	5/19/79	1/27/80	Expired (Logan)
			3/11/84	
Case Broderick	Kas.	3/18/84	3/24/84	Expired (Berry)

117 Governor Utah, 1871-75.
118 Justice N.M., 1871; justice Wash., 1871-75; chief justice Wash., 1875-79.
119 Justice N.M., 1870-71.

Nominee	Residence	Date of Nomination	Date of Commission	How succeeded
James B. Hays #	Wis.	12/14/85	8/2/86	Deceased
John Lee Logan	N.Y.	3/11/88	4/12/88	Statehood
Charles H. Berry	Minn.	7/9/88	7/19/88	Statehood
Hugh W. Weir #	Pa.	7/9/88	7/19/88	Removed
Willis Sweet [120]	Idaho	12/16/89	11/19/89 1/ /90	Statehood
James H. Beatty #	Idaho	12/16/89	11/21/89 1/ /90	Statehood

MONTANA: GOVERNORS

Nominee	Residence	Date of Nomination	Date of Commission	How succeeded
Sidney Edgerton [121]	Idaho	6/20/64	6/22/64	Resigned
Green Clay Smith	Ky.	6/13/66	7/13/66	Resigned
Nathaniel P. Langford *	Mont.	1/13/69		Unconfirmed
James Mitchell Ashley [122]	Ohio	4/5/69	4/9/69	Removed
Benjamin Franklin Potts	Ohio	12/16/69	7/13/70 7/13/74 7/13/78	Expired
John Schuyler Crosby	N.Y.	7/19/82	8/4/82	Resigned
B. Platt Carpenter	N.Y.	12/16/84	12/22/84	Suspended
Samuel Thomas Hauser	Mont.	12/10/85	7/3/85	Resigned
Preston Hopkins Leslie	Ky.	12/15/86	5/14/86 1/13/87	Removed
Benjamin F. White	Mont.	3/26?/89	3/27/89	Statehood

[120] U.S. attorney.
[121] Chief justice Idaho, 1863–64.
[122] Chairman House Committee on Territories, 1861–69.

MONTANA: SECRETARIES

Nominee	Residence	Date of Nomination	Date of Commission	How succeeded
Henry P. Torsey *	Me.	6/20/64	6/22/64	Declined
John Coburn *123	Ind.	2/21/65	3/3/65	Declined
Thomas Francis Meagher	N.Y.	12/19/65	8/4/65	Resigned; deceased 7/1/67
			1/26/66	
John P. Bruce *	Mont.	12/6/66		Rejected
James Tufts	Mont.	3/21/67	3/28/67	Removed
Wiley S. Scribner	Mont.	4/3/69	4/20/69	Suspended
Addison H. Sanders 124	Iowa	12/6/70	7/19/70	Withdrawn
James E. Callaway	Ill.	12/16/70	1/27/71	Resigned
			2/24/75	
James Hamilton Mills	Mont.	10/17/77	5/19/77	Resigned, expired
			11/8/77	
Isaac D. McCutcheon	Mich.	3/28/82	4/21/82	Resigned
John S. Tooker	Mich.	12/6/83	10/22/83	Resigned
			12/18/83	
William B. Webb	Mont.	12/17/85	9/29/85	Removed
			3/9/86	
Louis A. Walker	Mont.	4/1/89?	4/1/89	Statehood

MONTANA: JUDGES

Nominee	Residence	Date of Nomination	Date of Commission	How succeeded
Ammi Giddings	Conn.	6/15/64	6/22/64	Resigned (Munson)
Lorenzo P. Williston 125	Dak.	6/15/64	6/22/64	Expired (Knowles)

123 Justice Mont., 1884–85.
124 Register land office, Helena, 1870.
125 Justice Dak., 1861–64.

Nominee	Residence	Date of Nomination	Date of Commission	How succeeded
Hezekiah Lord Hosmer #	N.Y.	6/15/64	6/30/64	Expired
Lyman Ezra Munson	Conn.	3/10/65	3/11/65	Removed (Stafford); resigned
Henry L. Warren #		7/13/68	7/18/68	Removed; resigned
William M. Stafford *		7/15/68	7/15/68	Tabled (Dixon)
Hiram Knowles	Iowa	7/15/68	7/18/68	Resigned (Galbraith)
			7/13/72	
			12/12/72	
			12/12/76	
William W. Dixon *	Ky.	1/18/69	4/5/69	Unconfirmed (Symes)
George Gifford Symes	Mont.	3/26/69		(Murphy)
Lewis M. Burson * #	Tenn.	4/20/69		Withdrawn
John L. Murphy	Ohio	1/9/71	1/27/71	Suspended (Service)
Decius Spear Wade # 126	Mont.	3/14/71	3/17/71	Expired
			3/17/75	
			2/27/79	
			2/28/83	
Francisco G. Servis	Ohio	1/13/73	9/21/72	Resigned (Blake)
			1/21/73	
Henry Nichols Blake 127	Mont.	12/15/75	7/30/75	Expired (Conger)
			1/12/76	
William J. Galbraith	Iowa	5/19/79	6/23/79	Expired (DeWolfe)
			6/29/83	
			1/7/84	
Everton J. Conger	Ill.	1/7/80	1/19/80	Expired (Coburn)

126 Chief justice Mont., 1889.
127 Chief justice Mont., 1889, district attorney Mont.

Nominee	Residence	Date of Nomination	Date of Commission	How succeeded
John Coburn [128]	Ind.	2/15/84	2/19/84	Suspended (Pollard)
Charles R. Pollard *	Ind.	12/14/85		Rejected (McLeary)
James Harvey McLeary	Tex.	5/6/86	7/27/86	Resigned (Liddell)
Thomas Cummings Bach	Mont.	7/28/86	8/3/86	(to 10/5/89)
Newton Whiteside McConnell #	Tenn.	12/20/87	4/14/87 1/23/88	Resigned
Stephen DeWolfe	Mont.	12/20/87	1/23/88	Statehood
Moses J. Liddell	La.	2/27/88	3/5/88	Statehood
Decius Spear Wade * # [129]	Mont.	1/31/89		Unconfirmed
Henry Nichols Blake # [130]	Mont.	3/21/89	3/ /89	Statehood

WYOMING: GOVERNORS

Nominee	Residence	Date of Nomination	Date of Commission	How succeeded
Algernon Sidney Paddock * [131]	Neb.	7/25/68	4/7/69	Nomination reconsidered
Mathew F. Pleasants *	N.Y.	1/23/69	4/7/73	Unconfirmed
John Allen Campbell	Ohio	4/3/69		Resigned
John Milton Thayer	Neb.	2/10/75	2/10/75	Removed
John Wesley Hoyt	Wis.	3/11/78	4/10/78	Expired
William Hale	Iowa	7/19/82	8/3/82	Deceased 1/13/85
Francis Emroy Warren [132]	Wy.	2/25/85	2/27/85	Suspended
George W. Baxter	Wy.		11/5/86	Resigned by request

128 Secretary Mont., 1865.
129 Chief Justice Mont., 1871–87.
130 Justice Mont., 1875–80.
131 Secretary Neb., 1861–67; Utah Commission, 1882–86.
132 Governor Wy., 1889–90.

WYOMING: SECRETARIES

Nominee	Residence	Date of Nomination	Date of Commission	How succeeded
Thomas Moonlight	Kas.	12/8/86	12/20/86	Removed?
Francis Emroy Warren [133]	Wy.	3/26/89?	3/27/89	Statehood
Omar F. Roberts *	Ind.	7/25/68		Rejected
Henry M. Slade *	Ohio	1/23/69		Unconfirmed
Edward M. Lee	Conn.	4/3/69	4/7/69	Removed
Herman Glafcke [134]	Conn.	2/18/70	3/2/70	Removed
Jason Brevoort Brown	Ind.	3/18/73	3/24/73	Resigned 1/5/75
George W. French [135]	Me.	2/12/75	2/24/75	Expired
A. Worth Spates	Md.	1/7/79	2/24/79	Removed
Elliott S. N. Morgan	Pa.	12/17/79	3/10/80	Removed
	Wy.		3/26/84	
Samuel Davis Shannon	Wy.	1/4/88	4/9/87	Resigned
			1/16/88	
John W. Meldrum	Wy.	12/17/89	5/20/89	Statehood
			1/9/90	

WYOMING: JUDGES

Nominee	Residence	Date of Nomination	Date of Commission	How succeeded
Henry Z. Hayner *		1/23/69		Unconfirmed
John H. Howe * [136]	Ill.?	1/23/69		Unconfirmed

133 Governor Wy., 1885–86.
134 Postmaster Cheyenne, 1883.
135 Chief justice Dak., 1869–73; justice Dak., 1873.
136 Chief justice Wy., 1869–71.

Nominee	Residence	Date of Nomination	Date of Commission	How succeeded
William F. Pidgeon * [137]	Ind.	1/23/69		Unconfirmed
John H. Howe # [138]	Ill.	4/3/69	4/6/69	Resigned
William Theophilus Jones [139]		4/3/69	4/6/69	Resigned (Fisher)
John W. Kingman	N.H.	4/3/69	4/6/69	Renomination withdrawn; expired (Thomas)
Joseph W. Fisher	Pa.	2/23/71	2/28/71	Chief Justice (Carey)
#	Wy.	12/6/71	10/14/71	Resigned
			12/11/71	
			2/14/76	
Joseph Maull Carey [140]	Wy.	12/13/71	1/18/72	Expired (Blair)
Edward A. Thomas	N.Y.	3/18/73	3/20/73	Expired (Peck)
			4/13/73	
Jacob Beeson Blair	W. Va.	2/2/76	2/14/76	Expired (Saufley)
			2/11/80	
			3/24/84	
William Ware Peck [141]		10/17/77	5/31/77	Expired
			12/14/77	
James Beverley Sener #	Va.	12/11/79	12/18/79	Withdrawn
Solomon Newton Pettis * [142]	Pa.	3/9/80		
Samuel Chipman Parks [143]	N.M.	1/6/82	1/11/82	Expired (Corn)

[137] Secretary Idaho, 1868.
[138] Justice Wy., 1869.
[139] Delegate Wy., 1871-73.
[140] U.S. attorney, 1869-71; delegate Wy., 1885-90.
[141] Justice N.M., 1880.
[142] Justice Colo., 1861-62; justice N.M., 1880.
[143] Justice Idaho, 1863-65?; justice N.M., 1878-82.

Nominee	Residence	Date of Nomination	Date of Commission	How succeeded
John C. Perry #	N.Y.		3/11/84	Deceased
John W. Lacey #	Ind.	7/3/84	7/5/84	Resigned
Samuel Thompson Corn	Ill.	2/2/86	3/29/86	Expired (Clark)
William L. Maginnis #	Ohio	12/9/86	10/12/86	Removed
			1/13/87	
Micah C. Saufley	Ky.	3/12/88	4/2/88	
Willis Van Devanter #	Wy.	12/16/89	8/31/89	Statehood
			1/ /90	
Clarence Don Clark *	Wy.	3/31/90	4/ /90	Declined (Conaway)
Asbury B. Conaway	Wy.	6/6/90	6/ /90	Statehood

Appendix II

LIST OF TERRITORIAL DELEGATES
1861 to 1890

Name	Term [1]	Other Offices [2]
NEW MEXICO		
Miguel Antonio Otero (D)	1856–61	Secretary 1861
John Sebrie Watts (R)	1861–63	Justice 1851–54; chief justice 1868–69
Francisco Perea (R)	1863–65	
José Francisco Chaves (R)	1865–67	
Charles P. Clever (D)	1867–2/20/69	
José Francisco Chaves (R)	2/20/1869–71	
José Manuel Gallegos (D)	1871–73	Delegate 1853–55
Stephen Benton Elkins (R)	1873–77	U.S. attorney 1867
Trinidad Romero (R)	1877–79	
Mariano Sabino Peralta Otero (R)	1879–81	
Tranquilino Luna (R)	1881–3/5/84	
Francisco Antonio Manzanares (D)	3/5/1884–85	
Antonio Joseph (D)	1885–95	House Committee on Territories, 1885–89

[1] Full dates are given only when service did not begin or end with sessions of Congress, or upon admission.
[2] United States offices in the territories, other service as delegate, House Committee on Territories.

145

Name	Term [1]	Other Offices [2]
UTAH		
William Henry Hooper (D)	1859–61	Delegate 1865–73
John Milton Bernhisel (W)	1861–63	Delegate 1851–59
John Fitch Kinney (D)	1863–65	Chief justice 1854–57, 1860–63
William Henry Hooper (D)	1865–73	Delegate 1859–61
George Quayle Cannon (R)	1873–81	Committee on Territories, 1879–81
John Thomas Caine (D)	1/17/83–93	
Joseph Lafayette Rawlins (D)	1893–95	
Frank Jenne Cannon (R)	1895–96	
WASHINGTON		
Isaac Ingall Stevens (D)	1857–61	Governor 1861; governor Idaho 1863, delegate 1864–65
William Henson Wallace (R)	1861–63	Governor 1866–67
George Edward Cole (D)	1863–65	Register land office Olympia 1861–65
Arthur Armstrong Denny (R)	1865–67	Governor 1869–70; postmaster Wallula 1865–67
Alvan Flanders (R)	1867–69	Surveyor-general 1866–69, collector customs 1873
Selucius Garfielde (R)	1869–73	Justice Ore. 1853; justice Wash. 1854, chief justice 1858–61
Obadiah Benton McFadden	1873–75	Justice 1869–70, chief justice 1870–75
Orange Jacobs (R)	1875–79	
Thomas Hurley Brents (R)	1879–85	
Charles Stewart Voorhees (D)	1885–89	
John Beard Allen (R)	1889	
NEBRASKA		
Samuel Gordon Daily (R)	5/18/1860–65	U.S. marshal 1861–64, surveyor-general 1867–69
Phineas Warren Hitchcock (R)	1865–67	

Name	Term [1]	Other Offices [2]
		COLORADO
Hiram Pitt Bennet (R)	1861–65	Secretary 1867; postmaster Denver 1869–74
Allen Alexander Bradford (R)	1865–67	Justice 1862, delegate 1869–71
George Miles Chilcott (R)	1867–69	Register land office 1863–67
Allen Alexander Bradford (R)	1869–71	Justice 1862, delegate 1865–67
Jerome Bonaparte Chaffee (R)	1871–75	Committee on territories 1874–75
Thomas MacDonald Patterson (R)	1875–76	Committee on territories 1875–76
		NEVADA
John Cradlebaugh (D)	1861–63	Justice Utah 1858–60
Gordon Newell Mott (R)	1863–64	Justice Nevada 1861–63
		DAKOTA
John Blair Smith Todd (D)	1861–63	Delegate 1864–65
William Jayne (R)	1863–6/17/64	Governor 1861–63
John Blair Smith Todd (D)	6/17/1864–65	Delegate 1861–63
Walter Atwood Burleigh (R)	1865–69	Indian agent Greenwood 1861–65
Solomon Lewis Spink (R)	1869–71	Secretary 1865–69
Moses Kimball Armstrong (D)	1871–75	
Jefferson Parish Kidder (R)	1875–79	Justice 1869–75, 1879–83
Granville Gaylord Bennett (R)	1879–81	Justice 1875–78
Richard Franklin Pettigrew (R)	1881–83	Committee on territories 1881–83
John Baldwin Raymond (R)	1883–85	U.S. marshal 1877–82
Oscar Sherman Gifford (R)	1885–89	
George Arthur Mathews (R)	1889	

Name	Term [1]	Other Offices [2]
ARIZONA		
Charles Debrill Poston (R)	1864–65	Superintendent Indian affairs 1863–64
John Noble Goodwin (R)	1865–67	Chief justice 1863–64, governor 1864–65
Coles Bashford (Ind.)	1867–69	Secretary 1869–75
Richard Cunningham McCormick (Unionist)	1869–75	Secretary 1863–66, governor 1866–69
Hiram Sanford Stevens (D)	1875–79	
John Goulder Campbell (D)	1879–81	
Granville Henderson Oury (D)	1881–85	
Curtis Coe Bean (R)	1885–87	
Marcus Aurelius Smith (D)	1887–95	Delegate 1897–99, 1901–03, 1905–09
IDAHO		
William Henson Wallace (R)	2/1/1864–65	Governor 1863–64; governor Wash. 1861, delegate 1861–63
Edward Dexter Holbrook (D)	1865–69	
Jacob K. Shafer (D)	1869–71	
Samuel Augustus Merritt (D)	1871–73	Chief justice Utah 1894–96
John Hailey (D)	1873–75	Delegate 1885–87
Thomas Warren Bennett (Ind.)	1875–6/23/76	Governor 1871–75
Stephen Southmyd Fenn (D)	6/23/1876–79	
George Ainslie (D)	1879–83	
Theodore Frelinghuysen Singiser (R)	1883–85	Secretary 1880–83
John Hailey (D)	1885–87	Delegate 1873–75
Fred Thomas Dubois (R)	1887–90	U.S. marshal 1882–86; Committee on Territories 1889–90

Name	Term [1]	Other Offices
MONTANA		
Samuel McLean (D)	1865–67	
James Michael Cavanaugh (D)	1867–71	
William Horace Clagett (R)	1871–73	
Martin Maginnis (D)	1873–85	Committee on Territories 1877–79
Joseph Kemp Toole (D)	1885–89	
Thomas Henry Carter (R)	1889	
WYOMING		
Stephen Friel Nuckolls (D)	1869–71	
William Theophilus Jones (R)	1871–73	Justice 1869–71
William Randolph Steele (D)	1873–77	
William Wellington Corlett (R)	1877–79	
Stephen Wheeler Downey (R)	1879–81	
Morton Everel Post (D)	1881–85	Committee on Territories, 1883–85
Joseph Maull Carey (R)	1885–90	Chief justice 1871–76, U.S. attorney 1869–71

BIBLIOGRAPHY

A. MANUSCRIPT MATERIALS

Arthur, Chester Alan, Papers, 1881–85. Library of Congress.
Blase, Fred Woodward, "Political History of Idaho Territory, 1863–1890," M.A. dissertation. University of California, 1925.
Byers, William N., "History of Colorado, 1884." Bancroft Library.
Carey, J[oseph] M[aull], Interview, n.d. Bancroft Library.
Chandler, Zachariah, Papers, 1855–99. Library of Congress.
Fish, Hamilton, Papers, Letter Books, and Scrapbooks, 1831–93. Library of Congress.
Grant, Ulysses Simpson, Letter Books, 1869–77. Library of Congress. 4 vols.
Hallett, Moses, "Colorado Courts, Law, and Litigation in Early Times," Dictation, 1884, Bancroft Library.
Hayes, Rutherford B., Papers, 1865–93. Hayes Memorial.
Hoyt, John P. "Leading Events since the American Settlement of Arizona," Dictation, 1878. Bancroft Library.
Johnson, Andrew, Papers, 1831–91. Library of Congress.
Maginnis, Martin. Papers, 1873–85, 1891–1912; and Scrapbook, 1869–1900. Montana State Historical Society Library, Helena.
Owings, Nicholas H., Papers, 1872–99. University of Washington Library, Seattle.
Potts, Benjamin F., Letter Book, 1870–73. Montana State Historical Society Library.
Potts, Benjamin F., Scrapbook, 1867–79. Montana State Historical Society Library.
Routt, John L. "Territory and State," Dictation, 1884. Bancroft Library.
Safford, A[nson] P. K., "Narrative of A. P. K. Safford, Ex-Govr. of Arizona . . . ," Dictation, 1880. Bancroft Library.
Sanders, Wilbur Fiske. "The Courts of Montana." Unpublished notes, n.d. Bancroft Library.
————. Papers, 1864–1900. Montana State Historical Society Library.
————. "Sidney Edgerton, the First Governor of Montana," Dictation, 1885(?). Bancroft Library.
Sheldon, Lionel A., Dictation, n.d. Bancroft Library.
Squire, Watson C., Dictation, n.d. [ca. 1890]. Bancroft Library.
U.S. Department of Justice, Interior Department Accounts, 1861–80. National Archives.
———— Department of Justice, Letters to Judges and Clerks, 1874–1904. National Archives.
———— Department of Justice, Appointments Division, Appointment Letters. Vols. A–C, 1885–90. National Archives.

150

—— Department of Justice, Appointments Division, Appointment Papers, Territories, 1861–93. National Archives.

—— Department of State, Territorial Papers, 1861–73. National Archives.

—— Department of State, Appointments Division, Commissions of Judges, Vol. II, 1856–79, and Vol. III, 1879–88. National Archives.

—— Department of State, Appointments Division, Letters of Application and Recommendation, 1861–77. National Archives.

—— Department of the Interior, Appointments Division. Appointment Papers of Territorial Governors and Secretaries, 1873–93. National Archives.

—— Department of the Interior, Appointments Division, Letters of Appointment Sent, 1873–89. National Archives.

—— Department of the Interior, Appointments Division, Orders and Circulars, 1877–88. National Archives.

—— Department of the Interior, Appointments Division, Register of Appointments, Bureau Officers, Territorial and Miscellaneous, 1879–1908. National Archives.

—— Department of the Interior, Patents and Miscellaneous Division, Territorial Papers, 1873–90. National Archives.

—— Department of the Interior, Patents and Miscellaneous Division. Miscellaneous Letters Sent, Letter Books, fair copies, 1872–88; and press copies, 1871, 1876, 1883–84.

—— Treasury Department, A.B. Series, Letters from Executive Officers, 1831–69. Treasury Bldg., Secretary's Files.

—— Treasury Department. First Comptroller Correspondence, 1832–94. Treasury Bldg., Secretary's Files.

—— Treasury Department, Executive Correspondence, Solicitor, 1885. Treasury Bldg., Secretary's Files.

—— Treasury Department, Judiciary Correspondence. Treasury Bldg., Secretary's Files.

—— Treasury Department, Letters to Governors, State Officers, etc., press copies, 1862–78. Treasury Bldg., Secretary's Files.

—— Treasury Department, Letters from Executives of Territories, GS series, 1838–56. Treasury Bldg., Secretary's Files.

—— Treasury Department, Miscellaneous Correspondence. Treasury Bldg., Secretary's Files.

Valentine, Elvin L. "The American Territorial Governor," Ph.D. dissertation. University of Wisconsin, 1928.

Vilas, William F., Papers, 1883–1908. Wisconsin State Historical Society.

Wade, Benjamin F., Papers, 1832–78. Library of Congress.

Wallace, William Henson, Papers, 1853–91. University of Washington Library, Seattle.

Washington (Territory). Secretary, Copies of Letters Sent, fair copies, 1859–74; and press copies, 1863–67. University of Washington Library, Seattle.

Wheeler, William F., Letter Books, 1859–86. Montana State Historical Society Library.

——, Montana Penitentiary, letter, Wheeler to H. H. Bancroft, October 23, 1872. Bancroft Library.

Woods, G[eorge] L. "Recollections," n.d. Bancroft Library.

B. OFFICIAL DOCUMENTS

Arizona (Territory), *Acts, Resolutions and Memorials Adopted by the* [first to fifteenth] *Legislative Assembly of the Territory of Arizona.* 15 vols. Imprint varies, 1866–89.

———, *Report of the Acting Governor of Arizona.* Washington: 1881.

———, Legislative Assembly, *Journals of the Legislative Assembly of the Territory of Arizona* [first to twelfth sessions]. 12 vols. Imprint varies, 1866–83.

Carter, Clarence Edwin, ed., *The Territorial Papers of the United States,* Vols. I–II. Washington: Government Printing Office, 1934.

Colorado (State), *General Laws.* . . . Denver: Tribune Steam Printing House, 1877.

——— (Territory), *The Revised Statutes of Colorado . . . 1868.* Central City: David C. Collier, 1868.

———, *Laws . . .* [first to eleventh sessions]. 11 vols. Title and imprint vary, 1861–76.

Dakota (Territory), *General Laws . . .* [first to eighteenth sessions]. Title and imprint vary, 1862–89.

Democratic Party, *Official Proceedings of the National Democratic Convention, held in Chicago, Ill., July 8th, 9th, 10th and 11th, 1884.* . . . New York: Douglas Taylor's Democratic Printing House, 1884.

Hinds, Asher Crosby, *Hinds' Precedents of the House of Representatives of the United States, including References to Provisions of the Constitution, the Laws, and Decisions of the United States Senate.* 8 vols. Washington: Government Printing Office, 1907–35.

Idaho (Territory), *Laws of the Territory of Idaho . . .* [first to fifteenth sessions]. 15 vols. Title and imprint vary, 1864–89.

———, Legislative Assembly, *Journal of the Council . . .* [first to twelfth sessions]. 12 vols. Title and imprint vary, 1864–83.

———, Legislative Assembly, *Journal of the House of Representatives . . .* [first to twelfth sessions]. Title and imprint vary, 1864–83.

———, Supreme Court, *Reports of Cases Argued and Determined in the Supreme Court of Idaho Territory . . . 1866 to 1880.* San Francisco: A. L. Bancroft and Co., 1882.

Montana (Territory), *Acts, Resolutions and Memorials . . .* [first to fifteenth sessions]. 15 vols. Title and imprint vary, 1866–87.

———, Legislative Assembly, *Council Journal . . .* [first to sixteenth sessions]. 16 vols. Title and imprint vary, 1866–89.

———, Legislative Assembly, *House Journal . . .* [first to sixteenth sessions]. 16 vols. Title and imprint vary, 1866–89.

Nebraska (Territory), *Laws, Joint Resolutions, and Memorials . . .* [first to twelfth sessions]. 12 vols. Title and imprint vary, 1855–67.

———, Legislative, *Journal of the Council . . .* [first to twelfth sessions]. 12 vols. Title and imprint vary, 1855–67.

———, Legislative, *Journal of the House of Representatives . . .* [first to twelfth sessions]. 12 vols. Title and imprint vary, 1855–67.

Nevada (Territory), *Laws* . . . [first to third sessions]. 3 vols. Title and imprint vary, 1862–64.

———, Legislature, *Journal of the House of Representatives* . . . [first to third sessions]. 3 vols. Imprint varies, 1862–65.

New Mexico (Territory), *Laws* . . . [first to twenty-eighth sessions]. 28 vols. Title and imprint vary, 1852–89.

———, Legislature, *Journals of the House of Representatives* . . . [first to twenty-fifth sessions]. 25 vols. Title and imprint vary, 1851–94.

———, Legislature, *Journals of the Legislative Council* . . . [first to twenty-fifth sessions]. 25 vols. Title and imprint vary, 1851–94.

The Pacific Reporter Vol. XI. St. Paul; West Publishing Co., 1886.

Republican Party, *Official Proceedings of the Republican National Convention held at Chicago, June 3, 4, 5 and 6, 1884.* Minneapolis: Charles W. Johnson, 1903.

———, *Official Proceedings of the Republican National Convention held at Chicago, June 19, 20, 21, 22, 23 and 25, 1888.* Minneapolis: Charles W. Johnson, 1903.

Richardson, James D., comp., *A Compilation of the Messages and Papers of the Presidents, 1789–1897.* 10 vols. Washington: Government Printing Office, 1896–99.

U.S., *Revised Statutes of the United States.* . . . 2nd ed., Washington: Government Printing Office, 1878.

———, *The Statutes at Large of the United States of America* . . . [1789–1942], 56 vols. Title and imprint vary, 1845–1942.

———, Attorney-General, *Annual Report of the Attorney-General of the United States for the Year* [1861–90]. 30 vols. Washington: Government Printing Office, 1861–90.

———, Attorney-General, *Digest of the Official Opinions of the Attorneys-General of the United States, Comprising All of the Published Opinions Contained in Volumes I to XVI Inclusive, and Embracing the Period from 1789 to 1881,* comp. by A. J. Bentley. Washington: Government Printing Office, 1885.

———, Attorney-General, *Digest of Official Opinions of the Attorneys-General of the United States Covering Volumes 17 to 25, inclusive, 1881–1906,* comp. by James A. Finch, Washington: Government Printing Office, 1908.

———, Attorney-General, *Official Opinions of the Attorneys-General of the United States, Advising the President and Heads of Departments in Relation to their Official Duties.* . . . Vols. III–XIX. Washington: Government Printing Office, 1852–91.

———, Census Office, *Report on Valuation, Taxation, and Public Indebtedness in the United States, as Returned at the Tenth Census (June 1, 1880).* Washington: Government Printing Office, 1884.

———, Congress, *Annals of the Congress of the United States.* 42 vols. Washington: Gales and Seaton, 1834–56.

———, Congress, *Biographical Directory of the American Congress, 1774–1927.* . . . Washington: Government Printing Office, 1928.

U.S., Congress, *Congressional Globe.* 108 vols. Washington: Globe Office, 1834–73.

———, Congress, *Congressional Record.* 88 vols. Washington: Government Printing Office, 1873–1942.

———, Congress, *House Journals,* 1825–74.

———, Congress, *House Executive Documents,* 40 Cong., 2 Sess.

———, Congress, *House Reports,* 41 Cong., 2 Sess.; 46 Cong., 2 Sess.; 48 Cong., 1 Sess.; 49 Cong., 1 Sess.; 50 Cong., 1 Sess.

———, Congress, *Journal of the Executive Proceedings of the Senate of the United States of America.* . . . 30 vols. Washington: Government Printing Office, 1828–1909.

———, Congress, *Senate Executive Documents,* 40 Cong., Special Sess.

———, Congress, *Senate Journal,* 1842–63.

———, Congress, *Senate Reports,* 37 Cong., 3 Sess.; 38 Cong., 1 Sess.; 43 Cong., 1 Sess.; 46 Cong., 2 Sess.; 47 Cong., 1 Sess.; 50 Cong., 1 Sess.

———, Continental Congress, *Journals of the Continental Congress, 1774–1789.* . . . 34 vols. Washington: Government Printing Office, 1904–37.

———, Department of Justice, *Register of the Department of Justice and the Judicial Officers of the United States.* 10 vols. Washington: Government Printing Office, 1871–95.

———, Department of State, *Register of the Department of State.* . . . 12 vols. Washington: Government Printing Office, 1861–72.

———, Department of the Interior, *Annual Report of the Secretary of the Interior* (title varies). 63 vols. Washington: Government Printing Office, 1874–1936.

———, Department of the Interior, *Orders, Circulars, and Circular Instructions of the Department of the Interior, March, 1877, to February, 1885.* Washington: Government Printing Office, 1885.

———, Supreme Court, *United States Reports.* . . . 313 vols. Title and imprint vary, 1790–1941.

———, Treasury Department, *Decisions of the First Comptroller in the Department of the Treasury of the United States* . . . , ed. William Lawrence. Washington: Government Printing Office, 1881.

Utah, Supreme Court, *Reports of Cases in the Supreme Court of Utah* . . . 24 vols. Imprint varies, 1881–1902.

——— (Territory), *The Compiled Laws of the Territory of Utah* . . . Salt Lake City: Deseret News, 1876.

——— (Territory), *Laws of the Territory of Utah* . . . [third to twenty-ninth sessions]. Title and imprint vary. Salt Lake City: 1854–90.

Washington (Territory), *Laws of Washington Territory* . . . [first annual to eleventh biennial sessions]. Title and imprint vary, 1862–88.

——— (Territory), *Message of William A. Newell, Governor of Washington Territory.* Olympia: 1881.

——— (Territory), *Journals of the Council* . . . [first annual to eleventh biennial sessions]. Title and imprint vary, 1855–87.

——— (Territory), *Journal of the House of Representatives* . . . [first annual to eleventh biennial sessions]. Title and imprint vary, 1855–87.

Wyoming (Territory), *Session Laws of the Territory of Wyoming* . . . [first to eleventh sessions]. 11 vols. Title and imprint vary, 1870–[90].

——— (Territory), *Council Journal* . . . [second to eleventh sessions]. 10 vols. Title and imprint vary, 1872–90.

——— (Territory), *House Journal* . . . [second to eleventh sessions]. 10 vols. Title and imprint vary, 1872–90.

C. AUTOBIOGRAPHICAL WORKS

Baskin, R[obert] N. *Reminiscences of Early Utah.* [Salt Lake City: Tribune-Reporter Printing Co.,] 1914.

Bowles, Samuel. *Across the Continent: A Summer's Journey to the Rocky Mountains, the Mormons, and the Pacific States.* Springfield, Massachusetts: S. Bowles & Co., 1865.

Cullom, Shelby M. *Fifty Years of Public Service; Personal Recollections of Shelby M. Cullom.* Chicago: A. C. McClurg & Co., 1911.

Dana, Charles Anderson. *Recollections of the Civil War; with the Leaders at Washington and in the Field in the Sixties.* New York: D. Appleton, 1902.

Frémont, Elizabeth Benton. *Recollections of Elizabeth Benton Frémont.* I. T. Martin, comp. New York: F. H. Hitchcock, 1912.

———, Jessie Benton. *Far-West Sketches,* Boston: D. Lothrop Co., 1890.

Jacobs, Orange. *Memoirs of Orange Jacobs.* Seattle: Lowman & Hanford Co., 1908.

Jay, John. *The Correspondence and Public Papers of John Jay.* Henry P. Johnston, ed. 4 vols. New York: G. P. Putnam's Sons, 1890–91.

Jefferson, Thomas. *The Writings of Thomas Jefferson.* Paul Leicester Ford, ed. 10 vols. New York: G. P. Putnam's Sons, 1892–99.

Monroe, James. *The Writings of James Monroe.* Stanislaus Murray Hamilton, ed. 7 vols. New York: G. P. Putnam's Sons, 1898–1903.

Pettigrew, Richard Franklin. *Imperial Washington.* Chicago: Kerr & Co., 1922.

Roosevelt, Theodore, Jr. *Colonial Policies of the United States.* Garden City: Doubleday, Doran & Co., Inc., 1937.

Sloan, Richard E. *Memories of an Arizona Judge.* Stanford University: Stanford University Press, 1932.

Told by the Pioneers. Tales of Frontier Life as Told by Those Who Remember The Days of the Territory and Early Statehood of Washington. Works Progress Administration, Washington (State), comp. 3 vols. [Olympia?:] 1937–38.

Wallace, Lew. *Lew Wallace: An Autobiography.* 2 vols. New York: Harper & Bros., 1906.

Welles, Gideon. *Diary of Gideon Welles, Secretary of the Navy under Lincoln and Johnson.* John T. Morse, Jr., ed. 3 vols. Boston: Houghton Mifflin Co., 1911.

D. BIOGRAPHIES

Coolidge, Louis A. *An Old-Fashioned Senator: Orville H. Platt.* New York: G. P. Putnam's Sons, 1910.

Ellis, Elmer. *Henry Moore Teller, Defender of the West.* Caldwell, Idaho: Caxton Printers, 1941.

Pyle, Joseph Gilpin. *The Life of James J. Hill.* 2 vols. Garden City: Doubleday, Page & Co., 1917.

Sparks, Jared. *Life of Gouverneur Morris, with Selections from his Correspondence and Miscellaneous Papers.* 3 vols. Boston: Gray & Bowen, 1832.

Walter, Paul A. F., Frank W. Clancy, and M. A. Otero. *Colonel Jose Francisco Chaves, 1833–1924* [sic], Historical Society of New Mexico, *[Publications,]* no. 31, [Santa Fé:] 1926.

E. NEWSPAPERS

Bismarck: *Tribune* (title varies), 1873–81.

Cheyenne: *Daily Sun,* 1889.

————: *Weekly Leader,* 1875–90.

————: *Wyoming Weekly Herald,* 1876.

Colorado Springs: *Gazette and El Paso County News* (title varies), 1876–77.

Denver: *Rocky Mountain News,* 1861–71.

Helena: *Journal,* 1889.

Lander (Wyoming): *Wind River Mountaineer,* 1888.

Laramie: *Boomerang,* 1885.

New York: *Herald,* 1872.

————: *World,* 1889.

Rawlins (Wyoming): *Journal,* 1885.

Rock Springs (Wyoming): *Independent,* 1889.

St. Louis: *Republic,* 1892.

Santa Fé: *Daily New Mexican* (title varies), 1870.

————: *Gazette* (title varies), 1860–69.

Seattle: *Weekly Post-Intelligencer,* 1881–90.

Virginia City: *Montanian,* 1875.

Yankton: *Dakotian,* 1862.

F. ARTICLES

Ashley, Charles S. "Governor Ashley's Biography and Messages," *Contributions to the Historical Society of Montana,* VI (1907), 143–289.

Beardsley, Arthur S. "Compiling the Territorial Codes of Washington," *Pacific Northwest Quarterly,* XXVIII (1937), 3–54.

Bourne, Edward Gaylord. "A Trained Colonial Civil Service," *North American Review,* CLXIX (1899), 528–35.

Carpenter, K. W. "A Glimpse of Montana," *Overland*, San Francisco, II (1869), 378–86.

Dixon, W. W. "Sketch of the Life and Character of William H. Clagett," *Contributions to the Historical Society of Montana*, IV (1903), 249–57.

Ganaway, Loomis Morton. "New Mexico and the Sectional Controversy, 1846–1861," *New Mexico Historical Review*, XVIII (1943), 325–48.

Geary, John W. "Executive Minutes of Governor John W. Geary," *Transactions of the Kansas State Historical Society*, IV (1890), 520–742.

Goodloe, Green Clay. "Governor Green Clay Smith," *Contributions to the Historical Society of Montana*, VII (1910), 215–18.

"The Governorship of Utah, *Tullidge's Quarterly Magazine*, II (1000), 18–20.

Hosmer, J. H., ed. "Biographical Sketch of Hezekiah Lord Hosmer," *Contributions to the Historical Society of Montana*, III (1900), 288–99.

Humphries, Abram. "Removal of Territorial Judges," *American Law Review*, XXVI (1892), 470–71.

Irwin, John N. "Claims to Statehood: Arizona," *North American Review*, CLVI (1893), 354–59.

Jackson, William Turrentine. "Indian Affairs and Politics in Idaho Territory, 1863–1870," *Pacific Historical Review*, XIV (1945), 311–25.

Keen, Effie R. "Arizona's Governors," *Arizona Historical Review*, III (1930), No. 3, pp. 7–20.

L[ewis], W. D. "Albuquerque National Bank *v.* Perea," *American Law Register* (New Series), XXXII (1893), 262–66.

Mills, James Hamilton. "Reminiscences of an Editor," *Contributions to the Historical Society of Montana*, V (1904), 273–88.

Oliphant, Ethelbert Patterson. "Judge E. P. Oliphant," ed. James E. Babb, *Washington Historical Quarterly*, XI (1920), 254–65.

Pomeroy, Earl S. "The American Colonial Office," *Mississippi Valley Historical Review*, XXIX (1944), 521–32.

———. "Election of the Governor of Puerto Rico," *Southwestern Social Science Quarterly*, XXIII (1943), 355–60.

———. "Lincoln, the Thirteenth Amendment, and the Admission of Nevada," *Pacific Historical Review*, XII (1943), 362-68.

Poston, Charles D. "Building a State in Apache Land," *Overland* (2 Series), XXIV (1894), 87-93, 203-13, 291-97, 403-8.

"Removal of Territorial Judges," *American Law Review*, XXIV (1890), 308–11.

Schell, Herbert S. "Official Immigration Activities of Dakota Territory," *North Dakota Historical Quarterly*, VII (1932), 5–24.

Schneider, Eugene Curie. "Taxation in Dakota Territory," *South Dakota Historical Collections*, XIII (1926), 395–424.

Teetor, Henry Dudley. "Hon. Moses Hallett," *Magazine of Western History*, IX (1889), 613–14.

Thomas, Charles S. "The Pioneer Bar of Colorado," *Colorado Magazine*, I (1924), 193–204.

Turner, Frederick J. "The West as a Field for Historical Study," *Annual*

Report of the American Historical Association for the Year 1896, I (1897), 281–87.

Twitchell, Ralph Emerson. "Kirby Benedict," *Old Santa Fe*, I (1913), 50–92.

Wade, Decius S. "Self-Government in the Territories," *International Review*, VI (1879), 299–308.

Ward, Joseph. "The Territorial System of the United States," *Andover Review*, X (1888), 51–62.

G. REGIONAL, STATE, AND LOCAL HISTORIES

[Angel, Myron, ed.] *History of Nevada, with Illustrations and Biographical Sketches.* Oakland: Thompson & West, 1881.

Armstrong, Moses K. *The Early Empire Builders of the Great West.* Compiled and Enlarged from the Author's Early History of Dakota Territory in 1866. St. Paul: E. W. Porter, 1901.

Bancroft, Hubert Howe. *History of Arizona and New Mexico, 1530–1888*, *Works*, XVII. San Francisco: History Co., 1889.

———. *History of Nevada, Colorado, and Wyoming, 1540–1888*, Works, XXV. San Francisco: History Co., 1890.

———. *History of Utah, 1540–1887*, *Works*, XXVI. San Francisco: History Co., 1889.

———. *History of Washington, Idaho and Montana, 1845–1889*, *Works*, XXXI, San Francisco: History Co., 1890.

Fulton, Maurice Garland, and Paul Horgan, eds. *New Mexico's Own Chronicle. Three Races in the Writings of Four Hundred Years.* Dallas: Banks Upshaw and Co., 1937.

Hailey, John. *The History of Idaho.* Boise: Press of Syms-York Co., 1910.

Hawley, James H., ed. *History of Idaho, the Gem of the Mountains.* 4 vols. Chicago: S. J. Clarke Publishing Co., 1920.

History of Arizona Territory showing its Resources and Advantages. San Francisco: Wallace W. Elliott & Co., 1884.

Kingsbury, George W. *History of Dakota Territory.* 2 vols. Chicago: S. J. Clarke Publishing Co., 1915.

Roberts, B[righam] H. *A Comprehensive History of the Church of Jesus Christ of Latter-day Saints*, Century I. 6 vols. Salt Lake City: Deseret News Press, 1930.

Tullidge, Edward W. *The History of Salt Lake City and its Founders.* Salt Lake City: Edward W. Tullidge [1885].

H. TREATISES AND MONOGRAPHS

Arny, William Frederick Milton. *Interesting Items Regarding New Mexico.* Santa Fé: Manderfield & Tucker, 1873.

Dilla, Harriette May. *The Politics of Michigan, 1865–1878* (Columbia Studies in History, Economics and Public Law, XLVII, No. 1). New York: Columbia University Press, 1912.

Farrand, Max. *The Legislation of Congress for the Government of the Organized Territories of the United States, 1789–1895.* Newark: W. A. Baker, 1896.

Hunt, Gaillard. *The Department of State of the United States; its History and Functions.* New Haven: Yale University Press, 1914.

Hamilton, Patrick. *The Resources of Arizona.* Prescott, 1881.

Lindley, Curtis H. *A Treatise on the American Law relating to Mines and Mineral Lands* (3 ed.). 3 vols. San Francisco: Bancroft-Whitney Co., 1914.

Lord, Eliot. *Comstock Mining and Miners* (United States Geological Survey Monographs, IV). Washington. Government Printing Office, 1883.

McConachie, Lauros G. *Congressional Committees; a Study of the Origin and Development of our National and Local Legislative Methods.* New York: T. Y. Crowell & Co., 1898.

Meyerholz, Charles [Henry]. "Federal Supervision over the Territories of the United States," *Beiträge zur Kultur- und Universalgeschichte,* VI, 83–246.

Ritch, William Gillet. *Illustrated New Mexico* (3 ed.). [Santa Fé:] New Mexican Printing and Publishing Co., 1883.

Snow, Alpheus H. *The Administration of Dependencies. A Study of the Evolution of the Federal Empire, with Special Reference to American Colonial Problems.* New York: G. P. Putnam's Sons, 1902.

Trimble, William J. *The Mining Advance into the Inland Empire. A Comparative Study of the Beginnings of the Mining Industry in Idaho and Montana, Eastern Washington and Oregon, and the Southern Interior of British Columbia; and of Institutions and Laws based upon that Industry* (Bulletin of the University of Wisconsin, No. 638, History Series, III, No. 2). Madison: 1914.

Ward, Durbin. *On the Government of the Territories. The Constitutional Power of the General Government and the People in the Federal Territories.* Cincinnati: Daily Enquirer Steam Presses, 1860.

Willoughby, William Franklin. *Territories and Dependencies of the United States, their Government and Administration.* New York: The Century Co., 1905.

INDEX

161

Platt, Orville H., 87, 93
Poston, Charles D., 64, 87-88
Potts, Benjamin F., 36, 86, 105
Pratt, John, 85
President, 5, 6, 7, 9, 21, 26-27; *see also*
Appointments, and names of presidents
Printing, public, 12, 29, 31-33, 45, 87

Quay, Matthew S., 72

Railroads, 23, 47, 70, 71
Rawlins, John A., 68
Recommendations, types, 63 n.
Reconstruction, 91
Removals, 56, 67, 69, 70-72, 77
Resident appointments, 73-79
Resignations, 38, 55, 62
Resistance to appointed officers, 56-57, 101, 103
Richardson, Luther B., 79
Ritch, William G., 85
Roosevelt, Franklin D., 79 n.
Ross, Edward G., 24, 71-72

Safford, Anson P.-K., 102
"Sage-brush districting," 56-57
St. Clair, Arthur, 6, 96
Salaries, 28, 35-39, 101-2
Sanborn, William, 63
Schurz, Carl, 22, 24 n., 27, 47
Secretary, territorial, 28-29, 31-32, 42; acting, 29 n.
Self-government, 12, 97-99
Semple, Eugene, 86
Service, territorial, 62, 79
Seward, William H., 9, 10, 14, 22
Smith, Green Clay, 65
Sovereignty, territorial, 97-98, 100-1
Sparks, William A. J., 77
Spink, Solomon L., 85
Squire, Watson C., 23, 71, 72
State, Department of, 5, 6-15, 22, 96

States, political influence of, 67-68, 69
Stevenson, Edward A., 78 n.
Stewart, William M., 38, 104
Subsidies, 28-33, 34-35, 39-45, 49-50, 99-100

Taxes, 45-47
Teller, Henry M., 27
Territorial and Domestic Records Bureau, 7-8
"Territorial desk," 7, 8
Territories and Island Possessions, Division of, 106 n.
Todd, John B. S., 74, 85
Thomas, Arthur L., 71
Thompson, David P., 36, 67 n.
Treasury Department, 5, 8, 13-14, 25-26, 28-35, 42

Utah, 11, 21, 58, 59, 60, 75, 81, 106, 107

Vigilantes, 55, 60-61
Voorhees, Charles S., 86

Wade, Benjamin F., 64, 93
Waite, Charles B., 57
Waldo, Henry L., 38
Wallace, Lewis, 24 n., 69
War Department, 13, 25
Warren, Francis E., 23, 77, 78
Washington (Territory), 25, 45, 46, 57
Waters, Benjamin F., 55
White, Benjamin F., 79
Whitney, Oscar A., 69
Widener, P. A. B., 70
Wilkins, Turney M., 68, 69
Wisconsin, 3
Wolfley, Lewis, 73
Woolfolk, Alexander M., 105
Wyoming, 57, 65, 72 n., 77, 78-79

Zane, Charles S., 92 n.
Zulick, Conrad M., 73

AMERICANA LIBRARY

The City: The Hope of Democracy
By Frederic C. Howe
With a new introduction by Otis A. Pease

Bourbon Democracy of the Middle West, 1865-1896
By Horace Samuel Merrill
With a new introduction by the author

*The Deflation of American Ideals: An Ethical Guide
for New Dealers*
By Edgar Kemler
With a new introduction by Otis L. Graham, Jr.

Borah of Idaho
By Claudius O. Johnson
With a new introduction by the author

The Fight for Conservation
By Gifford Pinchot
With a new introduction by Gerald D. Nash

Upbuilders
By Lincoln Steffens
With a new introduction by Earl Pomeroy

The Progressive Movement
By Benjamin Parke De Witt
With a new introduction by Arthur Mann

*Coxey's Army: A Study of the
Industrial Army Movement of 1894*
By Donald L. McMurry
With a new introduction by John D. Hicks

Jack London and His Times: An Unconventional Biography
By Joan London
With a new introduction by the author

San Francisco's Literary Frontier
By Franklin Walker
With a new introduction by the author

Men of Destiny
By Walter Lippmann
With a new introduction by Richard Lowitt

Woman Suffrage and Politics:
The Inner Story of the Suffrage Movement
By Carrie Chapman Catt and Nettie H. Shuler
With a new introduction by T. A. Larson

The Dry Decade
By Charles Merz
With a new introduction by the author

The Conquest of Arid America
By William E. Smythe
With a new introduction by Lawrence B. Lee

The Territories and the United States, 1861–1890:
Studies in Colonial Administration
By Earl S. Pomeroy
With a new introduction by the author